PUBLICATIONS OF THE CENTER FOR JAPANESE AND KOREAN STUDIES

Chong-Sik Lee
The Politics of Korean Nationalism. 1963.

Sadako N. Ogata
Defiance in Manchuria: The Making of Japanese Foreign Policy, 1931–1932. 1964.

R. P. Dore
Education in Tokugawa Japan. 1964.

James T. Araki
The Ballad-Drama of Medieval Japan. 1964.

Masakazu Iwata
Ōkubo Toshimichi: The Bismarck of Japan. 1964.

Frank O. Miller
Minobe Tatsukichi: Interpreter of Constitutionalism in Japan. 1965.

Michael Cooper, S.J.
They Came to Japan: An Anthology of European Reports on Japan, 1543–1640. 1965.

POSTWAR
ECONOMIC GROWTH
IN JAPAN

Published under the auspices of
THE CENTER FOR JAPANESE AND KOREAN STUDIES
University of California, Berkeley

POSTWAR
ECONOMIC GROWTH
IN JAPAN

Selected Papers of the First Conference of the
TOKYO ECONOMIC RESEARCH CENTER
Edited by RYŪTARO KOMIYA
Translated by ROBERT S. OZAKI

1966
UNIVERSITY OF CALIFORNIA PRESS
Berkeley and Los Angeles

University of California Press
Berkeley and Los Angeles, California
Cambridge University Press
London, England
Translation © 1966 by The Regents of the University of California
Library of Congress Catalog Card Number: 66–22705
Printed in the United States of America

THE CENTER FOR JAPANESE AND KOREAN STUDIES of the
University of California is a unit of the
Institute of International Studies. It is the unifying organization
for faculty members and students interested in Japan and Korea,
bringing together scholars from many disciplines.
The Center's major aims are
the development and support of research and language study.
As part of this program the Center sponsors
a publication series of books concerned with Japan and Korea.
Manuscripts are considered from all campuses
of the University of California as well as
from any other individuals and institutions
doing research in these areas.

Editor's Preface

The rapidity of Japan's postwar economic growth has been a somewhat remarkable exception in modern economic history. Especially noteworthy is the continuation of accelerated growth after 1955, inasmuch as there was a widespread belief that the growth rate would inevitably slacken once Japan had completed the task of reconstruction and recovery from the War. This growth is seen, for example, in the per annum rate of increase in real GNP, which averaged 10.8 per cent for fiscal 1955–1961,* and in that of the manufacturing production index, which registered an incredible 16.1 per cent for 1955–1962.

Rapid growth was accompanied by some notable structural changes within the economy. In 1955, for instance, approximately 42 per cent of the total labor force was employed in agriculture; but due to the expansion of the nonagricultural sectors (especially manufacturing), the weight of farm labor was reduced to about 29 per cent by the end of 1962. On the other hand, the weight of the manufacturing industry in the National Income made a sizable leap from 24.8 per cent in fiscal 1955 to 30.8 per cent in fiscal 1960, and within the manufacturing industry machinery production showed the highest rate of growth. During 1955–1962 labor productivity rose at the annual average rate of 10.1 per cent in manufacturing, and 5.2 per cent in agriculture.

Accelerated growth has induced significant changes in income distribution as well. Assuming for the moment that, of distributive shares of National Income, returns to capital consist of rent, interest, dividends, corporate retained earnings, and half of non-agricultural proprietors' incomes, and that returns to labor comprise the other half of proprietors' incomes and compensation for employees, labor's share declined from 80.1 per cent in fiscal 1955 to 74.4 per cent in fiscal 1961. This should be interpreted as a re-

---

* Translator's note: The Japanese fiscal year runs from April 1st through the end of March of the following year.

flection of the rapid increase in investment activity and the steady rise in the weight of corporate income during the period. We must note, however, that the fall in labor's share occurred chiefly in the first half of the period, while after 1959 capital-labor ratios showed little change.

Similar shifts are observed in income-size distribution. According to the Government's *Employment Status Survey,* the pattern of income distribution showed a conspicuous tendency towards greater inequality from 1956 to 1959, but little further change occurred from 1959 to 1962. These recent trends should be viewed in the light of shifts in labor conditions since 1959. While excess supply has persisted in Japanese labor markets since the Meiji era, the expansion of the economy—especially the manufacturing industry—has finally induced a steady rise in wages in the traditional low-wage sectors; most conspicuous has been the rapid closing of wage-gaps between advanced industry and small- and medium-size businesses.

The real consumption level among urban wage- and salary-earners' households has, however, increased at the annual rate of 4.6 per cent from 1955 through 1962, a rate that is considerably lower than that of GNP for the same period. Increase in the rate of savings among the above households from 8.9 per cent in 1955 to 16.2 per cent in 1962, and the consumer goods price inflation since 1959 presumably account for this moderate rate of increase in real consumption expenditures. We must note, however, that the Engel's coefficient in cities declined from 46.9 per cent in 1955 to 39.0 per cent in 1962.

As one would expect, accelerated growth and concomitant structural changes have created many undesirable and difficult problems for the nation. Inflation of consumer goods prices that rose as much as 25 per cent in the four years from 1959 to 1963, two major balance-of-payments crises in 1957 and 1961, the stringent monetary policy that followed, excessive population concentration in major cities and the resultant critical housing shortage as well as impossible traffic congestion, the aforementioned sign of some tendency towards inequalization of income shares—all might be cited as outstanding examples.

In sharp contrast to the dynamism of the Japanese economy, relative retardation has thus far characterized empirical studies of postwar growth by Japanese academic economists. Causes of Japan's postwar growth, both as theoretical and policy issues, have been receiving the intensive attention of numerous economists outside Japan. Paradoxical as it may sound, however, few significant works have been conducted by Japanese economists them-

selves, with the possible exception of Professor Miyohei Shinohara's pioneering treatise, *Growth and Cycles in the Japanese
Economy,* and two or three others. At the same time, the climate
of opinion about growth in Japan has reflected certain conflicting
ideological biases—those who are critical of the government as well
as of the present Japanese economic system fondly underestimate
the nation's viability, placing incessant emphasis only upon negative aspects of growth, while the defenders of the present politico-
economic system tirelessly propagate the apparent success of government policies, especially the well-publicized Income-Doubling
Plan.

From a more dispassionate viewpoint, however, one simply cannot deny the positive aspects of extraordinary growth; and yet
there exist some doubts as to the extent to which the professed
government economic plans have truly contributed to postwar development. What have been the positive as well as negative effects
on growth and welfare of fiscal-monetary policy, balance-of-payments policy, protectionist measures, anti-monopoly acts pursued
by the government throughout the postwar years? How, and to
what extent, have these policy measures influenced capital accumulation, technological progress, changes in the industrial structure,
stabilization of cyclical fluctuations, improvement in external balance, and removal of monopoly elements from domestic markets?
Empirical studies on and evaluation of these policy problems remain an extremely important task for Japanese economists.

In view of the acute need for such studies, the Tokyo Economic
Research Center, a joint research organization whose membership
comprises those economics faculties at several universities in Tokyo
who specialize in economic theory, econometrics, and management
science, held its first conference on Japan's postwar economic
growth in January 1963. Preceding the conference, the Program
Committee, consisting of Masao Fukuoka, Moto-o Kaji, Ryūtaro
Komiya, Fujitarō Miyashita, and Mitsugu Nakamura, began its
planning in May 1962 and had completed, along with a schedule
of the conference, a tentative list of participants and the titles of
their papers by July of the same year. Participants were given approximately six months in which to work on their papers, and by
December the majority of the papers had been finished. Copies of
these papers were then distributed among all participants, including discussants. The Conference on Japan's Postwar Economic
Growth was held in January 1963, in Zushi City, Kanagawa Pre-
fecture, and lasted for four days in a congenial atmosphere of active debate and discussion.

Conferences of this sort are frequently held abroad, and their contribution to progress in academic research is universally recognized. Conferences of the National Bureau of Economic Research, annual meetings of the International Economic Association, two Income and Wealth Series (one in the United States and the other in Great Britain) are familiar to many of us. In Japan, however, few similar conferences have been held in the past because of insufficient funds as well as the isolationism and exclusionism practiced by leading universities. The Tokyo Economic Research Center plans to sponsor similar conferences in the future in order to encourage research and greater interchange of ideas.

This book is being published as an official record of the Zushi Conference and contains 11 out of 17 papers read at the conference and 10 comments thereon. Each paper was developed independently by its author but deals with a certain aspect of the central theme of the Zushi Conference, i.e., an empirical inquiry into the nature and causes of Japan's postwar economic growth. Furthermore, each chapter, to varying degrees, blends a survey of past important works in a given area and the author's new and original work. For example, chapters 2, 3, and 8 are by and large in the nature of surveys, whereas chapters 6, 7, 9, and 10 lean more towards discussion of original ideas and new research results. Although even the survey papers attracted much discussion, it was those papers which introduced original ideas that aroused the more intense controversy at the conference. The reader may have a glimpse of this in the comments on these papers.

Areas of initial disagreement that were later reconciled and dissolved after thorough discussions at the conference are not included in the comments. Only those views which remained dissentient even after extensive discussions appear as comments. The authors were given opportunities to rework their papers after the conference, and many of them incorporated comments into their revised and final versions before publication. Authors' replies to comments appear, by agreement, as footnotes in respective papers rather than as separate rejoinders following comments. It is hoped that both the comments and replies encourage further research and discussion in academic circles.

Problems yet unsolved concerning Japan's economic growth are numerous. We would be more than happy if publication of this book constitutes a modest step towards further advancement of empirical studies on the Japanese economy.

Finally, I, on behalf of the Program Committee for the Zushi Conference, take this opportunity to express our genuine thanks to the numerous individuals who have richly and generously contributed to the success of the conference, not only with their financial support, suggestions, and recommendations, but also with many other, visible and invisible, forms of assistance. My very personal thanks are extended to the authors of chapters and comments, without whose close cooperation my editing task would have been far more onerous, and to Mr. Kōshi Takeda of the Iwanami Publishing Company for his tireless efforts concerning the publication of this book. Last, but not least, my sincere gratitude goes to Mrs. Chigako Kaizuka and Miss Hiroko Yoshinobu for their competent secretarial service while this book was in preparation.

Ryūtaro Komiya

October 1963

Contents

PART IV.   BUSINESS FLUCTUATIONS AND
                 STABILIZATION POLICY

PART V.   MANAGEMENT

Tables

Figures

Translator's Introduction

Whereas many scholarly books and journal articles on Japan's postwar economy have already appeared in the English language, a large proportion of these have been written for the Western audience either by a limited number of Japanese authors capable of expressing themselves in another language or by Western specialists on the Japanese economy. Few of the growing number of significant treaties by Japanese scholars on the Japanese economy have thus far been made available to the West through translation.

This volume should prove of interest to students of the Japanese economy and of economic studies in Japan inasmuch as it is not a study by a single author but a collection of papers read at the first conference of the Tokyo Economic Research Center. The authors represent a cross-section of relatively young, non-Marxist or post-Keynesian economists in Japan. The reader will come across numerous comments in the book that are useful not only in understanding the Japanese economy but also in cultivating a deeper insight into the general problems of development and growth that occupy so much of our contemporary economic thought.

In a mixed economy, the private sector is influenced to varying degrees by the policies of the national government. In the case of Japan, however, the government seems to have played a disproportionately important role, compared with the experience of Western countries, in molding the pattern of her industrial growth after the War. Japan's postwar growth has been spearheaded by private investment in new plants and equipment, and the vigor of Japanese entrepreneurs has no doubt been another major factor. But no less contributory to the phenomenal industrial expansion has been the investment-orientation of fiscal-monetary policy pursued by the Japanese government. In chapter 1 Professor Ryūichiro Tachi examines how the monetary policy of the Bank of Japan and the fiscal policy of the Ministry of Finance have helped intensify and accelerate investment activity in the private sector.

1

The so-called "low interest-rate" policy created a state of excess demand over supply with respect to loanable funds. Thus, unlike their counterparts in the West, private firms borrowed heavily from commercial banks to finance their investments, while commercial banks in turn resorted to the Bank of Japan as the ultimate supplier of credit. Seeking investment funds, growth firms in strategic industries were favored by the preferential monetary-fiscal measures of the government, many of which differed little from subsidies to those firms. The "easy-money-with-surplus-budget" principle not only provided a basis for the preferential credit policy of the Bank of Japan, but it also enabled the government to allocate sizeable sums for public loans and investments directed towards the objective of growth.

Tax policy in a mixed economy involves the delicate task of collecting enough tax revenue to finance the building of sufficient social overheads and other requirements of a modern state and, at the same time, controlling the level and manner of taxation so that the prospect of growth in the private sector will not be unduly jeopardized. In chapter 2 Professor Sei Fujita discusses the evolution of tax policy in Japan since the Shoup Reform. He observes that a series of special measures has been adopted by the government in order to encourage saving in the nation and capital accumulation among large firms, but many of these measures—allegedly adopted for the purpose of accelerating growth—were tantamount to outright subsidies. The author points out that under the particular tax policy of the Japanese government large corporations have been favored over small businesses, while a greater inequity has resulted from the distribution of tax burdens in favor of investors and at the expense of consumer welfare. Critical inadequacy of social overheads in the nation and the undue complexity of the present tax system are other consequences of the government's policy.

During the decade of the 1950's, Japanese economic growth had proceeded without secular inflation—a remarkable record in view of her average annual growth rate during that period of some 9 per cent in real terms. There were cyclical upswings in both the consumer and wholesale price indexes, but the economy did not experience any persistent inflationary trend. However, in 1959 the consumer price index began to rise at the conspicuous rate of 5 to 6 per cent per annum, and the trend has persisted despite the continuing stability of the wholesale price index. In chapter 3 Professor Hiroshi Niida gives an appraisal of the inflation and a survey of the views of Japanese economists on the issue. The trend in the consumer price index is conditioned by the prices of those products that are largely supplied by the relatively backward sectors of the Japanese economy, such as small businesses, services, and agriculture. While the level of demand for consumer goods and services has been rising rapidly, reflecting the growth-induced increase in income, supply has not been keeping pace on account of the low productivity of those sectors. At the same time, a labor shortage brought about by the sustained expansion of the economy has in recent years been causing wage inflation even in the backward sectors. The recent consumer-price inflation may be viewed as a consequence of the continuing inefficiency and low productivity in these sectors especially at the retail level, combined with rising labor costs.

The government's protectionism with respect to agriculture and the foods industry seems to be another factor in the inflation. The price of Japanese rice is almost twice as high as the international price, and many processed foods in Japan are more expensive than abroad. Since more than 30 per cent of the overall increase in the consumer price index is attributable to food prices, it is perhaps no exaggeration to say that the protectionist policy of the government has been one of the main causes of the recent inflation.

Economic growth of a country may assume an export-oriented pattern insofar as internal growth is led by the expansion of the export sector. On the other hand, export expansion itself may be an effect of internal growth. According to a popular thesis in trade-and-growth theory, rapid growth of an import-dependent country is prone to lead to a deterioration of the external balance because, while accelerated internal growth raises the level of required imports, world demand for the country's products may not increase fast enough to avoid an emerging deficit in the balance of payments. In chapter 4 Mr. Hisao Kanamori challenges this theory as overly pessimistic and suggests an alternative model in the light of Japan's postwar experiences in external trade that places greater emphasis on the positive effects of growth upon external equilibrium. Growth has raised the level of Japanese imports, but it has also induced expansion of her exports. According to Kanamori, Japanese export expansion was mainly due to internal factors, such as the higher rate of labor-productivity increase over money wages, the entry of new goods into Japanese exports reflecting vigorous innovations in the home market, and the shift of the industrial structure toward heavy-and-chemical goods for which world demand has been increasing rapidly. All of these, he argues, are the results of Japanese economic growth itself.

Professor Tatemoto in his comment complains, however, that Kanamori's definition of the balance-of-payments equilibrium is confusing, and that if we adhere to the trade balance as the basis for evaluating Japan's external balance, Kanamori's argument will break down completely. This comment is remindful of the recent controversy concerning deficits in the U.S. balance of payments. In the case of Japan, the overall balance has been favorable over the long run, and the magnitude of her foreign exchange reserves has shown an upward secular trend primarily because of special procurements by the U.S. government in Japan (during the early 50's) and the inflow of foreign capital (in more recent years). The merit of Kanamori's thesis seems to depend upon how we decide to interpret these nontrade credit items in appraising Japan's balance of payments.

The recessions which occurred in Japan prior to 1964 followed a certain recurrent pattern. Accelerated growth of the economy induces a rapid, short-run increase in imports of industrial materials. As exports continue to expand at a more modest pace, the balance of payments deteriorates to a point at which the government is compelled to invoke a stringent, deflationary policy. The rate of growth is sufficiently reduced so that external equilibrium is restored. Then the tight-money policy is removed, and domestic investment activity begins to gather momentum. The economy proceeds to repeat the next round of cyclical fluctuations. In chapter 5 Professor Masao Fukuoka develops a model of Japan's cyclical growth which should interest the mathematically minded. He applies Hicks' trade-cycle model to the Japanese experiences and adopts the balance-of-payments ceiling as a major restriction upon Japan's cyclical growth, whereas the labor-supply constraint assumes a similar role in Hicks' model.

A challenging problem in growth economics is the identification of the determinants of labor shares in different countries. Is there a law pertaining to the relationship between the stages of economic development and labor shares? Can we generalize about the ways in which labor shares affect the pace of economic growth? Do larger labor shares necessarily imply a lower rate of saving and a slower speed of capital accumulation? In chapter 6 Professor Kōtaro Tsujimura argues that one factor in Japan's growth has been the optimal labor shares, large enough to sustain a required level of consumer demand and yet small enough so that a sufficiently high rate of saving and capital formation could be maintained. The optimal labor shares in turn were a result of the particular employment structure in Japan, characterized by the high elasticity of labor supply from labor-surplus backward sectors to modern sectors, coupled with Japan's reliance upon foreign technology,

technology which is initially developed in the West independently of the domestic factor proportions and the indigenous input-price structure within the Japanese economy. Tsujimura incorporates Arthur Lewis' model of unlimited supply of labor and Alexander Gerschenkron's catching-up thesis on borrowed technology into his theory of Japanese labor shares.

Economic growth induces shifts in the pattern of income distribution. In Japan a declining trend in labor shares has been observed. Some have attributed it to low wages resulting from an over-supply of labor relative to capital. Still others have hypothesized that the annual proportional wage-increase system which tends to make young workers' compensations too small in terms of their productivity, together with the increasing number of young and female workers in the Japanese employment markets, provides one major explanation. In chapter 7 Professor Masao Baba conducts a series of statistical tests to examine the impact of labor unions on labor shares and concludes that the impact of unions is not as significant as is commonly believed, and that the rapid pace of capital accumulation centering around private investment in new plant and equipment in large-scale manufacturing firms seems to provide a better explanation for the observed falling trend in Japanese labor shares.

Since investment is financed by saving, continual capital accumulation presupposes a sufficiently high rate of saving. The high propensity of the Japanese to save has aroused the curiosity of many observers. Explanations abound and extend from the naive to the sophisticated. On the naive side, for example, frugality as a traditional Japanese virtue is often cited as a major cause. To say that the Japanese save because they are frugal, however, is too tautological to make much economic sense. Other explanations such as the unequal income distribution, the large weight of self-employed, the modest coverage of social security programs, and the impact of the particular compensation-employment system in Japan are scrutinized by Professor Komiya in chapter 8. He maintains that many of the commonly accepted views fail to meet empirical tests, and that extra income in the form of bonuses and the underdevelopment of the consumer-credit market afford more plausible explanations for the high rate of saving in Japan.

The number of econometric models of the Japanese economy has been steadily increasing in recent years. Professor Mori's simulation analysis of fluctuations and growth of the Japanese economy for the period 1955–1960 (chapter 9) is indicative of the above trend and may be regarded as an example of the pioneering works in econometric research being conducted in postwar Japan. The future will no doubt witness an even greater application of quantitative methods to empirical studies of the Japanese economy.

In the context of a mixed economy it is often not easy to determine whether the apparent fulfillment of a certain objective is attributable specifically to government policy. The Japanese economy grew at a phenomenal rate during the postwar period. It does not necessarily follow, however, that this was the direct effect of the government's policy on growth. The more strategic reason may be found elsewhere. In chapter 10 Professor Kaizuka examines the stabilization effect of Japanese fiscal policy upon aggregate economic activity as well as upon external-balance positions. Contrary to prevalent belief in Japan, he concludes that the government's fiscal policy has been either fairly stabilizing or neutral vis-à-vis the private sector.

In the last chapter Professor Noda evaluates the role of entrepreneurs in Japan's postwar economic growth. The Zaibatsu dissolution, the breakdown of the military-industrial complex and the controlled economy of the prewar era, and the Occupation's political and economic reforms have brought about a competitive environment and a new social climate that are more conducive to the flourishing of vigorous entrepreneurship than those before the War. He argues that the remarkable postwar growth records of the Japanese economy are, to a large extent, ascribable to the energetic conduct of Japanese corporate executives.

Translation of a technical work in economics is not as formidable a task as translation of foreign literature. Given the structural differences between Japanese and English, however, I have encountered considerable difficulties. Some of my solutions are undoubtedly not to the liking of the authors, but I only hope they will condone the shortcomings that may remain. Throughout I have been most concerned with the readability of the text from the standpoint of the Western reader. I make no claim, though, to have violated Edward G. Seidensticker's dictum that it is illegal to compose better prose than the original. I must also admit that I did not possess enough virtuosity to bring out in the English text the stylistic differences of the Japanese authors.

In the course of translation I accumulated far more debts to many individuals than I had ever anticipated. I am deeply grateful to Professor Henry Rosovsky, former director of the Center for Japanese and Korean Studies at the University of California, Berkeley, who not only encouraged my undertaking but also made invaluable arrangements for my project at the center.

Professor Ryūtaro Komiya of the University of Tokyo, editor of the book, held a visiting professorship at Stanford University during the academic year 1964–1965. His tenure at Stanford enabled me to see and consult him on many occasions; I express my genuine thanks for his comments and suggestions. I am indebted to Professors Sei Fujita, Hiroshi Niida, and Kazuo Noda and to Mr. Hisao Kanamori, who were kind enough to answer through correspondence my questions about their chapters. Professor Kiyoshi Nagashima of the Prefectural University of Osaka graciously assisted me, while he was a visiting scholar at the University of California, Berkeley, in the translation of certain economic terms used in Japan and in the pronunciation of Japanese names. The onerous task of typing the manuscript was cheerfully and competently executed by Miss Frances Hammond of the Center for Japanese and Korean Studies at the University of California, Berkeley. My father, Professor Shigeru Ozaki, of Aoyama Gakuin University, Tokyo, was generous enough to send across the Pacific various dictionaries which helped my translation immeasurably. Finally, my wife, Cecilia, went far beyond the call of duty in editing and proofreading the entire first draft. To all these individuals I express my sincere gratitude. They are in no way responsible, however, for the contents of this volume.

PART I

Public Finance and Monetary Policy

I

Ryūichiro Tachi:
Fiscal and Monetary Policy*

INTRODUCTION

Many articles have been written on the causes of the rapid post-war recovery and subsequent development of the Japanese economy. There seems to be a consensus that Japan's postwar growth, in contrast to the export-oriented economy of West Germany, has been largely induced by accelerated private investment—principally, investment in plants and equipment.[1] On the other hand, there exist divergent views as to why investment expenditures managed to grow at what appear to be almost abnormal rates.

As many authors point out, a series of innovations and technological advances have helped to sustain continual growth in private investment.[2] But no less important is the role played by the postwar economic policy (particularly fiscal and monetary policy) of the Japanese government; we might even contend that postwar growth cannot be fully understood without first considering the nature and characteristics of the fiscal and monetary measures adopted by the government. Although granted that in a "mixed" economy, such as Japan's, growth and fluctuations cannot be purely independent of government

* This paper is a part of work conducted at the University of Tokyo Center for Japanese Industry Studies. The author expresses his thanks to Kenjirō Ara, Noboru Kamakura, Ryūtaro Komiya, and Sei Fujita for their useful comments at the meeting of the Money and Banking Association and at the Zushi Conference, and to the University of Tokyo Economic Research Fund and the Committee for Savings Promotion for their financial support.

[1] For example, see *Keizai Hakusho*, fiscal 1960, pp. 27–28. However, Professor Miyohei Shinohara has written: "An important clue to understanding Japanese growth lies in the rate of her export expansion," and "a search for the secret of Japanese growth without examining her exports is doomed to failure"—thus emphasizing the importance of exports in explaining Japanese postwar growth. See Miyohei Shinohara, *Kōdo Seichō no Himitsu* (Nihon Keizai Shimbun-sha, 1961), p. 33. But Table 7 in this chapter illustrates a considerable difference between West Germany and Japan on this point. For a critique of the Shinohara thesis, see Giichi Miyazaki, "Katō-kyōsō no Ronri to Genjitsu," *Ekonomisto*, special issue, October 10, 1962, pp. 102–103.

[2] For example, Osamu Shimomura, "Keizai Seichō no Tadashii Haakuno Tameni," *Nihon Keizai no Seichō Ryoku* (Kinyū-zaisei Jijō Kenkyū-kai, 1959), p. 231.

policies, there seems reason to believe that in the case of Japan the government has assumed a disproportionate share of influence relative to the experiences of other countries.

In this paper we shall first examine a simple theoretical model to be used as a frame of reference for discussions in the following sections on the ways and means of fiscal and monetary policy in the postwar context, with special reference to the manner in which the policy has affected Japan's growth. This paper, however, does not deal with the closely related and extremely important problem of what economic as well as social forces have supported the policy of the government.

GROWTH AND A POLICY MODEL

Production is induced by demand. Without demand, therefore, economic growth cannot be expected. In the absence of an inflationary gap, a policy towards the creation of sufficient, effective demand is a prerequisite of growth policy in general. It should be noted that we speak here not so much of components of effective demand—such as personal consumption expenditures (C), private investment (I), and government expenditures (G)—as of *sufficiency* of that effective demand. As long as the condition of sufficient demand is met,[3] the higher the rate of capital accumulation, the faster will be the rate of growth.[4] This suggests the importance of a growth policy, be it with respect to public or private sectors, that suppresses consumption in order to encourage investment expenditures. Let us examine this point in greater detail. Under a mixed economic system, C, I, and G are all dependent upon fiscal and monetary policy parameters. Let $\overline{Y}$[5] stand for the full-employment-level output that can be produced in a unit of time with a given set of technology and resources (labor and capital) and without inflation, G for government spending determined in accordance with a fiscal policy, t and t' for tax policy parameters, and i for the monetary policy parameter. Then, for the economy to achieve a stable growth,

$$\overline{Y} = C(\overline{Y}, t, [i]) + I(\overline{Y}, t', i) + G \qquad (1)$$

[3] As will be examined later, it is not easy to fulfill this condition over the long run.

[4] As is well known, the growth rate = output coefficient (reciprocal of the marginal capital coefficient) × the rate of accumulation. Therefore, the growth rate depends upon the rate of accumulation as well as the output coefficient. We assume here, however, that the capital coefficient (or its reciprocal, the output coefficient) remains constant within a time period in question or changes only slightly. The capital coefficient varies from country to country; but in a given country it varies only slowly over a period of time if the effects of cyclical fluctuations are removed.

[5] Keynes himself has pointed out the possibility of a series of semi-critical points at which an increase in effective demand is bound to induce wage and price inflation even before factors become fully employed. (J. M. Keynes, *The General Theory of Employment, Interest, and Money* [1936], chapter 21.) Keynesian semi-inflation and creeping inflation are, of course, serious problems associated with growth. We assume, however, that no conspicuous inflation is to occur prior to the point of full and complete factor utilization.

must be established. In the first term of the right side of the equation i appears in a bracket because, in an economy where consumer finance is well-developed and extensive, the government's selective monetary policy can affect consumption expenditures via influence over down-payment ratios, terms of payment, and the like.

We can rewrite (1) as

$$\overline{Y} - C(\overline{Y}, t, [i]) - G \equiv S + (T - G) = I(\overline{Y}, t', i) \qquad (2)$$

In (2), T stands for tax and other revenues to the government. We may consider G (total government expenditures) as consisting of G_C (government consumption expenditure) and G_I (government invest-ment expenditure). Since $G = G_C + G_I$, (2) can be rewritten as

$$\overline{Y} - C(\overline{Y}, t, [i]) - G_C \equiv S + (T - G_C) = I(\overline{Y}, t', i) + G_I \qquad (3)$$

$S + (T - G_C)$ corresponds to gross savings in the National Income statistics.

Let us assume that the government attempts to promote capital accumulation and growth by way of an easy-credit policy, authoriza-tion of higher depreciation charges, an increase in government invest-ment expenditures, and so forth. Investment will naturally rise. But unless the government simultaneously implements a policy towards encouraging savings, *ex ante* investment in the left side of (3) will exceed ex ante saving in the right side of (3), thus generating an infla-tionary gap. This implies that the government has the double-edged task of encouraging private and public investments while suppressing private and government consumption expenditures in order to promote capital accumulation without inflation and external imbalance. This, in short, is the essence of the principle of "easy money with surplus budget," often advocated as an approach to effective growth policy.[6]

The success of such policy depends, first of all, upon the degree to which private investment responds to changes in policy parameters, such as money supply, the rate of interest, legal depreciation rates, and corporate income tax rates. If private investment fails to respond, the successful implementation of growth policy cannot be hoped for. As is well known, a negative view on the effectiveness of monetary policy has persisted since the 1930's. More recently, however, we have witnessed a tendency to reconsider this view. For example, studies, such as one by Meyer and Kuh and the Radcliffe Report, seem to indicate that the importance of the liquidity position (e.g., the quick ratio à la Meyer and Kuh) for investment decision-making is much

---

[6] The same emphasis appears also in Paul A. Samuelson, "The New Look in Tax and Fiscal Policy," *Federal Tax Policy for Economic Growth and Stability*, Joint Economic Committee Report (1955), pp. 229–234. Generally speaking, it is more difficult to measure the output effect of government investment expenditure than that of private investment expenditure. Still, we find it hard to accept the view that there are basic qualitative differences between the two. Government investment should be differentiated from government consumption, and the former should be treated together with private investment.

greater than previously believed.[7] No similar empirical studies have
been conducted to substantiate this thesis with respect to Japan. But
we may safely assume that the government's "low interest-rate" policy
has had a considerable impact upon postwar investment behavior in
Japan.

With regard to the direct effects of corporation taxes upon investment, we can give no simple, categorical answers, inasmuch as they
involve complex problems of tax incidence and distribution of risks.
We are certain, however, that government measures such as the Special
Depreciation System and the Accelerated Depreciation Act have favored growth industries and have contributed to the expansion of
private investment activity in general.[8]

A second problem affecting the success of the easy-money-with-surplus-budget approach to growth policy is that (a) in the short run,
due to the labor-shortage-induced rise in wages as the economy approaches a full-employment level, the country may suffer a cost-pushed
inflation unless technological progress makes possible sufficient capital
substitution for labor, while (b) in the long run, the country may
witness a gradual slackening of growth rates along with a decline
in population. The third difficulty is that in the long run capital
accumulation results in higher labor productivity and hence in a
stronger international competitive position of the country; but in the
short run accelerated investment necessary for capital accumulation
is prone to induce a deterioration in the balance of payments. The
fourth problem concerns the danger that the vigorous investment
promotion policy is bound to generate inflationary gaps, since it is
likely to touch off a spiral of "induced" investments.

Finally, let K be the stock of capital, and $I(Y, K, i, t')$ be the
investment function. If $\dfrac{\partial I}{\partial K} < 0$, whenever there is a small decline
in the rate of income growth, the increase in the stock of capital
tends to exert a negative pressure on investment. Then, unless the
investment elasticity with respect to policy parameters such as i and t'
is very high, and/or unless the government undertakes an extraordinarily rigorous investment promotion policy via fiscal and monetary
measures (the lowering of i and t' as well as an increase in G_I), there is
imminent danger of slackening investment and slower growth rates.
The likelihood of this danger, it should be noted, is particularly
strong in a period where the level of replacement demand is low

[7] Cf. J. Meyer and E. Kuh, "Acceleration and Related Theories of Investment,"
Review of Economics and Statistics (August 1955), pp. 217–230; J. Meyer and E. Kuh,
The Investment Decision (1957); and *Report of the Committee on the Working of
the Monetary System* (1959), chapter 6.

[8] For this point, see Richard Goode, *The Corporation Income Tax* (1951), p. 216;
Evsey D. Domar, "Depreciation, Replacement, and Growth," *Economic Journal*,
Vol. 63 (March 1953), 1–32, and "The Case for Accelerated Depreciation," *Quarterly
Journal of Economics*, Vol. 67 (November 1953), 493–519; and Robert Eisner, "Ac-
celerated Amortization, Growth, and Net Profit," *American Economic Review*, Vol.
66 (November 1952), 533–544.

(hence the necessity for greater net investment), following a phase of accelerated investment and growth.[9]

As the foregoing simple analysis indicates, the problems surrounding fiscal and monetary policy with respect to growth are many. From a macro-viewpoint, however, those problems center around one question: How to achieve a balance between the stabilizing factors in the left side of equation (3) and the investment factors in the right side of equation (3) in order to maintain a continually high rate of growth?[10]

The Role and Characteristics of Postwar Fiscal and Monetary Policy

Many excellent papers have been written on postwar fiscal and monetary policy. However, they tend to concentrate on the separate roles and characteristics of fiscal as against monetary policy. What seems needed is a more unified analysis of the overall impact of fiscal-monetary measures upon postwar growth. In the following sections we shall attempt such an integrated approach in examining growth aspects (1) of fiscal policy, (2) of monetary policy, and (3) monetary aspects of fiscal policy.

Characteristics of Postwar Fiscal Policy

We may first point out as a main characteristic of postwar fiscal policy that since the 1949 Dodge Recommendations the Japanese government has consistently adhered to a policy of "sound" public finance. The interpretation of "soundness," however, has not necessarily remained the same; for example, the government initially placed emphasis upon the overall balance as the criterion of soundness, while in later years the balance in the General Account (Ippan Kaikei) came to be emphasized instead. Issuance of government-guaranteed bonds by public corporations, although widely accepted now, used to be regarded as unsound. Despite these variations in the nuances of the policy, we notice that, insofar as the General Account is concerned, the government since 1949 has upheld the rule of "sound" financing, in both theory and practice, in that it has persistently tried to adjust

[9] Professors Tadao Uchida and Tsunehiko Watanabe have recently estimated the plant-and-equipment investment function on the basis of quarterly data, 1951–1956, and have found that the beginning stock of fixed capital is positively correlated with investment in the following period. From this they maintain that excess plant capacity will not emerge in Japan at least for some time. (Tadao Uchida and Tsunehiko Watanabe, "Nihon Keizai no Hendō," *Riron Keizai Gaku*, Vol. 9, Nos. 3–4, pp. 20–29.) However, they have somewhat ignored the supply side of fixed capital, and we have some doubts whether theirs can be appropriately called the plant-and-equipment investment function.

[10] A treatise on the duality in fiscal policy for a growing economy is found in John G. Gurley, "Fiscal Policy in a Growing Economy," *Journal of Political Economy* (December 1953), pp. 523–535.

the volume of current operating expenses within the limits of current revenues.

Although the scale of public finance has been increasing, thanks to the ever-rising demand for government spending (see Table 1-1), the

TABLE 1-1

THE SIZE OF PUBLIC FINANCE, TAX VALUES, AND REDUCTION RATES

Fiscal year	(1) The size of public finance[a] (100 million yen)	(2) Ratio of (1) to national income (per cent)	(3) Tax values[b] (100 million yen)	(4) Tax burdens[c] (per cent)	(5) Ratio of tax reduction to natural increase in tax revenue to the central government[d] (per cent)
1934–1936 average	43	29.9	19	12.9	
1951	11,366	25.1	9,954	22.0	100.1
1952	13,663	26.9	11,508	22.6	28.2
1953	16,294	28.3	12,786	22.2	58.3
1954	17,467	29.0	13,000	21.6	20.6
1955	17,149	25.5	13,184	19.6	92.9
1951–1955 average		26.9		21.6	
1956	18,106	23.7	15,367	20.1	0
1957	20,019	24.2	17,290	20.9	37.5
1958	22,090	25.9	17,348	20.4	24.8
1959	24,398	24.3	19,833	19.8	12.2
1960	28,536	24.1	25,457	21.5	△ 2.8
1956–1960 average		24.4		20.5	
1961[e]	31,443	23.3	30,736	22.8	16.5
1962[f]	36,336	25.4	31,827	22.2	20.5

SOURCES: (1), (2), (3), (4) from Keizai-tōkei Kenkyū Kai, *Keizai Shihyō*, first half, fiscal 1962 edition, pp. 324–325. (5) from *Kunino Yosan* and Zeisei Chōsakai, *Zeisei Chōsakai Tōshin oyobi sono Shingi no Naiyō to Keika no Setsumei*, special edition, 1960, p. 10.

[a] Sum of expenditures from *Ippan Haikei* and *Chihō Futsū Kaikei* (adjusted for double-counting).

[b] Sum of National Taxes (including profits of government monopolies) and Local Taxes (excluding subsidies, transfer payments, grants-in-aid).

[c] Ratio of the value of total tax payment to the National Income.

[d] "Natural increase" refers to the excess of actual tax revenue (in *Ippan Kaikei*) in a given fiscal year over the projected tax revenue at the end of the preceding fiscal year, before tax reductions are effected. "Tax reduction" refers to a net decrease in tax revenue during the first fiscal year following a tax reform. △ indicates a tax increase.

[e] Estimates.

[f] Appropriations.

ratio of public expenditures to the National Income has actually decreased relative to the prewar average (1934–1936; unless otherwise stated, the prewar average mentioned in the remainder of this paper refers to this period). With respect to tax policy, almost every year has witnessed a reduction in tax rates since the Shoup Recommendations; but because of the strong demand for government spending, the amounts of reduction were within the confines of natural increase (often only a fraction thereof) in government revenue. Consequently, the tax burden (the ratio of tax revenue to the National Income) has been quite high relative to the prewar average, as is shown in Table 1-1, although lower than in the period immediately following the war. A sign of further increase has been observed in recent years. A decline in the ratio of public expenditures to the National Income, combined with a rise in the tax burden relative to the prewar period, may be said, then, to be one important, major characteristic of fiscal policy, oriented towards the balanced-budget doctrine, in postwar Japan.

Such policy, which discourages the expansion of public expenditures (especially of a consumptive nature) as well as private consumption expenditures by not allowing maximum tax reductions, has undoubtedly added to the rise in the gross saving ratio (the ratio of gross

TABLE 1-2

COMPOSITION OF DOMESTIC SAVINGS
(per cent)

Fiscal year	(1) Capital consumption allowances	(2) Retained corporate earnings	(3) Personal savings	(4) Government surplus	(5) Savings ratio[a]
1934–1936 average	38.7	9.7	67.7	−3.2	19.0
1951	16.8	12.9	43.1	27.2	30.6
1952	21.4	11.7	41.1	20.2	27.4
1953	23.9	15.0	26.5	19.9	27.9
1954	31.9	13.3	31.9	17.4	23.4
1955	31.2	13.1	39.9	15.3	25.4
1951–1955 average	25.0	13.2	36.5	20.0	
1956	26.9	18.0	33.1	17.4	31.8
1957	29.0	13.5	34.0	21.3	31.6
1958	36.5	11.7	41.4	21.9	27.3
1959	28.6	17.1	35.3	18.8	35.0
1960	27.3	18.9	33.5	21.9	38.2
1956–1960 average	29.7	15.8	35.5	20.3	

SOURCE: Economic Planning Agency, *Kokumin Shotoku Hakusho.*
[a] Ratio of Gross Domestic Savings to GNP.

savings to the National Income). In Table 1-2 we observe that, of the components of gross savings, surplus in the government's Current Account has risen most conspicuously relative to the prewar period, and this seems to illustrate the role played by postwar fiscal policy in raising the gross saving ratio.

The second characteristic of postwar fiscal policy is that the weight of investment expenditures in total public expenditures has been notably large. Table 1-3 shows the weight of investment expenditures in

TABLE 1-3

WEIGHT OF CAPITAL EXPENDITURES
IN GOVERNMENT PURCHASE OF GOODS
AND SERVICES[a](per cent)

Fiscal year	
1934–1936 average	17.1
1951	42.7
1952	41.0
1953	45.6
1954	41.2
1955	44.6
1951–1955 average	43.0
1956	42.5
1957	44.4
1958	46.3
1959	48.7
1960	49.9
1956–1960 average	46.4

SOURCE: *Kokumin Shotoku Hakusho.*
[a] Includes the central and local governments, Special Accounts, Government Enterprises (Seifu Kigyō), and Public Corporations (Kō-sha).

the government's purchase of goods and services (including the Special Account, government enterprises, and public corporations). We notice that, in contrast to the prewar average rate of 17 per cent (the highest was 23.3 per cent in 1930), postwar weight of investment expenditures in government spending ranges from 40 to 50 per cent. These are much higher than those of many foreign countries.

We may cite, as a third characteristic of postwar fiscal policy, the "Special Depreciation" provision (whose origin actually goes back to wartime) and other tax incentive measures, as well as preferential treatments. All of these measures are designed to promote investment, although the corporation income tax rate, along with personal income tax, has risen as compared with that of the prewar years.[11]

Characteristics of Postwar Monetary Policy

One major characteristic of postwar monetary policy has been a deliberate, low interest-rate policy coupled with more direct quantitative controls. After the Korean War, the demand for private investment rose rapidly. However, Japanese firms, having lost much of their own investible funds during the course of postwar inflation, were forced to seek funds from external sources. As private investment demand mounted, the government, fearing renewed inflation, adopted a stringent policy with respect to the supply of funds to private firms, strictly controlling—by direct as well as indirect measures—the flow of funds, except to those firms classified as belonging to the category of "important industries." Under these circumstances, the rates of interest should have risen, if we were to follow the laws of supply and demand in the loanable funds market. But the government, concerned with lessening the burden of the national debt as well as enhancing the international competitive strength of Japanese export firms, continued to pursue the so-called "low interest-rate" policy; the interest rates remained at a level considerably lower than would have been realized under the condition of a freer interplay of supply and demand forces in the money markets. Consequently, there were a large number of "unsatisfied borrowers," on the one hand, and, on the other, selected firms with sufficient funds acquired externally at low rates that were the beneficiaries of preferential treatment under the "loan rules" (yūshi junsoku) of the government.

The postwar, low interest-rate policy thus differed considerably from a more traditional, easy-credit policy because it attempted to keep the interest rates low not through a sufficient increase in the money supply, but rather by limiting the supply of loanable funds while regulating the legal, maximum loan rates and terms of issuance of corporate bonds under the Emergency Interest Rates Adjustment Act and other similar legislative means. In essence—one might argue —this policy, insofar as its results were concerned, differed little from one of direct government subsidies to priority firms. It also was a policy that gave a strategic advantage to investments within large-scale industries.[12]

Under the above type of monetary policy, the interest rate could

---

[11] For a discussion of the depreciation systems in postwar Japan and a survey of the present system, see Zeisei Chōsakai, *Tōmen Jissensubeki Zeiseikaisei ni kansuru Tōshin oyobi sono Shingi no Naiyō to Keika no Setsumei* (December 1960), pp. 169–186; and chapter 2 in this book by Mr. Fujita.

[12] A discussion of the low interest-rate policy is found in Ryūichiro Tachi and Ryūtaro Komiya, "Wagakuni no Kinyū Seisaku wa Ikani Arubekika," *Keizai Hyōron* (May 1961).

no longer effectively serve its adjustive function with respect to supply of and demand for funds in the financial markets, and the level
of demand for investment funds remained persistently high. As a
result, commercial banks and other financial intermediaries were
led to take advantage of this situation with frenzy—actively lending
voluminous funds, especially to priority firms and promising enterprises, so as to establish closer ties therewith—but often without due
consideration for the cash positions of lenders themselves, as well as
for the solvency position of borrowing corporations. This, in turn, led
to the financial institutions chronically resorting, in order to cope with
the funds shortage, to the Bank of Japan as an ultimate supplier of
loanable funds.

Although an increase in discounts and advances at the Bank of
Japan often acts as an indicator of a tight money supply, we must also
note that the same increase may more aptly be a sign of an ease in
the tight-money situation outside the bank.[13] In fact, as long as city
rates are higher than discount rates at the Bank of Japan, we may
expect a continuing flow of investment funds from the bank. Of course,
the Bank of Japan has been making use of its tools of control, such as
the High Rates Adoption System (Kō-ritsu Tekiyō Seido) and the
Regulation at the Window, but we have reason to suspect that these
tools were not fully utilized under the pressure of the low interest-rate
policy.

Whatever was the intent of the Bank of Japan itself, it is difficult
to deny that much of the voluminous private investment funds was
actually financed by the Bank's credit. It is inaccurate to describe
Japan's postwar monetary policy as an easy-money policy in the traditional sense of that term. Nevertheless, it was an easy-money policy
insofar as it was aimed at fostering particular industries and enterprises by encouraging investments therein; this was accomplished by
channeling to them, under the priority system, large volumes of
investible funds, much of which was financed by the Bank of Japan
credits.

Monetary Aspects of Fiscal Policy

The monetary aspect of Japanese public finance appears in the
balance in the National Account (Kokko Shū-shi). However, inasmuch
as the coverage of this account is comprehensive, including postal

---

[13] See W. L. Smith, "The Discount Rate as a Credit Control Weapon," *Journal of
Political Economy* (April 1958), pp. 171–177. Central bank discounts, of course, provide a monetary ease; and this point becomes clear as one considers what would
happen if, in the absence of discounts, needed funds all had to be supplied from
within the money markets. However, if a comparison is made with the case of a
new supply of funds via open-market operations, we notice that central bank discounts can exert greater control over commercial banks. We may presume that one
of the reasons why the discounts have been heavily relied upon for the supply of
money in the postwar years is the Bank of Japan's desire to retain a sufficient capacity to control the money markets and to prevent inflation in the economy.

savings, two Special Accounts (one for foreign exchange dealings and the other for food management), Public Loans and Investment Accounts, and the like, it is difficult, without proper adjustments, to compare the National Account balance with the surplus in the Current Account (Seifu Keijō Yojō) or with the difference between total government revenues and total government expenditures.[14] For this reason, it is rather misleading to view the National Account balance as an indicator of the government's influence over the markets for goods and services. But it is this account that perhaps exerts the most significant impact upon private finance, since the government's cash transactions are primarily handled through this account. As a matter of fact, the patterns of private finance in Japan follow closely the monthly, seasonal, and cyclical variations in the National Account. In recent years the surplus in the National Account, along with "overloan," has been showing a chronic tendency to increase.

We observe in Table 1-4, however, that the net receipts in public-finance funds from the private sectors have been more than offset by the amounts of the Bank of Japan discounts to the private sectors—the implication of which is little different than if the government had used the National Account surplus to redeem privately held government securities. However, to the extent that the flow of funds from the government to the private sectors as a result of redemption of government bonds may be used for consumption rather than for investment, it seems plausible to contend that, in actual practice, the government's channeling of funds from the National Account to the Bank of Japan and back to the private sectors as Bank discounts has been far more conducive to the acceleration of investment activity in the nation.[15]

A recent trend in Public Loans and Investment (Zaisei Tōyūshi), another area of fiscal policy involving direct government influence over the money supply, has shown a shift of emphasis from investment to welfare expenditures; but up to 1957–1958 public loans and invest-

[14] Postal savings are included in personal savings in the National Income statistics, but not in government revenues.

[15] If the National Account surplus is used to retire government bonds, its effect depends upon the distribution of those bonds: (1) if most bonds were held by the central bank, there would be little flow of funds to the public; (2) if bonds were held by financial intermediaries, there would be a return flow of funds to the public via those intermediaries; (3) if bonds were held by individuals or firms, there would be the same return flow of funds to the public. However, the investment effect of (3) is presumably smaller than it is in the case of (2) because a greater portion of the returned funds is likely to be spent on consumption. Therefore, the maximum promotion effect upon private investment can be expected when the National Account surplus is used to retire bonds previously held by the financial intermediaries or when central bank discounts in the same amount are issued to those intermediaries. Since, in postwar Japan, the majority of government bonds were held either by the Bank of Japan or by various government agencies, the retirement of those bonds did not result in the return flow of funds to the public. Long-term government bonds are often in direct competition with funds for private plant-and-equipment investments. Therefore, the retirement of these long-term bonds, in general, is more investment-inducive than that of short-term bonds.

TABLE 1-4

Shifts in Government Supply of and Demand for Cash[a]

(100 millions of yen)

Item	Fiscal year												Total
	1950	1951	1952	1953	1954	1955	1956	1957	1958	1959	1960	1961	
Government Accounts	312	−354	−24	−949	1,902	2,766	−1,634	−2,597	2,510	1,333	−46	−4,973	−1,754
General Account	−567	−1,176	−871	−368	1,218	−2	−1,008	−1,082	638	−354	−2,757	−2,789	−9,112
Foods Management Special Account	−579	208	661	717	−57	1,069	1	−381	−63	174	324	25	2,099
Foreign Exchange Account	1,458	614	186	−1,298	741	1,699	−633	−1,134	1,935	1,513	2,387	−2,209	5,259
Issuance of the Bank of Japan Notes	850	613	584	186	−39	440	914	225	676	1,203	2,004	2,171	9,827
Government Cash Balance	538	967	608	1,135	−1,941	−2,326	2,548	2,822	−1,834	−130	2,050	7,144	11,581
Bank of Japan Discounts	191	999	634	1,261	−1,652	−2,248	2,491	3,118	−1,759	134	2,206	6,860	12,235

Source: Bank of Japan, *Economic Statistics of Japan*.

[a] A minus sign denotes a surplus in the government account or the government sector's net absorption of the nation's money supply.

ments were heavily geared towards the promotion of private investment, especially plant-and-equipment investment by large corporations (see Table 1-5).[16]

TABLE 1-5

USES OF PUBLIC LOANS AND INVESTMENT
(per cent)

Item	Fiscal year									
	1953	1954	1955	1956	1957	1958	1959	1960	1961	1962
Housing, Public Health, Welfare, etc.	38.2	41.4	45.1	43.8	51.3	51.5	49.3	47.2	49.9	51.2
Highways, Conservation, etc.	32.7	31.0	32.1	37.0	27.7	27.3	29.8	31.3	30.4	29.8
Important Industries	29.1	25.9	15.8	14.1	20.1	21.2	15.2	13.6	10.0	9.5
Export Promotion	...	1.7	7.0	5.1	0.9	...	5.7	7.9	9.7	9.5

SOURCE: Economic Planning Agency, *Keizai Hakusho*, fiscal 1962, pp. 364–365.

We may summarize our preceding discussions by saying that postwar fiscal-monetary policy has been characterized by the government's
attempt to promote private investment via the low interest-rate policy,
Special Depreciation Allowances, Public Loans and Investment System, and the like, and also by its endeavor, through "sound" fiscal
policy, to further capital accumulation in the country. It appears
reasonable to suspect that this investment-oriented, fiscal-monetary
policy has been one of the significant factors responsible for the fast

TABLE 1-6

SHIFTS IN THE COMPOSITION OF GROSS NATIONAL EXPENDITURES
(per cent)

Fiscal year	Personal consumption expenditures	Government purchases of goods and services	Gross domestic capital formation	Gross domestic private capital formation
1934–1936 average	65.5	15.5	19.0	15.8
1951–1955 average	60.4	10.4	27.6	18.8
1956–1960 average	58.0	9.7	31.8	23.4

SOURCE: *Kokumin Shotoku Hakusho.*

growth of the Japanese economy (see Table 1-6). Table 1-7 clarifies
this point through an international comparison of the GNP components for the decade of 1950's. We notice that in slow-growing countries, such as the United States and Great Britain, the weight of

[16] A detailed survey of the role of public loans and investment in capital formation
in postwar Japan is found in S. Endo, "Zaisei Tōyūshi no Taishō," *Kinyū Zaisei
Kōza*, Vol. 3 (Yūhikaku, 1961), pp. 67–116. His views, however, differ somewhat
from the author's.

TABLE 1-7

COMPOSITION OF GROSS NATIONAL EXPENDITURES AND INTERNATIONAL
COMPARISON OF REAL GROWTH RATES
(per cent)

| Country | Composition of gross national expenditures (1951–1960 average in current prices) | | | | | |
	Personal consumption expenditures	Government consumption expenditures	Gross domestic fixed capital formation	Increase in inventory	Exports of goods and services	Imports of goods and services
Japan	59.2	10.1	23.4	6.2	13.6	12.3
West Germany	58.3	15.0	21.5	2.3	21.2	19.2
Italy	67.3	12.9	20.2	0.8	12.7	14.2
France	66.3	14.4	17.1	1.1	13.8	13.9
U.S.A.	63.3	18.2	16.5	1.1	4.6	4.4
U.K.	66.3	17.4	14.3	1.3	21.0	21.7

| Country | Average annual (real) growth rates (1951–1959 average) | | | | |
	GNP	Personal consumption expenditures	Government consumption expenditures	Gross domestic fixed capital formation	Exports of goods and services[a]
Japan	8.3	6.5	6.1	17.8	6.5
West Germany	7.3	7.4	4.9	10.1	13.5
Italy	5.7	4.3	6.8	8.4	8.5
France	4.2	4.1	3.0	5.5	7.4
U.S.A.	2.8	3.3	3.2	2.1	2.2
U.K.	2.6	2.7	0.9	5.7	3.8

SOURCES: *Kokumin Shotoku Hakusho* and U.N., *Yearbook of National Accounts Statistics.*
[a] Figures in this column are in current prices.

consumption expenditures (inclusive of government consumption) is relatively large, while that of gross capital formation (especially fixed capital formation) is rather small. In contrast to these, the records of such fast-growing nations as Japan and West Germany show a relatively small weight of consumption expenditures along with a considerably larger weight of gross domestic capital formation (especially fixed capital formation). Japan, in particular, demonstrates conspicuously small weights of government consumption expenditures and personal consumption expenditures relative to other countries; and this, together with her extremely high rate of gross domestic capital formation, seems to illustrate the impact on growth of the investment-centered, fiscal-monetary policy of the Japanese government.

Given the *ex post* nature of these statistical figures, one might be tempted to argue that the fall in the weight of government consumption expenditures has been merely a reflection of the rapid expansion of Japanese GNP induced by active private investment, which in turn was strongly supported by the rise in government spending. However, in view of the absence of heavy military expenditures in the postwar years, which considerably lessened government consumption demand, and in view of a series of investment-promotion policies in the postwar context, it seems more plausible that the decline in the weight of government consumption has been due to something more real than such an apparent cause as a statistical mirage in the GNP data.

We now turn to some problems that have been associated with growth policy. (We should note that at the outset much of the "growth" policy was not formulated as such.)

MONETARY PROBLEMS IN GROWTH POLICY

Cycles in Postwar Japan and the Role of Monetary Policy

Inflationary or deflationary gaps cannot, at least in theory, be problems in growth policy, provided that economic variables always respond to changes in policy parameters and that the government is capable of effectively implementing the proper anti-cyclical measures at the right time. But erroneous timing and other policy errors, as well as the unresponsiveness of economic variables to policy parameters, can lead to an actual rate of growth that is higher than the warranted rate in the Harrod sense,[17] with resultant problems such as balance-of-payments deficits, prolongation of delivery terms, and price inflation. This has actually taken place in postwar Japan. Table 1-8 reveals the three rounds of balance-of-payments crises and the following stringent monetary policy in 1954, 1957, and 1961.

Excessive private investment was the prime cause of these cyclical fluctuations. But the role of monetary policy in the course of these events deserves mention. While fiscal policy (especially tax policy) has had some stabilizing effects on business fluctuations,[18] monetary policy—as many observers have pointed out—seems to have actually helped intensify fluctuations in the sense that the auto-corrective mechanism in the money markets was considerably impaired by the government's advocacy of the low interest-rate doctrine.[19]

---

[17] See R. F. Harrod, *Toward a Dynamic Economics* (1949), Lecture 3.

[18] For this point, see Economic Planning Agency, *Keizai Hakusho*, fiscal 1962, pp. 30–31—especially Figure 35. Our contention, however, is that discretionary fiscal policy did not have a significant stabilizing effect. In addition to the above *Keizai Hakusho*, see also chapter 10 of this book by Keimei Kaizuka.

[19] The auto-corrective mechanism here refers to a self-adjusting process within the money market whereby a balance-of-payments deterioration and an increase in tax revenue induced by fast growth tighten the money supply, which in turn leads to higher interest rates. The same process works conversely when there is a slowing down of growth.

TABLE 1-8

ANNUAL RATES OF GROWTH IN GROSS NATIONAL EXPENDITURES AND MONEY SUPPLY[a]
(per cent)

Item	Fiscal year									
	1952	1953	1954	1955	1956	1957	1958	1959	1960	1961
(1) Gross National Expenditures (in current prices)	15.3	16.5	7.7	10.7	10.1	12.5	−1.5	20.7	16.2	22.5
(2) Real Gross National Expenditures[b]	10.9	9.5	3.2	11.2	7.3	9.4	0.0	18.3	13.0	16.1
(3) Foreign Exchange Reserves[a]	0	0	−85	31	174	−417	337	460	502	−338
(4) Money Supply	25.7	15.7	3.0	13.5	19.8	4.1	12.0	16.6	20.6	17.9
(5) Cash Supply	12.1	9.5	−1.2	7.1	14.5	4.5	5.9	16.1	18.8	20.3
(6) Deposit-Currency Supply	34.2	19.2	5.0	16.3	21.8	4.1	14.4	16.7	21.3	17.0

SOURCES: *Kokumin Shotoku Hakusho*, fiscal 1951, and *Economic Statistics of Japan*, 1956 and 1961.

[a] Change in the balance at the end of year in millions of dollars.

[b] Real gross national expenditures for 1951 and 1952 are in 1934–1936 prices. Those for 1953 and later years are in 1955 prices.

[c] No comparable figures available due to a different calculation method employed before 1954.

The fifth and sixth rows in Table 1-8 list the annual rates of increase in currency in circulation and deposits at commercial banks, respectively. We observe, first, that in the recovery and upswing phases of the cycles (e.g., 1955–1956 and the second half of the 1958–1960 period) deposits somewhat led currency in circulation. Second, even at times when the balance of payments deteriorated (e.g., in 1953 and 1961) there were no signs of a slowdown in the rate of increase in deposits, and the rate fell sharply only after the adoption of strict monetary control measures. The first observation is consistent with the commonly known time lag between the creation of bank deposits, as city banks expand their loans, and the subsequent rise in demand for currency induced by the increase in production as well as consumption activities. The second observation refers to the recursive pattern of city-bank behavior during the cycles in Japan, in which a mere worsening of the external balance usually fails to bring a halt to the momentum of an investment boom, and bank loans continue to expand until and unless the Bank of Japan finally invokes a series of stringent, tight-money measures centered around the Regulation at the Window.

Under the present fractional reserve system, the banks' demand-deposit creation induces, only after a certain time lag, a subsequent rise in demand for currency, which in turn affects the liquidity position of the banks. However, it is often difficult to tell whether the observed deterioration in the banks' liquidity position is merely temporary or of a more serious, permanent nature. This uncertainty is one reason for the banks' propensity to add to economic instability.[20]

Let us make further related observations on finance in postwar Japan.

(1) Intense oligopolistic competition among city banks in search of stable relationships with large corporations and leading combines has at times made it difficult for them to use restraints, and they have often indulged in excessive credit extension.

(2) Much of the rising demand for new currency necessitated by continual growth was met by the Bank of Japan credit. As this process, together with the low interest-rate policy of the government, became habitual and "built-in," city banks became increasingly insensitive to and uncritical of their own liquidity positions.

(3) In the absence of a well-developed bonds market, the terms of corporate bonds flotation were bound to be arbitrary and haphazard. Prior to the launching of the Corporate Bonds Investment-Trust (Shasai Tōshi-Shintaku), practically all new corporate bonds were sold to commercial banks,[21] and they were, in effect, little different from bank loans.

(4) With a greater liberalization of foreign capital transactions, an

---

[20] See Ryūichiro Tachi, "Keiki Hendō to Kinyū," *Shisō* (November 1962).

[21] It used to be common practice that upon issuance of corporate bonds, dealers, city banks, and the like, after consulting with issuing firms. would allocate quotas

increasing number of city banks have been showing an intense desire to acquire foreign short-term loans,[22] particularly during the tight-money periods.

These developments are believed to have been causing an overall decline in the auto-corrective mechanism in the Japanese money markets.[23]

The Overloan[24]

We shall now turn to a brief examination of the remaining problems, such as the so-called "overloan," business firms' "over-borrowings," the resultant closer ties and integration between city banks and corporations, and unbalance between the short- and long-term rates.

The persistent use of the overloan throughout the course of postwar development has been largely due to the aforementioned investment-oriented (as against West Germany's export-oriented) pattern of growth under the government's "sound" fiscal policy, coupled with the low interest-rate principle that has often made it necessary for many firms to borrow from commercial banks to finance their transactions balances. These banks in turn had to rely heavily upon credits from the Bank of Japan, and, as a result, the Bank of Japan discounts became an increasingly intact institution. In other words, investment-induced growth has meant a steady rise in the degree to which business firms depend upon commercial banks and commercial banks rely upon the Bank of Japan.

Let us pursue this point a little further. The supply of money must increase to correspond with economic growth. But in present-day Japan the sources of increase in the money supply are restricted to three kinds: (1) a deficit in the government budget; (2) a positive net receipt in the international balance of payments; and (3) "credit creation" by city banks. Of these three, the positive net receipt in the balance of payments approximately corresponds, under the existing

---

of those bonds among themselves. The quota of public corporation bonds distributed among all banks in the country used to amount to as high as 70 to 80 per cent prior to the establishment of the Public Corporate Bonds Investment-Trust; but it fell to 44.7 per cent in 1960, and to 64.5 per cent in 1961.

[22] There was a conspicuous increase in the influx of short-term foreign capital after the opening of the nonresident free-yen accounts in 1960. Later, especially in 1961, with the tightening of domestic money markets, Japanese foreign-exchange banks began actively to borrow short-term foreign capital, consisting largely of Euro-dollars. Some banks even began to charge high premium rates on their foreign-exchange loans.

[23] See *Keizai Hakusho*, fiscal 1962, p. 29.

[24] We follow the definition of overloan as "the phenomenon referring to the persistence of excessive lending by commercial banks that is primarily supported by the Bank of Japan credit," as it appears in Kinyū Seido Chōsakai Tōshin, *Overloan no Zesei* (1963).

system, to an excess payment (in yen) to the Special Account for Foreign Exchange Transactions. As we saw earlier, there has been little increase in the money supply due to deficits in the government budget. On the contrary, Table 1-9 shows that there has been a surplus in the government budget in recent years. The positive foreign-exchange balance has been an important source of money supply except when the external balance deteriorated (e.g., in 1953–1954, 1957 and 1961); but, in comparison with West Germany, the supply from this source has been modest, certainly not sufficient to keep up with the pace of economic growth. This leaves only the third source of money supply —commercial banks' credit creation—and the rising private demand for money has had to be met largely by city-bank credits, mostly in the form of bank loans.

Business firms became exceedingly dependent upon bank loans to finance not only their new investments but also their ever-expanding transactions balances. Commercial banks, on the other hand, desirous of establishing firm relationships with leading corporations and combines, found it difficult to restrain their lending activity in view of such strong demands for loans and thus frequently found themselves not only "loaned-up" but also actively engaged in borrowing from the Bank of Japan to offset the mounting cash shortage that developed when deposits were withdrawn. This then was the major cause of the persistence of overloan.[25]

The unique circumstances surrounding the sources of money supply, as well as the institutionalization of overloan, helped popularize the notion that the overloan is a necessary evil that accompanies fast economic growth, persuading banks to adopt an easy attitude towards their lending practice on the one hand, and easing the reluctance of business firms to rely more upon external means to finance their investments on the other hand.

Economic growth that continued at a rate much faster than the government had anticipated brought about an unexpected increase in tax revenue and government surplus, which meant a critical shortage of funds on the part of both firms and commercial banks; the Bank of Japan, as we have already seen, was also drawn into this vicious circle of an endless search for investible funds. The Bank of Japan discounts have increased approximately in proportion to the excess of cash demand over its supply (see Table 1-4); when superficially viewed, this gives the impression that the Bank of Japan has been the sole supplier of necessary currency, the demand for which kept rising with growth. The above, however, is merely an *ex post* relationship, and we should not fail to identify the three (more fundamental) factors, hidden beneath that relationship, which are responsible for the overloan— namely: (1) the low rate policy that promoted private investment; (2)

[25] We cannot apply to postwar Japan a textbook explanation that an expansion of the Bank of Japan credit induces that of city-bank credit. More aptly, it is the other way around; an expansion of city-bank credit induces an increase in money demand, which in turn necessitates a rise in the Bank of Japan credit.

TABLE 1-9

CAUSES OF CHANGE IN THE MONEY SUPPLY
(100 millions of yen)

| Fiscal year | Change in money supply | Kinds of money | | General fiscal expenditures[b] | Foreign exchange balance | Causes of change in the money supply | | | | |
| | | Cash[a] | Deposit currency | | | Credit creation | | | | |
						Total[c]	Loans and discounts	Securities	Time deposits	Bank debentures
1952	3,240	592	2,648	313	384	2,543	7,771	763	−4,579	−434
1953	2,520	518	2,002	457	−493	2,556	7,214	1,139	−4,546	−508
1954	555	−70	625	1,187	−325	−307	3,467	621	−3,733	−280
1955	2,551	421	2,130	1,354	1,591	−394	4,378	901	−4,534	−209
1956	4,244	946	3,298	−607	475	4,376	10,051	1,070	−5,907	−190
1957	1,056	295	761	−1,014	−2,313	4,383	12,050	1,660	−8,048	−480
1958	3,213	450	2,763	498	2,006	709	10,469	1,731	−9,793	−641
1959	4,971	1,294	3,677	613	1,731	2,627	13,786	1,731	−11,620	−1,133
1960	7,208	1,752	5,456	−1,259	1,884	6,583	19,442	5,207	−14,953	−1,284
1961	7,531	2,250	5,281	−2,087	−1,458	11,076	23,928	8,599	−19,388	−1,245
Total	37,089	8,448	28,641	−545	3,482	34,152	113,156	24,609	−86,736	−6,404

SOURCE: Bank of Japan, *Economic Statistics of Japan.*

a "Cash" refers to bank notes and subsidiary currency outside financial institutions.

b "General fiscal expenditures" refer to those from the National Fund (Kokko) to the public, plus the newly issued subsidiary currency (Hojo-Kahei).

c Components of "credit creation" do not necessarily add up to their totals due to the omission of "others" from the table.

easy-credit policy on the part of commercial banks; and (3) the government's upholding of the "sound" fiscal principle.[26]

Although some people have maintained that disparities in the rates structure, along with the overloan, constitute another major monetary problem separate from government policy, it seems more plausible to argue that the problem can be examined more effectively within the context of the aforementioned low interest-rate policy of the government—to the extent that we can interpret that policy as the government's attempt to control the money supply and to deliberately manipulate the rates structure. In other words, if we were to follow market principles, there are only two things the monetary authority can do: (1) determine the rates structure and let the supply of funds be adjusted by the market mechanism; or (2) control the money supply and let the market mechanism determine the rates structure. To control the money supply and the rates structure simultaneously is not only undesirable but impossible. The fundamental reason for the emergence of disparities in the rates structure in Japan is that the government's low interest-rate policy was intended to regulate simultaneously money supply and the rates, despite the above dictum of the market. In short, the inflation of call rates and the widening of gaps between nominal and effective rates has been induced by the same mechanism that will generate black-market prices under rationing and price controls. To state the matter paradoxically, one might say that the disparities in the rates structure have arisen because of the defiance of economic laws against artificial barriers of control. It follows then that any future attempt by the government to correct such disparities by artificial means of regulation, without due consideration for the above market principles, will merely call forth a repetition of past errors.[27]

[26] I have discussed elsewhere the causes of overloan; hence, I shall not pursue this point any further. See, e.g., Ryūichiro Tachi, "Sengo Waga Kuni no Kinyū Kōzō jō no Jakkan no Mondaiten ni tsuite," *Suzuki Takeo Kyōjū Kanreki Kinen Ronbun Shū* (Tōyō Keizai Shimbun, 1963).

[27] For a more detailed discussion of this point, see Ryūichiro Tachi, "Kinyū Seido Chōsakai 'Overloan no Zesei ni tsuite no Tōshin' o meguru Shomondai," *Keizai Gaku Ronshū*, Vol. 29, No. 2 (July 1963).

2

Sei Fujita:
Tax Policy

Since the Second World War most countries have come to rely heavily upon fiscal policy as a means of achieving stable economic growth. The importance of public expenditures to solidify a nation's social overheads such as roads and port facilities, and of government spending to promote research and development in science and education has been particularly emphasized. Under normal circumstances, however, before a government can allocate the resources necessary for such public works without generating inflation, there must be found some way(s) in which to divert those resources from the private sectors of the economy. Borrowing from the private sectors, and taxation, are two standard approaches, but excessive reliance upon the former involves the danger of hampering private capital formation. Therefore, most government expenditures are usually financed by taxes; yet this approach also suffers a disadvantage in that it may seriously discourage private investment and savings. Even work incentives and the morale of management may be impaired by high tax rates. From the viewpoint of a growth policy, then, the optimal tax system is one that will provide sufficient resources for public works designed to enhance social welfare but will, at the same time, minimize any hindering effects that it might have upon the economic growth of the nation. Furthermore, it must offer a positive incentive to those private economic activities that are most conducive to growth.

On the basis of these criteria, how can we appraise the Japanese tax system since the Shoup Recommendations (1949)? That is the main concern of this paper. We shall first take a brief look at the evolution of the tax system since the Shoup Recommendations, to be followed by an examination of the recent framework of individual taxation and the forms by which business income is taxed (particularly the taxation of corporate income). Lastly, we shall discuss some harmful effects of the recent tax policy in order to clarify what problems remain to be solved in the Japanese tax system.

EVOLUTION OF THE TAX SYSTEM SINCE THE SHOUP RECOMMENDATIONS

The Shoup System

The Shoup Recommendations[1] that laid the foundations of the present Japanese tax system placed extremely heavy emphasis upon the equity principle and direct taxes—principally individual and corporate income taxes.[2] The Recommendations also devoted considerable attention to the objective of stable growth.[3] For example, the Asset Revaluation System, recommended by the Shoup Mission and implemented by the Japanese government, had a pronounced effect upon capital accumulation among business firms. We must note, however, that a series of preferential treatments—the antithesis of the principle of equitable taxation—that were later developed and adopted by the Japanese government as a powerful weapon for growth strategy, were not contained in the original Shoup Recommendations. Income taxes, constituting the core of the Shoup System, were patterned after the net worth accretion theory, the principle of consolidated income tax, and the fiction theory of the legal entity.[4] The first two of these three basic criteria had already been adopted in the income tax reform of 1947,[5] but their application and incorporation became more thorough and extensive in the tax reform of 1950.

[1] Shoup Mission, *Report on Japanese Taxation*. To be referred to as the Shoup Report in later pages.

[2] For a survey of the Shoup Recommendations and the following tax reforms, see Yoshio Hayashi, *Sengo Nihon no Sozei Kōzō* (Yūhikaku, 1958), part 2, chapter 1; Takeo Suzuki, *Gendai Zaisei Shi*, Vol. 2, Nos. 1 and 2 (the University of Tokyo Press, 1960); Nihon Sozei Kenkyū Kyōkai, *Sengo Nihon no Zeisei* (Tōyō Keizai Shimpo-sha, 1959), Vols. II and IV; Tetsu Hashimoto, "Zeisei Kaikaku no Jakkan no Mondaiten," *Keizai Gaku Ronkyū*, Vol. 13, No. 3 (1959); and other sources cited in these works.

[3] The Shoup Report (p. 19) emphasized the importance of income taxes for their built-in stabilizing effects. The report also recommended the lowering of maximum rates in the income tax structure and the introduction of a wealth tax (i.e., the net worth tax to be levied against high property-income earners). These were meant to alleviate the harmful effects upon production and investment motives of excessively high progressive income tax rates (*ibid.*, p. 82).

[4] The net worth accretion theory refers to the notion that, assuming that a certain individual spent zero amount on consumption during a given period of time, the net increase in the value of his assets should be regarded as his income for that period. In accordance with this view, not only such regular and recursive incomes as interest and salaries but incomes of a more temporary kind such as capital gains should be classified as taxable income (see H. C. Simons, *Personal Income Taxation* [University of Chicago Press, 1938]; and W. Vickrey, *Agenda for Progressive Taxation* [New York: Ronald Press, 1947]). The consolidated income principle refers to a tax system under which progressive rates are applied to the total of a given individual's incomes: salary, interest, dividends, and the like. Under the legal entity doctrine a corporation, for tax purposes, is regarded as an entity separate from its owners. The denial of this thesis means, then, that all income of a corporation is interpreted as belonging to its shareholders.

[5] Nihon Sozei Kenkyū Kyōkai, *Sengo Nihon no Zeisei*, pp. 6–8.

Under the 1950 reform, for example, temporary incomes, like retirement income, forestry income, and capital gains, could be averaged out over several years; but their total was to be added to all other incomes before the application of the income tax rates.[6] Moreover, capital gains taxation was expanded to cover gratuitous transfers of assets by inheritance or gift. Under the previous system the taxpayer had been permitted to separate interest income from other income and elect 60 per cent withholding at source, but this system was abolished on the premise that it violated the principles of consolidated income taxation.

The third basic criterion, the entity legal fiction theory, was thoroughly adopted in Japan for the first time in the Shoup tax system. In other words, standing on the interpretation that the corporate income tax is merely a form of broad taxation at source against a shareholder's share of the profits of a corporation, a credit (called a "deduction from tax") of 25 per cent of dividends received against the amount of individual income tax—computed in accordance with the consolidation of these dividends with other income—was recognized, while the preexisting system of withholding at source against dividend income was abolished.[7] On the other hand, from the standpoint that the retention of corporate earnings means postponing taxation of the income attributable to the shareholders, 2 per cent interest tax per annum was levied against the undistributed profits of corporations (in the case of family-owned corporations, 7 per cent against the amount of their retained earnings after the first 500,000 yen). In addition, dividends received by one corporation from another were not to be included in income, and the corporation tax on liquidation income was repealed.

The Tax System since 1951

Reforms since 1951 may be said to be a series of additions to, and partial revisions of, the Shoup System. The need for lessening the burden of individual income taxes, in particular, has been emphasized. Almost every year has witnessed an increase in basic exemptions and exemptions for dependents, as well as a reduction in the progressive rates. Consequently, the exemption point up to which income is tax-free has risen markedly, while the effective rates have become considerably lower than before. Table 2-1 shows changes in real, tax-free income (in 1960 prices) of a wage-salary earner's family of five with three children.

According to this table, tax-free income in 1960 was approximately 2.6 times as much as it was in 1950. This rate of increase is higher

[6] Prior to 1950 a half of these temporary incomes was to be added to other incomes as a simplified means of avoiding an unfairly excessive tax assessment resulting from a mechanical application of the effective progressive rates.

[7] A 15 per cent deduction on dividends was allowed as early as 1948. This, however, was a provisional arrangement designed primarily to encourage stock investments.

than that for both real personal income and real personal consumption expenditures on a per capita basis (about 2.0 times). Particularly notable is the rate of increase from 1950 through 1953. It is clear from the table that the effective income tax rate (the ratio of income tax to income before tax) has considerably declined in the 1950's. To illustrate this trend, we have calculated from the government's *Family Budgetary Survey Report* (*Kakei Chōsa Hōkoku*) shifts in real income tax rates for workers' families (the national average for all city wage- and salary-earners' families); the results show that the rate decreased from approximately 6.6 per cent in 1953 to 3.4 per cent in 1960. Furthermore, during 1954–1959 the individual income tax continued to decrease each year even in terms of its absolute value.

Another noteworthy aspect of the individual income tax system since 1950 is the government's initiation of a series of special measures for personal savings promotion and other policy objectives. This meant some conspicuous modifications of the basic framework of the Shoup System, and much of the original logical consistency in the system was lost. During 1952–1954, for example, the government began to discard the principle of consolidated income taxation by setting separate rates for retirement income, interest income, and income from forestry. In 1953 capital gains on securities were made tax-free, and revival of the previous system of taxing one-half of other capital gains as well as of all temporary incomes meant a partial abandonment of the net worth accretion theory. Again, restoration of withholding at source against dividend income (fiscal 1951) and the policy-oriented increase in the rate of the dividend credit (1955) were inconsistent with the fiction theory of the legal entity. That aspect of the reform of the Shoup System which pertains to the policy objective of promoting personal savings will be dealt with in the next section.

Corporation tax rates were raised during the Korean boom, and although they have been gradually lowered in subsequent years, the extent of the reduction has been far less than it has been in the case of individual income taxes (see Table 2-2). We must note, however, that some significant changes have taken place in the corporate tax system itself. Abolition of the interest tax on undistributed profits (of ordinary corporations in 1951, and of family-owned corporations in 1954), revival of the corporation tax on liquidation income (in 1953), and an overall reduction in the rates structure are examples of those changes which signify a retreat from the position taken by the fiction theory. The prior method of adjusting double taxation of dividend income at the shareholder's level was partially revived in 1961 by adopting the device of reducing the corporate tax rate on income later paid out as dividends. Furthermore, the government has initiated a series of incentive measures specifically designed to promote tech- nological progress and rationalization of business firms by remolding rules and regulations that affect capital consumption allowances, cumulation of internal savings, and the raising of investible funds by the corporations. These incentive measures will be discussed in greater

TABLE 2-1

SHIFTS IN REAL TAX-FREE INCOME, 1950–1962
(A wage-salary earner's family with three children)

Fiscal year	Tax-free income in 1960 prices (ten thousand yen)	Annual rates of increase (per cent)
1950	12.7	...
1951	15.5	22.4
1952	18.5	18.7
1953	20.8	12.6
1954	22.2	6.7
1955	24.1	8.8
1956	24.9	3.0
1957	27.5	10.5
1958	28.3	2.9
1959	32.5	14.8
1960	32.8	1.0
1961	37.1	13.2
1962	36.3	−2.1

SOURCE: Taxable minimum incomes shown in Table 26 (p. 33) in *Zeisei Chōsakai Tōshin Bessatsu*, December 1961. Adjusted for the 1960 all-city consumer goods prices.

detail in a later section of this paper. In the area of indirect taxes, except for an increase in the gasoline and light-oil taxes, there had been few significant changes prior to fiscal 1962, when the rates on liquor, commodities, and entertainment were considerably reduced.

Let us now examine how these changes in the tax structure have influenced the size as well as the composition of tax revenue in the course of the nation's economic growth. For the decade 1950–1960 the rates of increase in various components of the national tax revenue were: 1.77 times for the income tax; 3.26 times for the indirect taxes; and 6.84 times for the corporation taxes.[8]

The rate of increase for income tax revenue was the lowest of the three because there were frequent major income tax reductions during this decade. The high rate exhibited by the corporation tax revenue is a reflection of the fact that during this period corporation income increased 6 times over—in sharp contrast to personal income and personal consumption expenditures, both of which increased approximately 3 times over.

Figure 2-1 illustrates changes in the composition of national tax revenue induced by the differential rates of increase in its components. Inasmuch as the weight of direct taxes other than the income tax and the corporation tax (e.g., inheritance tax, revaluation tax, and the like) in the national tax revenue is negligible, we may safely presume that the "other taxes" in Figure 2-1 consist mostly of indirect taxes.

[8] Zeisei Chōsakai, *Shingi no Naiyō oyobi Keika no Cetsumei* (December 1961), p. 24, Table 20.

TABLE 2-2

CHANGES IN CORPORATION TAX RATES[a] SINCE 1950

Fiscal year of reform

1950	1952	1955	1957	1958	1961
35%	42%	35% for an annual income of less than 500,000 yen	35% for an annual income of less than 1,000,000 yen	33% for an annual income of less than 2,000,000 yen	33% for an annual income of less than 2,000,000 yen
					24% for dividends
		40% for income after the first 500,000 yen	40% for income after the first 1,000,000 yen	38% for income after the first 2,000,000 yen	38% for income after the first 2,000,000 yen
					28% for dividends

SOURCE: Nihon Sozei Kenkyū Kyōkai, ed. *Zeisei Kenkyū Sankō Shiryō Shū*, various fiscal years.

[a] Tax rates for annual income of ordinary corporations.

This implies that, contrary to the intent of the Shoup Mission, there has been a decline in the relative importance of direct taxes—as against indirect taxes—in the sphere of individual taxation. Essentially the same can be said of the composition of tax revenue inclusive of

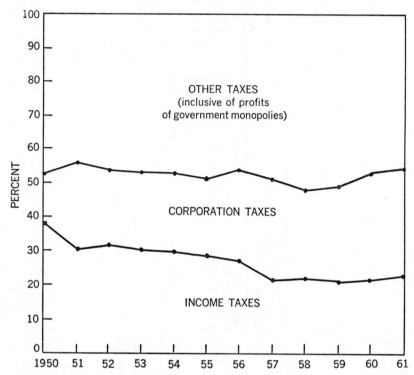

Fig. 2-1. Composition of national tax revenue, 1950–1961. Source: adapted from Nihon Sozei Kenkyū Kyōkai, ed. *Zeisei Kenkyū Sanko Shiryō Shū,* various fiscal years.

local taxes.[9] A shift in emphasis from direct to indirect taxes may then be identified as a major characteristic of tax policy in the 1950's.

If we combine the corporation tax and the income tax, the ratio of that sum to total national tax remains little changed in 1963 relative to 1950. Since, however, the elasticity of income tax revenue with respect to the National Income is believed to be higher than that of the consumption tax,[10] the weight of direct taxes in 1963 would have

[9] If we include local taxes, the ratio of indirect taxes to direct personal taxes was 98.6 per cent in 1950, and for 1960 is estimated to be 175.9 per cent. (*1961-nen Zeisei Chōsakai Tōshin Bessatsu,* p. 19, Table 16.)

[10] Under the assumption that there were no tax reforms, annual average rates of increase in the components of the national tax revenue for 1950–1960 are estimated to have been: 32.3 per cent for the income tax at the origin; 16.2 per cent for the declared income tax; 24.6 per cent for the corporation tax; 15.7 per cent for indirect taxes; and 21.8 per cent for the total tax revenue. As against these, the average rate of increase in the National Income was 13.1 per cent. (*1961-nen Zeisei Chōsakai Tōshin Bessatsu,* p. 14, Table 13.)

been much greater had there been no major income tax reductions.

The ratio of tax revenue (inclusive of local taxes) to the National Income during the decade of the 1950's remained stable within a range of 20 to 22 per cent. Behind this stable ratio lay, however, a series of reforms that considerably altered the original structure of the Shoup System. Of numerous factors, both economic and political, that motivated those reforms,[11] perhaps the most significant for our purpose is the extreme importance attached by the government to the goal of accelerated economic growth during the era following the peace treaty. How, and to what extent, has the Japanese tax policy affected growth over the past ten years or so? We shall now deal with this question, examining first the effects of individual taxation.

THE STRUCTURE OF INDIVIDUAL TAXATION

Effects on Personal Savings

One significant factor behind Japan's rapid growth after the war is the high ratio, relative to other countries, of her gross national savings to the GNP (or GDP). Most noteworthy is the rate of personal savings, which has been extraordinarily high in comparison with that of other advanced countries.[12] The average propensity to save (expressed as a ratio of personal saving to disposable personal income) was approximately 15 per cent for the decade of the 1950's and was in the neighborhood of 16 per cent for the period 1950–1961 (see Table 8-2 in chapter 8 of this book). These propensities are considerably higher than those in other leading, industrialized countries (see Table 8-1 in chapter 8). The propensity during the second half of the 1950's was greater than it was in the first half, and it showed a persistent upward-rising tendency throughout the entire decade.

In what way has tax policy contributed to the positive trend in personal savings? We shall first focus our attention on the effect of the increased dependency upon indirect consumption taxes in the area of individual taxation and on the effect of the introduction and solidification of savings promotion measures within the framework of income taxes.

It is generally believed that the progressive income tax tends to discourage saving to a greater extent than do the more indirect kinds of personal tax. This belief is usually supported by the following three arguments.[13]

[11] Cf. M. Bronfenbrenner and K. Kogiku, "The Aftermath of the Shoup Tax Reforms," *National Tax Journal* (September and December, 1957); and Sei Fujita, "Shotoku Kazei no Seijiteki Genkai," *Handai Keizai Gaku*, Vol. 11, Nos. 1-2 (1961).

[12] Cf. U.N., *World Economic Survey*, 1960, 1961, chapter 1; R. Komiya, "Sengo Nihon no Shihon Chikuseki Ritsu," *Keizai Kaku Ronshū*, Vol. 29, No. 2 (July 1963); and chapter 8 of this book.

[13] See R. Goode, "Taxation of Savings and Consumption in Underdeveloped Countries," *National Tax Journal* (December 1961), pp. 306–311.

(1) With respect to the distribution of tax burdens in terms of income brackets, the progressive income tax usually gives a greater burden to high-income earners than do indirect consumption taxes. If we assume that any tax will decrease saving by an amount equal to the product of the tax value times the marginal propensity to save, and that the marginal propensity to save is an increasing function of income, it follows, then, that the higher the degree of dependence of a given tax system upon the progressive income tax, the greater will be the decline in total personal savings induced by a given amount of tax.

(2) With respect to a given income bracket, the greater the average propensity of an individual to save, the less the burden of the consumption tax he must bear. On the other hand, in the case of the income tax, the average propensity to save is not itself directly affected by the tax value.[14] To the extent we can assume that those taxpayers who have a high average propensity to save also tend to have a high marginal propensity to save, we may hold that the progressive income tax is more prone to hamper personal saving than are indirect taxes.[15]

(3) The progressive income tax reduces the rate of real (after-tax) yield on savings as the marginal tax rate goes up. In the case of the consumption tax, however, the postponement of consumption simultaneously means the postponement of tax payment; the rate of real yield on present saving for the purpose of future consumption remains unaffected. Present saving with no specific intent as to its future uses

---

[14] Assuming that those taxpayers whose average propensity to save is low tend to have a larger number of dependents than the average, the tax burden and the average propensity to save move in the same direction.

[15] These two arguments assume that the following household consumption function is relevant with respect to both the indirect consumption tax and the income tax. $C = a + c(Y - T)$ where C = consumption in factor prices, a = constant, c = marginal propensity to consume, Y = personal income, T = tax. It is questionable that the indirect tax can be incorporated into this sort of consumption function. Therefore, we may formulate an alternative household consumption function based upon the Brown formula. (E. C. Brown, "Analysis of Consumption Taxes in Terms of the Theory of Income Determination," *American Economic Review* [March 1950], pp. 74–89.)

$$C = a + \frac{cY}{1 + T_i/C}$$

where T_i = the indirect tax, and it is assumed that the price level in the absence of the consumption tax equals 1. According to this consumption function, the value of a decrease in saving due to the given indirect tax equals:

$$T_i \left(1 - c \times \frac{Y}{C + T_i} \right)$$

This value should be viewed as a decreasing function of income, even if c is constant and independent of the income level. It is at low income brackets, where saving is zero $(Y = C + T_i)$, that the above value equals the value of decrease in saving, $T_d(1 - c)$, induced by the same amount of income tax (rather than indirect tax). The Brown function implies then that the progressive income tax has a greater negative effect on saving than the indirect tax, even under the assumption of constant marginal propensity to consume.

is actually encouraged by the consumption tax because such saving enables the taxpayer to avoid the tax. The differential effects of the consumption, as against progressive income, taxes become particularly conspicuous in the higher income brackets where the marginal income tax rates are higher. Assuming that the interest elasticity of personal savings by those who belong to the high-income brackets is sufficiently high, the substitution effect between saving and future consumption is conducive to a higher rate of saving under the consumption tax than under the progressive income tax.

Negative effects on savings of the progressive income tax can be alleviated by reducing tax rates on interest income from savings or on the saved portion of personal income. However, unless counteracted by a set of rules limiting gains to the wealthy from such reductions, these measures lead to a shift in the distribution of tax incidence in favor of those in the high-income brackets. For the money balance as well as the average propensity to save are usually an increasing function of personal income. From the viewpoint that these special reductions tend to prevent dissaving due to the fall in the rate of real (after-tax) yield on savings that would occur under the regular progressive tax, it is often held that these measures are more effective in inducing savings than is the lowering of the progressive rates.

We have already observed that tax reduction policy in the 1950's meant primarily a reduction in the income tax with a resultant increase in the weight of indirect consumption taxes in the domain of personal taxes. Another aspect worthy of notice is that during the same period the government also introduced a series of measures for personal savings promotion. A summary of these measures appears in Table 2-3. The government's attempt in this direction was intensified from 1953 through 1955. However, there has, to some degree, been a reversal of this policy since the hearing of the Ad Hoc Committee for Tax System Investigation, held at the end of 1956.[16] On the other hand, some other measures have actually been strengthened during this time; and under the fiscal 1963 reform the rate of tax collection at the origin with respect to interest and dividend incomes was reduced by 50 per cent. We may contend then that even at present these savings promotion measures are in force to a not insignificant degree.

Inasmuch as postal savings, as well as savings via the National Savings Association (Kokumin Chochiku Kumiai), are tax-exempt, only a very small fraction of total personal deposit-savings has been subjected to the interest tax.[17] Concerning stock investment, an exemption for the capital gains on securities has provided a strong incentive. Moreover, the dividend credit system for those investors whose dividend income was to be added to all other incomes and the reduction in the rate of withholding tax for those who could escape the "con-

[16] See *Rinji Zeisei Chōsakai Tōshin* (December 1956), pp. 80–88.
[17] See *1961-nen Zeisei Chōsakai Tōshin Bessatsu*, p. 438, Table 282.

TABLE 2-3

SPECIAL MEASURES FOR PERSONAL SAVINGS PROMOTION

Separate taxation of interest income and rates reduction (Special Measures Act— Tokubetsu Sochi Hō)	The Shoup System—the consolidated tax (the withholding tax rate 20%) 1951—Revival of the Selective Withholding System, 50% 1953—Separate taxation of interest income at 10% 1954—Long-term saving deposit tax lowered to 5% 1955—All interest income made tax-exempt 1957—Revival of 10% separate interest tax on short-term saving deposits 1959—Revival of 10% separate interest tax on long-term saving deposits 1963—Both of above separate rates changed to 5%
Exemption of postal savings interest tax (Income Tax Act— Shotoku-zei Hō)	Maximum tax-exempt (since 1920) postal savings per deposit Fiscal year: 1950 1952 1955 1957 1962 Value (yen): 30,000 100,000 200,000 300,000 500,000
Exemption of interest tax under the National Savings Association Act	Established in 1941. Tax-free deposits are the same as maximum postal savings above. (Replaced with the Tax-Free Small Savings System in 1963.)
Special provisions for dividend tax (Special Measures Act)	The Shoup System—25% of dividends deductible. No withholding. 1951—Revival of the withholding system, 20% 1954—The withholding tax rate reduced to 15% 1955—The withholding tax rate reduced to 10% Dividend deduction raised to 30% 1957—Dividend deduction lowered to 20% (10% for dividends after the first 10 million yen) 1962—Together with the reduction of the corporation tax on paid dividends, the dividend deduction lowered to 15% (7.5% for dividends after the first 10 million yen) 1963—The withholding tax rate reduced to 5%
Tax exemption on capital gains (Income Tax Act)	The Shoup System—the consolidated income tax Exempted since 1953
Income tax exemption on life insurance (Income Tax Act)	Maximum value of life insurance premium deductible from the income tax Fiscal year: 1951 1952 1953 1954 1955 Value (yen): 2,000 4,000 8,000 12,000 15,000 1957 1962 22,500 32,500
Savings deduction (Special Measures Act)	With respect to specified long-term savings, 3% of the amount of savings in a given year (not exceeding 6,000 yen) deductible Established in 1958, repealed at the end of fiscal 1959

SOURCES: Adapted from *1961-nen Zeisei Chōsakai Tōshin Bessatsu* and Nihon Sozei Kenkyū Kyōkai, *Sengo Nihon no Zeisei*, etc.

solidated income taxation" have created additional incentives for stock investment.

The income tax exemption allowed on life insurance (see Table 2-3) has been the sole example of a tax exemption applied to the saved portion of personal income. Two other similar measures—the National Bonds Exemption System (1953)[18] and the Savings Exemption —were primarily in the nature of experiments by the government. The life insurance exemption was used by more than half of all tax-payers in 1959,[19] and it is believed that this system has been contributing to the popularization of life insurance in the country.

These tax-incentive measures for personal savings promotion, together with a rise in the weight of indirect taxes in the sphere of personal taxes, presumably worked in favor of those in the high-income brackets (as against those in the lower income brackets) from the standpoint of the distribution of personal tax burdens.[20] There is also little doubt that much of the negative effect of the progressive tax on saving was removed by these measures. In short, changes in the tax structure during the decade of the 1950's appear to have moved in the direction of raising the rate of saving out of disposable personal income.[21]

It is difficult to prove this proposition, however, either in theory or by empirical testing. For example, there remains much uncertainty as to whether the marginal propensity to save differs significantly from one income bracket to another. We are also in a state of relative ignorance concerning the elasticity of saving by the wealthy with respect to the progressive income tax rates affecting the rate of real yield on savings. In Table 8-2 (in chapter 8) we fail to detect any clear, upward trend in savings during 1953–1955, the period when savings

[18] National Bonds here refer to those issued to finance expenditures from the Industrial Investment Special Account (Sangyō Tōshi Tokubetsu Kaikei). Individuals and corporations purchasing these bonds were allowed special tax deductions.

[19] *1961-nen Zeisei Chōsakai Tōshin Bessatsu*, p. 445, Table 289.

[20] The income tax rates in 1950 for a family of 5 (a couple and 3 children) were 7.33 per cent, 32.70 per cent, and 43.33 per cent for annual incomes of 150,000 yen, 500,000 yen, and 1 million yen, respectively. Since per capita personal income approximately tripled from 1950 to 1960, 450,000 yen, 1.5 million yen, and 3 million yen may be regarded as the 1960 equivalents of the above three 1950 income levels. The 1960 income tax rates at these equivalent income levels were 2.2 per cent, 16.08 per cent, and 25.08 per cent, respectively. Thus, the income tax burden has diminished to the greatest advantage of the low-income brackets. This observation, however, must be weighed against the fact that indirect consumption taxes in Japan work regressively because they refer predominantly to the consumption of liquor, sugar, and cigarettes (see *1961-nen Zeisei Chōsakai Tōshin Bessatsu*, p. 88, Table 52). In view of the regressiveness of the indirect taxes and in view of the government's savings promotion measures, it seems reasonable to hold that the reduction in personal tax burdens has been greater for high-income brackets than for low brackets.

[21] To the extent we can assume that the ratio of saving to income of the independent proprietors and professionals is higher than that to wage-salary income, we may contend that the increasingly lenient assessment favoring the former (relative to the initial rates in the Shoup System) has helped raise the overall rate of personal savings.

promotion measures were most actively instituted by the government. Furthermore, an examination of the ratios of net increase in personal saving deposit to disposable personal income for various fiscal years does not reveal any clear evidence to uphold the proposition that the tax system with respect to interest income had a definitive effect on the rate of deposit-saving against disposable personal income.[22] The rapid increase in the level of per capita real disposable income from 1955 on seems to be a more appropriate explanation of the concomitant rise in personal savings.[23] It is, of course, inconceivable that the rate of personal saving will continue to increase indefinitely in the future. It *is* conceivable, however, that once the economy has reached a path of sustained, rapid growth, the rate of savings will remain at a high level over a long period of time.

The belief in the efficacy of the tax-incentive system to promote savings and the notion that a high rate of saving is vital to the nation's growth are still widely held in both political and financial circles. Our analysis seems to indicate, however, that the effectiveness of such tax measures has been somewhat exaggerated; and the continuation of such measures appears unwarranted in the light of the extremely high level of gross national saving over the past several years.[24]

Effects on Work Incentives

The progressive income tax introduced by the Shoup Mission may have considerably diminished the work incentives of wage-earners as well as those of proprietors. If this were the case, the subsequent shift in emphasis towards indirect taxes and a comprehensive reduction in tax rates during the 1950's meant an abatement of the subjective burden of the tax for the general public; and this, coupled with the lowering of real rates of progression, must have added to the nation's productive activity. There are, however, as in the case of wage-reduction effects, many conceptual difficulties associated with the identification of effects of taxation on the labor supply.[25] With respect to the managerial and professional classes, we must consider not only legal and illegal means of evading taxes to which these people have access but also non-pecuniary incentives that assume an important role for these categories of taxpayers.[26] Even if the tax policy of the

[22] For this point, see Sei Fujita, "Seisaku Genzei ka Ippan Genzei ka," *Kinyū Journal*, Vol. 4, No. 4 (April 1963), p. 56.

[23] This point is stressed in the U.N. *World Economic Survey*, 1960, pp. 26–27, 35–37. There have appeared many other explanations of the high rate of saving in Japan compared to other countries. E.g., see chapter 8 of this book.

[24] It is dubious whether additional preferential measures introduced in fiscal 1963 with respect to interest and dividend incomes were appropriate or necessary.

[25] One reason for this difficulty is the inverse relationship between the income effect and substitution effect with respect to the demand for leisure.

[26] There are two excellent papers by G. F. Break that examine the effects of the income tax on work incentives: "Income Taxes, Wage Rates and the Incentive to Supply Labor Services," *National Tax Journal* (December 1953), pp. 333–352; and "Income Taxes and Incentives to Work," *American Economic Review* (September 1957), pp. 529–549.

1950's had any positive effects at all on growth via the enhancement of work incentives, it is doubtful that such effects have been significant.

The Consumption Tax and Economic Growth

In the domain of indirect consumption taxes, two measures have been enacted that we may presume have contributed to economic growth. One is the commodity tax on durable consumption goods. In the past the government delayed the application of a commodity tax to "new" durables until their domestic market expanded to a sufficiently large scale, and thereafter deliberately low rates were levied.[27] This has resulted in some notable unbalance within the commodity tax rates structure from the standpoint of the tax-absorption capacity of buyers. Viewed from the aspect of growth, however, these preferential tax measures toward those new durable goods whose price-elasticity of demand is high undoubtedly contributed to rapid growth by enhancing the firms' expansion as well as cost reductions, which in turn led to further industrialization of the country and a rise in Japanese exports.

A second consumption tax measure that is believed to have contributed to growth is the use of gasoline and light-oil taxes for highway construction. Revenues from them have been steadily increasing. The Extraordinary Measures Act (Rinji Sochi Hō) of 1953 provided that revenue to the central government from the gasoline tax (introduced in 1949) be used specifically for improvement of the nation's roads and highways. The local highways tax and light-oil tax were instituted in 1955 and 1956, respectively, for the construction and maintenance of local roads and highways. The rates of these three taxes were raised by sizeable margins in 1957, 1959, and 1961, and the revenues therefrom have been rapidly increasing in recent years.

With these expanding financial resources as a background, the government launched a Five-Year Highway Improvement Plan in 1954 with an appropriation of 260 billion yen. In the Second Five-Year Plan (introduced in 1958) the appropriation was raised to 1 trillion yen. In the Third Five-Year Plan (1961) the budgeted work expenditures reached a magnitude of 2.1 trillion yen. Consequently, the amount of expenditures on highway construction has been rising at an accelerated pace (see Table 2-4). The government's endeavor to remove the bottleneck in highway transportation, thus far, has been only a partial success. But without the series of government measures designed to develop and modernize gasoline taxes and coordinate them

---

[27] For example, there were no taxes on transistor radios prior to fiscal 1959 and none on stereo sets until fiscal 1962. The rate of tax on small (14-inch) radio sets was 15 per cent till the middle of 1956 (20 per cent since then), while the rate on tape-recorders for the first two years was 5 per cent, and the rate on small automobiles has been 15 per cent from fiscal 1954 to the present. On the other hand, the 30 per cent rate on cameras and electric fans was lowered to 20 per cent in fiscal 1962.

TABLE 2-4

GASOLINE TAX, LIGHT-OIL TAX, AND HIGHWAY CONSTRUCTION EXPENDITURES

Fiscal year	(1) Tax revenue[a]	(2) Highway construction expenditures	(3) Annual rates of increase in (2) (per cent)
	(100 millions of yen)		
1954	293	610	...
1955	332	626	2.6
1956	409	745	19.0
1957	669	1,049	40.8
1958	783	1,372	30.8
1959	1,108	1,758	28.1
1960	1,391	2,113	20.2
1961	1,902	3,156	49.4
1962[b]	2,264	4,149	31.5

SOURCES: Tax values in (1) were calculated from Nihon Sozei Kenkyū Kyōkai, *Zeisei Kenkyū Sankō Shiyrō Shū.* (2) and (3) are from Kensetsu Shō, *1963-nen Kensetsu Hakusho*, p. 322, Table 6.

[a] Sum of gasoline tax, local highways tax, and light-oil tax.

[b] Appropriations.

with highway projects, it is certain that the congestion of roads and highways, bad as it is, would have been far worse today.

CORPORATION TAX AND ECONOMIC GROWTH

During the decade of the 1950's, approximately 21 per cent (on the average) of the Japanese GNP has been allocated for Gross Private Domestic Capital Formation (see Table 2-5). As we have already observed, the high rate of personal saving has been one of the significant factors responsible for such a high level of private investment. However, about one-half of capital formation has been financed by gross savings within the business sector; the average ratios of retained earnings of corporations and of capital consumption allowances to the GNP during the 1950's were 4.2 per cent and 7.6 per cent, respectively. Capital consumption allowances have shown a steady upward trend in their ratios to the GNP. A similar trend was seen in the ratio of depreciation to sales among major business enterprises in the period 1951–1955.[28]

The ratio of corporate retained earnings to after-tax corporate incomes was, on the average, as high as about 80 per cent on the basis

[28] According to a survey by the Mitsubishi Economic Research Institute, the average depreciation-sales ratio among some 600 firms registered at the Tokyo Stock Exchange rose from 1.84 per cent in the first half of 1951 to 3.60 per cent in the second half of 1955. The ratio by types of business also showed a similar upward trend. (Mitsubishi Economic Research Institute, *Kigyō no Seichō to Shūekisei* [1962], p. 101, Table 4-1, and p. 104, Table 4-3.)

TABLE 2-5

THE RATIOS OF GROSS DOMESTIC PRIVATE CAPITAL FORMATION, CAPITAL
CONSUMPTION ALLOWANCES, AND CORPORATE RETAINED EARNINGS TO GNP,
1950–1961
(per cent)

Fiscal year	(1) Gross domestic private capital formation	(2) Capital consumption allowances	(3) Corporate retained earnings
1950	20.7	5.2	4.9
1951	23.0	5.1	3.9
1952	19.7	5.9	3.2
1953	18.9	6.7	4.2
1954	15.5	7.5	3.1
1955	16.7	7.9	3.3
1956	24.4	8.5	5.7
1957	23.7	9.2	4.3
1958	18.3	10.0	3.2
1959	26.2	10.0	6.0
1960	29.0	10.4	7.2
1961	32.8	11.6	6.8

SOURCE: *1961-nendo Kokumin Shotoku Hakusho.*

of National Income statistics; consequently, its ratio to the GNP was also notably high relative to those in other countries.[29] How has the business tax (particularly the corporation income tax) affected these patterns in the internal cumulation of investment funds by the corporations?

Development of the Depreciation Systems

There are three major actions that the government has taken since the Shoup Recommendations to improve the depreciation allowances for corporations. They are: (1) the Asset Revaluation System; (2) allowance of higher depreciation rates; and (3) provision for "special" depreciations. Of these three, the third action was intended primarily to promote investment for "rationalization" of firms. We shall first discuss measures (1) and (2).

The Asset Revaluation System was one of the most important recommendations made by the Shoup Mission.[30] Its purpose was to make proper adjustments in the tax rates for nominal profits and capital

[29] CF. U.N. *World Economic Survey*, 1960, p. 31 (Table 1-12); R. Komiya, "Sengo Nihon no Shihon Chikuseki Ritsu," *Keizai Gaku Ronshū*, pp. 33–34; and chapter 8 of this book.

[30] For the Asset Revaluation System, see Shoup Report, pp. 123–131 and Appendix C; S. Davidson and Y. Yasuba, "Asset Revaluation and Income Taxation in Japan," *National Tax Journal* (March 1960), pp. 45–58; Yoshio Hayashi, *Sengo Nihon no Sozei Kōzō*, part 2, chapter 2; and Katsunosuke Moroi, "Kotei-shisan no Saihyōka ni tsuite," *Keizai Gaku Ronshū*, Vol. 19, Nos. 6–7 (1950).

gains of business firms attributable to the postwar inflation, as well as
to encourage capital accumulation through improvement of the depreciation systems. The first revaluation was attempted in 1950; but
since the nation at that time was still in the midst of a "stabilization"
crisis following the Dodge Recommendations, and because the revaluation was voluntary as well as subject to a 6 per cent tax applicable to
the revaluation gains, there was only a limited response from the
business firms. Meanwhile, the price level rose considerably, thanks to
the Korean boom. The firms were given several opportunities for revaluation over the subsequent years. Particularly important is the
Corporate Capital Accumulation-Asset Revaluation Special Measures
Act of 1954, under which asset revaluation above a certain limit by
large corporations became mandatory together with reduction of the
revaluation tax and the fixed-asset tax.

As a result, the net increase in the book value of revalued corporate
assets reached a magnitude of 1,343.5 billion yen.[31] Most of this increase is believed to be in depreciable assets. The aforementioned increase in the ratio of depreciation to the GNP or to sales was probably greatly influenced by these asset revaluations.

Let us now turn to the legal depreciation methods with respect to
fixed assets of the business firms. There is an extremely close correspondence between the book value of the depreciations allowed by the
firms and the depreciation value in the tax accounting sense when the
two are compared in terms of their averages over business cycles. Allowance for faster depreciation, in general, reduces the tax amount on
gross profits; at the same time there will be a nominal decline in net
profits after tax and depreciation. This effect is permanently visible in
a growing firm. Therefore, the tax-reduction measure which allows for
faster depreciation, when compared with an alternative of general reduction in the rate of corporate income tax, is usually believed to be
more effective in discouraging external distribution of profits and in
encouraging internal savings by the business firms. Faster depreciation
also reduces investment risks; and the postponement of tax payment
on returns from the investment means a gain through time discount
to the firm. These effects must necessarily promote investment activity.[32]

The depreciation system in the present corporation tax was established as a result of the Shoup Recommendations, and the useful life
tables were completed in 1951. The life span of fixed capital, for depreciation purposes, was reduced, on the average, by 20 per cent under
the new system. Pressure coming from the business circles in later years
for a further reduction led to the government's reworking the whole
schedule in 1962, and a 20 per cent reduction was applied to the depreciation period for machinery and equipment. The legal deprecia-

[31] Mitsubishi Economic Research Institute, *Kigyō no Seichō to Shūekisei*, p. 108,
(Table 4-4).

[32] See Sei Fujita, "Kōsoku Shōkyaku to Kigyō Tōshi," *Osaka Daigaku Keizai Gaku*,
Vol. 9, No. 1 (1959), pp. 133–155, and the bibliography therein.

tion rates allowed in Japan prior to this most recent reform are considered to be higher than those generally approved in the United States and Great Britain—although not as high as those in West Germany.[33] The latest reform is specifically designed to promote capital accumulation and to encourage plant modernization, and it seems reasonable to speculate that the reform will have considerable influence on gross business savings in the future.

Encouragement of the Retention of Earnings

The minimum anticipated net return required to persuade a firm to invest out of its internal saving is generally lower than that on investment to be financed by external means. In addition, a sufficient internal saving enables the firm to borrow more easily from outside sources. Particularly in the case of small- and medium-size firms, external financing involves not only higher interest expenses but also greater risks of losing their managerial control than it does in the case of large corporations. This implies then that the encouragement of internal savings by small- and medium-size businesses is vitally important for their growth and development.

Two measures have been taken since the Shoup System in order to promote corporate retained earnings. One of these was a general reduction in the corporate tax on retained earnings of corporations (especially family-owned corporations). Under the Shoup System, as we noted earlier, there was an interest tax on the cumulated retained earnings in each accounting year. Considered detrimental to internal savings, the interest tax applicable to general corporations was repealed in 1951 and that on family-owned corporations in 1954. Since 1954 the special (interest) tax, to be levied only when a family-owned corporation's cumulated internal saving exceeds a certain limit, has remained; but the eligibility conditions for exemption of this tax were considerably relaxed under the reforms of 1954, 1961, and 1963.

Another important measure adopted during the 1950's to encourage internal savings was the introduction of various tax-free reserves or allowances within the corporation. Of these, the Reserve for Bad Debts (made tax free in 1950), the Reserve for Inventory-Valuation Losses (1951), and the Allowance for Retirement Compensations (1952) have been most extensively adopted by the firms throughout different industries.[34]

A glance at the legal limitations on the amounts which may be entered in or accumulated in the various tax-free provisions and

[33] Zeisei Chōsakai, *Dai-ichiji Tōshin no Shingi no Naiyō oyobi Keika no Setsumei* (to be referred to as *1960-nen Zeisei Chōsakai Tōshin Bessatsu* in the following pages) (December 1960), pp. 176–177.

[34] Other examples of tax-free reserves and allowances are: (1) Reserve for Abnormal Risks (in casualty insurance); (2) Reserve for Droughts (in electrical power supply); (3) Reserve for Defaults (in commodities and securities markets); (4) Reserve for Export Losses (abolished in 1960); and (5) Allowance for Extraordinary Repairs (in shipbuilding and steel mills).

allowances reveals that up to the *Report of the Temporary Tax System Investigation Commission* at the end of 1956 the trend was towards gradual relaxation, while since then the tendency has been to increase restrictions.[35] Accordingly, as is shown by columns (1) and (2) in Table 2-6, the rate of accumulation was extremely high in the first half of the 1950's. Although these reserves are usually classified as liability accounts on a firm's balance sheet, it can be said that they actually function as equity capital. The National Income statistics include the net increase in these reserves in corporate retained earnings, and, as indicated in column (3) of Table 2-6, their percentage of total retained

TABLE 2-6

THE TAX-FREE RESERVES AND ALLOWANCES OF THE CORPORATIONS
1950–1959

Fiscal year	(1) Net increase (100 million yen)	(2) Cumulative total (100 million yen)	(3)[a] Ratio of net increase (1) to total retained earnings (per cent)
1950	112	112	5.8
1951	91	202	4.2
1952	694	896	35.3
1953	1,010	1,906	34.0
1954	1,106	3,012	47.5
1955	1,042	4,054	38.1
1956	1,257	5,310	23.6
1957	969	6,280	22.3
1958	917	7,197	27.7
1959	1,140	8,337	15.1

SOURCE: (1) and (2) from Nihon Sozei Kenkyū Kyōkai, *Zeisei Kenkyū Sankō Shiryō Shū.*
[a] Corporate retained earnings for (3) are from the National Income statistics.

earnings reached close to 40–50 per cent around the middle of the last decade. It will perhaps be premature to assess, solely on the basis of this ratio, the effect of the Tax-Free Reserve System; but, nevertheless, the introduction and wide adoption of the system seem to have had some definite, positive effect on the rate of corporate savings during the first half of the 1950's.[36]

[35] For a survey of changes in these systems, see *1960-nen Zeisei Chōsakai Tōshin Bessatsu*, pp. 281–308.
[36] Suppose there were, instead, a reduction in the corporation income tax equivalent to the loss in tax revenue to the government as a result of the introduction of the Tax-Free Reserves-Allowances System. Since the level of corporate demand for investment was high, much of the resultant increase in corporate profits would have been retained; but the higher rate of profit which appears in the book under the assumption of the corporate income tax reduction, would have exerted greater pressure for an increase in dividend, as well as wage, payments.

External Sources of Owned Capital

The ratio of owned capital to total assets in Japanese business enterprise dramatically declined from the wartime through the period of postwar inflation, and there was little sign of its upturn at the time of asset revaluation (see Table 2-7).[37] The decline was attributable to

TABLE 2-7

OWNED CAPITAL RATIO
IN MAJOR CORPORATIONS

Fiscal year	Owned capital ratio (per cent)
1934–1936	61
1951, first half	37
1952, first half	36
1953, first half	35
1954, first half	39
1955, first half	39
1956, first half	37
1957, first half	33
1958, first half	33
1959, first half	31
1960, first half	29

SOURCE: Mitsubishi Economic Research Institute, *Hompō Jigyō Seiseki Bunseki.*

the fact that the accelerated rate of capital accumulation by corporations called forth an ever-increasing degree of dependence upon external funds, while borrowing from commercial banks and financial intermediaries, as a method of external financing, was not only much simpler and easier but also more advantageous to the firms than was the more orthodox equity financing. In order to restore a more balanced pattern in corporation finance, the government implemented the mandatory Asset Revaluation measure in 1954, and, at the same

[37] When comparing the postwar owned capital ratio with prewar or foreign data, we must remember that there are two factors that tend to make this ratio in Japan rather misleadingly low. One is that many lands owned by Japanese corporations have been—and continue to be even today—very insufficiently evaluated. Another factor is that various tax-free reserves are often included in externally supplied capital. According to the Zeisei Chōsakai (the Association for Taxation Studies), the recalculated value of 31 per cent for the first half of 1959 in Table 2-7 is 37 per cent, adjusting for the land value as of the third Asset Revaluation and reclassifying tax-free reserves as part of internally supplied capital. Similarly, the recalculated value becomes 43 per cent (in lieu of the above 31 per cent) if the land revaluation be made in terms of its current value. See *1960-nen Zeisei Chōsakai Tōshin Bessatsu*, p. 116 (Table 46). Owned capital ratios of major industries in other countries are: 61 per cent for the United States (1956); 66 per cent for Great Britain (1959); and 42 per cent for West Germany (1958). *Ibid.*, p. 115 (Table 45).

time, lowered the corporation tax on that part of corporate profits which corresponds to dividends on newly subscribed stocks—with respect to dividends paid on stocks issued prior to the end of January 1957, corporations were allowed a tax write-off when the dividend rate was less than 10 per cent over a period of two years following the date of stock issuance. This measure expired as of the time limit for its applicability, and the weight of owned capital showed signs of continual decline. In 1961 the corporation tax on that portion of corporation income which was to be paid out as dividends was reduced from 38 to 28 per cent for ordinary corporations (and from 33 to 24 per cent for small corporations).

To the extent that these measures contributed to the firms' greater reliance on owned capital funds and, thus, their greater financial stability, we might hold that they have also added to the nation's economic growth. With respect to the aforementioned 10 per cent tax exemption on dividends of new stocks, the qualification that the exemption was allowed for only two years following the stock issuance (prior to January 1957) must have had some positive effect on the timing of the firms' issuance of new stocks. However, there is no clear evidence that the measure has actually helped popularize equity financing among Japanese corporations.[38] Furthermore, the corporation tax reduction on paid dividends had the negligible effect of lowering the cost of raising external funds (including tax) from 196.9 to 174.5 for each 100 dividend payments.[39] These experiences strongly suggest that a more wholesome pattern of capital formation by Japanese corporations cannot be hoped for without first removing the numerous direct and indirect causes of the firms' "over-borrowing." Inasmuch as many of these causes have little to do with the tax system *per se*,[40] new and stronger tax measures alone will not solve the problem. Nevertheless, a not insignificant result may be expected if the government corrects the somewhat excessive preferential treatment presently given to interest income and, at the same time, allows corporations to write off up to (say) an 8-per-cent dividend rate through a revision of the present corporation tax.[41]

[38] During the period of four years (1954–1957) in which the new stock dividend tax exemption measure remained in effect, paid-in funds amounted to 819.5 billion yen. Payments in the two four-year periods preceding and following the above four years (1954–1957) were 418.9 billion yen and 1,997.6 billion yen, respectively. Of the amount of 819.5 billion yen (1954–1957), as much as 138.8 billion yen was paid in during the last two months of the effective period. (Tokyo Shōken Gyō Kyōkai, *Shōken Gyō Hō.*)

[39] *1960-nen Zeiseido Chōsakai Tōshin Bessatsu,* p. 161 (Table 62).

[40] Besides the accelerated rate of growth of corporations that could not be sufficiently financed by internal funds alone, we may cite as other factors responsible for over-borrowing: the fact that individuals in Japan typically save only small amounts in the form of deposit-saving; managerial indifference to the hazards of over-borrowing; loan rates that were often considerably lower than dividend rates; and the absence of a well-established custom of selling securities at current prices.

[41] There is no need to implement this reform as a special tax measure. With respect to the non-family-owned corporation, all that is necessary is to interpret

Promotion of Technological Progress and Protection of New Industries

From the growth-policy standpoint, the importance of promoting technological progress and assisting the development of new industries cannot be overstressed. The recent, dramatic expansion of private investment—it should be noted—has been but a reflection of waves of new innovations and the concomitant rapid advancement of modern industry. What has been the role of tax policy during the 1950's in this process of Japanese industrial development? We may first consider the selective, accelerated depreciation system. This type of policy has been widely used in many countries after the war as a means of encouraging investment by firms. In Japan, the Special Depreciation System, introduced in 1951 with respect to "important machinery," and another Special Depreciation System, established in 1957 and applicable to "machinery for rationalization of firms," are two cases in point.[42] The sum total of depreciations under these two systems in fiscal 1960 amounted to only a small fraction of the total depreciation by all corporations; but in the area of investment-goods industries, such as iron and steel, automobiles, and industrial machines, there were many large corporations in which the depreciation under the special systems accounted for as much as 30–40 per cent of total depreciation.[43]

Under the 1961 Tax Reform that pronounced general shortening of the statutory useful life-years for fixed assets, the special depreciation allowances for "important machinery" were abolished, and the initial additional allowances for "machinery for modernization" were reduced to one-third of the acquisition cost.

The Special Depreciation for Research and Development (1952) and the Special Depreciation for Innovational Tools and Equipment (1958) carry important implications for growth; but the amount covered under these systems did not reach any significant proportions. The two systems permitted the firms to recover invested funds in a very short period of time and were unified into the Special Depreciation System of fiscal 1961 that allowed for a one-third depreciation within the first year.[44] A corporation has an option of either writing off as loss or depreciating, over a five-year period, special research and development expenses other than those which cover acquisition of

dividends to be essentially in the nature of interest, as they really are in Japanese context. This may necessitate a removal of the present Dividends Exemption System; but such action should not cause any adverse effects in the stock market, provided it is done gradually and with proper timing.

[42] There are many other special depreciation allowances (not mentioned in this paper) for mining machines and equipment, mine shafts, forest conservation, new rental housing, and so forth.

[43] *1960-nen Zeisei Chōsakai Tōshin Bessatsu,* p. 315 (Table 112).

[44] A special 10 per cent depreciation allowance during the first year is granted for those facilities which are used for "development" research, and which are not subject to separate approval under the fiscal 1961 system.

fixed assets. In addition, donations to those research organizations which have been approved by the Minister of Finance are deductible from the corporation income.[45]

In Japan the ratio of research expenditures in science and technology to the National Income is considerably lower than it is in the United States and Great Britain.[46] In the second half of the 1950's, however, the ratio of research expenditures in private industries to sales or plant-and-equipment investments has risen conspicuously.[47] At least a part of this rise may be ascribed to the series of aforementioned preferential tax systems favoring research and development. Inasmuch as Japan's future growth depends upon further development of domestic technology, additional (direct and indirect) fiscal measures for the encouragement of technological progress will be extremely important.

Another measure that has been employed as a means of assisting the growth of new industries is the Strategic Commodities Tax Exemption System (Jyūyō Bussan Menzei Seido).[48] This system granted a tax exemption to incomes earned by specified industries from the sales of "strategic" commodities, effective for the first three years after the beginning of production or upon completion of new manufacturing facilities. This was tantamount to an open subsidy to these industries. The origin of the system goes back to the prewar period, but, as Table 2-8 illustrates, the magnitude of tax-exempt incomes grew steadily during the first half of the 1950's. Synthetic textiles, chemical fertilizers, and plastics are examples of major items that have been "subsidized" under the system; however, we must note that many other favored commodities could hardly be described as "new products." Recently, the government has revised the system to include *only* "new products" and imposed a limit upon the tax-exempt income that can be cumulated by a firm as well as upon the time period in which the exemption is legally allowed.

One quite serious flaw in this system is that it fails to function as an effective "subsidy" except when the firm manages to earn a high rate of net profit within a short period of time. As a result, many firms in Japan have tended to acquire "new products" and already-tested techniques from abroad in lieu of developing them at home on their own initiative. If new product development at home is to be

[45] For other preferential tax measures related to research expenditures, see Akira Uchino, *Nohon no Kenkyū Tōshi* (Jitsugyō Kōhō Sha, 1962), pp. 193–199.

[46] Ratios for fiscal 1960 were: 1.6 per cent in Japan; 3.0 per cent in the United States; 2.6 per cent in Great Britain; 2.3 per cent in the Soviet Union; 1.8 per cent in West Germany; 1.6 per cent in France. (*Ibid.*, p. 249.)

[47] Ratios of research expenditures to net sales in 1953 and 1960 were as follows (in percentage; figures in parentheses are those for 1960): all industries, 0.4 (1.0); electrical machinery, 0.7 (2.5); transport equipment, 0.3 (1.4); precision instruments, 1.9 (1.6); manufacturing, 0.4 (1.1); and chemicals, 0.6 (1.9). (*Ibid.*, p. 147, Table 30.) The ratio of research expenditures to plant-and-equipment investment in the manufacturing industry—according to a survey by the Japan Development Bank—increased from 4.7 per cent in 1957 to 8.1 per cent in 1960. (*Ibid.*, p. 162, Table 39.)

[48] In 1961 the name was changed to *Shinki Jyūyō Bussan Menzei Seido.*

intensified, it seems necessary that some further measures of special depreciation and subsidies be added to the present system.

Export Promotion

After the war the Japanese government was compelled to adopt a stringent deflationary policy several times over because of balance-of-payments difficulties. Direct tax measures to promote exports as a part of the overall growth policy, therefore, have been a major concern to the government. Of such measures introduced during the 1950's, perhaps the most important is the Export Income Deduction System of 1953.

This system was patterned after the Export Promotion Act of West Germany. At first, the system allowed export dealers to deduct from their income 1 per cent of the value of their export transactions, and producers of exported goods to deduct 3 per cent of total revenue from the sales of those goods, provided the amount did not exceed 50 per cent of their net income from such sales. In 1955 the income limit for deduction purposes was raised from 50 to 80 per cent. The 1957 revision allowed additional deductions to be applied to the excess of current exports over 150 per cent of total exports in the preceding year.[49] Furthermore, under the 1959 revision firms were enabled to write off 50 per cent of revenue (but not exceeding 50 per cent of net income) from technology exports. Table 2-8 shows that these steps to strengthen the Export Income Deduction System, together with a rapid expansion of exports, have increased the value of tax-exempt export income.

Table 2-8 clearly indicates that under the Export Income Deduction System both Japanese export dealers and producers of export goods were heavily subsidized by the government.[50] Meanwhile, bitter complaints arose abroad; and in 1961 the government was forced to repeal the "additional deductions" permitted under the 1957 revision. Progress in trade liberalization is making it increasingly difficult for the Japanese government to continue the Export Income Deduction System.[51] The government should perhaps give greater attention in the future to the problems of improving export finance and insurance, while encouraging modernization of Japanese firms through tax meas-

[49] The deduction rates were: 1.5 per cent for dealers; 4.5 per cent for producers; 7.5 per cent for plant exporters. The amount of export income corresponding to the excess export (as defined in the text) becomes the maximum amount to be exempted.

[50] In some instances, more than 80 per cent of dealers' export income and more than 50 per cent of producers' were actually tax-exempt. See *1960-nen Zeisei Chōsakai Tōshin Bessatsu*, p. 327 (Table 116).

[51] In the fall of 1961 the government allowed, as an emergency measure to cope with the balance-of-payments "crisis," additional depreciation for firms whose current exports exceed those in the preceding year. The theory behind this system lacks definitional clarity and logical consistency. It will most likely be an object of controversy in the future.

TABLE 2-8

TAX-EXEMPT CORPORATION INCOMES UNDER THE
STRATEGIC COMMODITIES TAX-EXEMPTION SYSTEM AND THE
EXPORT INCOME DEDUCTION SYSTEM, 1950–1959
(100 millions of yen)

Fiscal year	(1) Strategic commodities exemption	(2) Export income deduction
1950	10	...
1951	36	...
1952	73	...
1953	101	14
1954	107	40
1955	142	83
1956	196	166
1957	272	236
1958	119	198
1959[a]	120	324

SOURCE: Nihon Zeisei Kenkyū Kyōkai, *Zeisei Kenkyū Sankō Shiryō Shū.*
[a] Preliminary estimates.

ures as a means of increasing the international competitive strength of Japanese exports. No less important, if we are to expect a balanced and continual development of overseas markets for Japanese exports backed by high business incentives, is an effective fiscal-monetary policy to prevent excessive booms in the domestic economy.

Many other measures, apart from those mentioned above, have been taken to promote economic growth[52]—although they cannot be examined within the space of this paper. The foregoing survey is sufficient to conclude, however, that one outstanding characteristic of the business tax system since the Shoup Recommendations is that the Japanese government has relied chiefly upon a series of "special" measures, rather than upon a general reduction of tax rates, as a means of encouraging corporate savings and investment, assisting the modernization of firms, and promoting the nation's exports.

SOME RECOMMENDATIONS CONCERNING RECENT TAX POLICY

In this paper we have examined some major aspects of postwar tax policy designed to promote economic growth. Some measures have undoubtedly made a significant contribution to accelerated growth. On the other hand, we have reason to believe that recent tax policy

[52] For example: special tax provisions with respect to liquidation income arising from mergers of certain machines manufacturers where such mergers are believed to strengthen and stabilize the firms' positions (1961); Special Depreciation System to promote industrialization in the underdeveloped areas of Japan (1961); the Special Depreciation System to encourage modernization in, as well as improve, the international competitive capacity of, small- and medium-size businesses (1963). We must wait longer to see the effects of these measures.

has also been causing various difficulties within the economy. Let us take a brief look at some of those difficulties which appear particularly serious.

(1) Each year has witnessed an endless series of partial revisions in the individual as well as the corporate income taxes, not to mention incessant reforms and repeals of numerous special measures. Consequently, the tax system has lost much of its stability and logical consistency and has become complex and difficult to understand. This has imposed an undue strain upon taxpayers who are required to expend more time and energy than ever before for the sheer purpose of fulfilling their tax-payment obligations. At the same time, such a system has provided greater opportunities for tax evasion. As a result, a notable decline in tax-payment incentives has been observed, while the Tax Bureau has been suffering an inflation of administrative costs as well as added difficulties in fair and equitable execution of the tax system.

(2) There has emerged a serious unbalance in the distribution of tax burdens.[53] As a result of various personal savings promotion measures, property income is frequently taxed more lightly than employee compensations. And inasmuch as the majority of special measures under the corporation tax system work in favor of large corporations, more often than not the real tax rates on large corporations are lower than those on small businesses. This tendency was particularly conspicuous during the first half of the 1950's.[54] Tax-payment incentives have deteriorated among many firms, while growth and development of small businesses have been seriously hampered.

(3) Through various special measures the income-tax as well as the corporation-tax base has been lowered; as a result, the statutory tax rate applied to the taxable portion of income has been considerably higher than it would have been in the absence of such lowering of the base.[55] This has encouraged business to search for legal and illegal means of tax evasion. It should be noted that the higher tax rate in this context involves the danger of initiating a certain vicious circle, in that it is prone to generate new political pressure from interest groups for another round of special tax measures.[56]

(4) The popular belief that taxation hinders capital accumulation in the private sectors, coupled with the common notion that the weight

---

[53] See Yoshio Hayashi, *Sengo Nihon no Sozei Kōzō*, part 2, chapter 3.

[54] According to calculations made by the Association for Taxation Studies (Zeisei Chōsa Kai), in 1952 the effective corporation tax rate on large firms with more than 10 million yen of capital was, on the average, 32.3 per cent in contrast to 42.7 per cent on smaller firms. In 1958, the former was 31.3 per cent, and the latter 38.0 per cent. (*1960-nen Zeisei Chōsakai Tōshin Bessatsu*, p. 108, Table 40.)

[55] For example, under the Special Tax Measures of fiscal 1954, the reduction in the corporation-tax base reached the magnitude of 130 billion yen, or as much as about 25 per cent of corporation incomes on the basis of National Income statistics.

[56] For a discussion of this "vicious circle" in the case of the U.S. individual income tax, see J. A. Pechman, "Erosion of the Individual Income Tax," *National Tax Journal* (March 1957), pp. 1–25.

of taxation in Japan is "excessive" relative to other advanced countries, has led the Japanese government to fail to provide sufficient public expenditures for education, public health, housing, and social security.

(5) In the process of lowering the burden of taxes levied on individuals, the government relied chiefly upon the income tax, rather than indirect taxes, for the purpose of individual-tax reductions, and these reductions were often made at most inappropriate times. Consequently, the tax system as a whole has failed to function effectively as a built-in stabilizer.[57]

These adverse effects seem to have been induced largely by the government's obsession with rapid growth, since it has, throughout the 1950's, indulged in a series of revisions and reforms of the original Shoup System as well as of "special" measures—all professedly directed towards the goal of accelerated growth. Removal of these harmful effects presupposes, *inter alia*, a major policy reorientation on the part of the government. Particularly important is a shift in emphasis towards the objectives of economic stability and a more equitable distribution of tax burdens. For example, the principle of consolidated income taxation should receive a wider application than it does today, while much greater attention ought to be paid to the proper timing of changes in exemptions, tax rates, and the like.

No less urgent is a major reexamination and reorganization of the entire tax system so that the system will become much simpler and easier to understand—and less burdensome to follow than it is today from the taxpayers' standpoint. This proposition obviously involves many difficult problems. Questions concerning determination of the "correct" relative weight of direct taxes as against indirect taxes in the case of personal taxes, reorganization of present indirect taxes in connection with general sales taxes, pros and cons of adopting the corporate entity doctrine as the basis of individual as well as corporate income tax systems—these are but some of those problems. With respect to "special" measures under the present system, those which have become obsolete or those whose effectiveness has not been demonstrated should be abolished as soon as possible; and those which should be continued on a permanent basis may best be incorporated into the income-tax and/or corporation-tax laws rather than being allowed to remain as "special" measures.

Any new preferential tax treatment ought to be introduced with the utmost care. No such treatment should be contemplated unless there is sufficient evidence that it will provide a more effective solution than the alternative of a general, non-discriminatory tax reduction, or that it will clearly be a better alternative than those afforded by monetary policy or by revision of government-expenditures programs. A particular policy objective, for which such preferential treatment

---

[57] The tax-free reserve system that allows firms to cumulate their reserves in a boom and to deplete them in a recession, as well as the special depreciation system enabling firms to practice accelerated depreciation during the first year, tends to reduce cyclical fluctuations in corporation income tax revenue to the government.

is contemplated, should be regarded as only a part of—but not the whole—criterion for judgment. As we have seen, any preferential tax measure is apt to induce a multitude of difficulties, especially in connection with problems of tax base and distribution of tax burdens. It is clear from our experiences that the government will find it politically arduous to repeal any preferential measure once it has been introduced. These other problems, besides the specific policy objective, must therefore be duly considered.

3

Hiroshi Niida:
Price Problems*

INTRODUCTION

Inflation of consumer goods prices accompanying Japan's rapid growth since 1959 has aroused lively discussions among many Japanese economists. This paper is a survey of those discussions up to March 1963.

There are three major problems of inflation on which discussants have focused their attention. One of them is how to explain the notable disparity between consumer and wholesale price indexes that has been observed in recent years. Despite the stability of, or even minor falls in, wholesale prices, consumer prices have been rising about 5.6 per cent annually over the past several years. This sizeable disparity between the two indexes is a rather unique feature of the Japanese inflation, and we may go so far as to say that unless this phenomenon, rather uncommon in other countries, first be properly analyzed, we cannot hope to understand fully the recent price problems in the Japanese economy.[1] The second problem is how to appraise, from the

* At the Zushi Conference I read a paper entitled, "Cost-Inflation Riron no Tembō to Nihon-keizai no Bukka Mondai" ("The Cost-Inflation Theory and Price Problems in Japan"). This chapter is a revised version of that part of the above paper which considers Japanese price problems. I expect the first half of the paper to be published elsewhere in the near future under the separate title, "Cost-Inflation Riron no Tembō." I am grateful for suggestions received at the conference and through personal correspondence with R. Komiya, T. Negishi, T. Watanabe, and several others. The work for this paper was financially supported by the University of Tokyo Economic Research Fund and the Central Committee for Savings Promotion.

[1] The phenomenon of disparity between wholesale and retail prices is not restricted to Japan; as is shown in the tabulation below, the same is observed in practically all advanced countries. But the unique characteristics of Japanese price behavior are: (1) the extent of disparity, which is much greater than in other countries; and (2) the fact that since 1954 the wholesale price index has not shown any upward trend. We suspect that, given the exceedingly high rate of growth and wide wage-gaps between the advanced and traditional sectors in the Japanese economy, inflation problems in Japan differ in many respects from those in other

policy standpoint, the recent inflation of consumer goods prices in connection with economic growth and to determine whether price stability should be regarded as one of the important policy objectives. The third problem is what price policy should be selected in view of the so-called "dual economy" in Japan. In this paper we shall attempt a survey of discussions concerning these three problems, following a sequence of three headings: diagnosis; appraisal; and prescription.

Before we begin, let us consider, in brief, the prime causes of change in the relative price structure. For simplicity, we exclude foreign trade and assume a closed economy where perfect competition prevails. In our case a change in the relative prices of goods depends upon one, or a combination, of the following three events:

(1) Change in tastes and preferences of the consumers.
(2) Change in factor endowments.
(3) Change in the production function.

The first change affects both demand for goods and the supply of labor. It induces shifts in the aggregate demand curve as well as in the aggregate labor-supply curve, which in turn will result in a formation of different relative prices. The second and third are changes in the supply factors that determine relative prices and are likely to significantly affect the process of economic growth. The second event refers to exogenously given changes in the availability of factors of production—hence, to the production-possibility curve, or the transformation curve. So long as factor proportions in different industries are not the same, *ceteris paribus*, relative changes in the supply of various factors of production will not cause a uniform, proportional change in the production-possibility curve. In general, an increase in the supply of a factor will lower its price, which in turn will stimulate production of goods in which the content of that factor is large; finally, there will be a relative decline in the price of the goods in question. Change in

countries. Data for selected years are shown for wholesale (W) and consumer (C) prices indexes in various countries:

	1954		1958		1962	
	W	C	W	C	W	C
France	81	83	100	100	113	119
West Germany	92	92	100	100	103	109
Italy	98	91	100	100	101	109
U.K.	97	86	100	100	100	110
U.S.A.	93	93	100	100	100	105
Japan	108	98	100	100	101	118
India	90	87	100	100	115	112
Mexico	77	70	100	100	109	111

SOURCE: U.N., *Yearbook* and *Monthly Bulletin of Statistics*. The base year shifted to 1958.

the production function pertains to technological progress. The rates of productivity increase usually differ from one industry to another, and factor proportions in different industries will change as a result of non-neutral patterns of change in technology. In the process of growth a productivity increase in one sector may lead or lag vis-à-vis other sectors. For example, productivity has been rising much faster in the manufacturing industry—particularly among large corporations —than it has in the service sector including retail trade. Under perfect competition this means that the prices of outputs of the manufacturing industry will fall, other things being equal, relative to prices of products produced in other sectors where the productivity increase has not been as rapid.[2] Viewed from the aspect of factor proportions and provided that technological progress is "biased," [3] differential rates of productivity increase in different industries lead to relative changes in production costs depending upon factor proportions in those industries. If technological progress is capital-using rather than capital-saving, the capital-intensive industry will suffer a rise in production cost as well as in the price of its output relative to other industries where the degree of capital-intensity is lower.

From the foregoing analysis it is clear that even relative prices of inputs are ultimately determined by (1), (2), and (3) above. In view of the wide wage-gaps in Japan, however, we may add a fourth cause of changes in relative prices in the output market: (4) Change in relative prices of inputs.

If the price of a certain input rises relative to other inputs, the production cost in an industry which employs a large proportion of that input will increase—and so will the price of output in the same industry.

These four changes, then, are the main causes of fluctuations in relative prices. With respect to the last three we observe that the differential rates of productivity increase and heterogeneous factor proportions perform an important role on the supply side of the market. Fluctuations in absolute prices of commodities in the real world, reflecting changes in their relative prices, assume either the form of a money price increase in the sector where the relative price has risen, or a money price decrease in the sector where the relative price has fallen—or a combination of the two. What particular form the fluctuations will assume, in reality, depends upon the mechanism for determining absolute prices. On the basis of these preliminary considera-

[2] Even if duality-induced wage-gaps exist (i.e., perfect competition does not prevail in the labor markets), as long as perfect competition persists in the goods market, prices of goods produced in the higher-productivity sector will fall relative to prices of goods made in the lower-productivity sector—provided wage-gaps remain constant during a period of productivity increase.

[3] Under perfect competition, labor-saving technological progress induces a greater increase in marginal product of capital relative to marginal product of labor, which will lead to a fall in the relative share of labor; similarly, capital-saving technological change will reduce the share of capital. Neutral or unbiased technological change implies that relative shares remain constant.

tions we shall now proceed to survey the discussions on the Japanese inflation.

DIAGNOSIS

In explaining the stability of wholesale prices and the inflation of consumer prices, economists seem to agree on the causes of disparities between the two. The common argument emphasizes the differential rates of productivity increase in different industries as the explanation for the gaps between wholesale- and consumer-price indexes. Productivity in the manufacturing industry (particularly among large-scale firms) has been rising in recent years much more rapidly than it has in the various service sectors, inclusive of small retail stores. It follows then that prices of goods in the high-productivity sectors can fall relative to those in the low-productivity industries.

Approximately 80 per cent of items included in the wholesale price index consist of manufactured goods at the wholesale level. On the other hand, the consumer price index comprises not only retail prices of those goods which are included in the wholesale price index but also prices of those which do not generally enter into the wholesale index, such as fresh foods, rent, transport cost, gas, city water, education, medicine, haircuts, commercial laundry, public baths, and so forth. Consequently, the wholesale price index, heavily weighted by manufactured goods, is bound to fall relative to consumer prices.[4]

This argument then explains the disparities observed in Japan between the wholesale- and consumer-price indexes by applying the theory of differential relative prices as a reflection of differential industrywise productivities. Productivity gaps among goods and services whose prices constitute the consumer-price index, however, are no less conspicuous than those at the wholesale level. There are certain retail sectors where productivity rises relative to other retail sectors; similarly, productivity of certain goods at the wholesale level may fall relative to other wholesale goods. It may not be legitimate, therefore, to mechanically employ this simple theory of differential relative prices as an explanation for the apparent gaps between wholesale and retail prices.[5] Yet this approach is not an unreasonable one if we can prove

[4] Cf. R. Komiya, "Keizai Seichō to Bukka Mondai" and "Zoku-Keizai Seichō to Bukka," *Nihon Keizai Shimbun*, January 31–February 5, and May 10–May 15, 1961, respectively; T. Yoshino, ed. *Keizai Seichō to Bukka Mondai* (Shun-jū Sha, 1962); a review of the preceding book by R. Komiya in *Keizai Gaku Ronshū*, Vol. 29, No. 1 (April 1963).

[5] It is, of course, important to attempt a theoretical explanation of the gaps between the two price indexes in Japan. But from the standpoint of the theory of equilibrium, it seems rather meaningless to try to explain differences between wholesale and retail prices, let alone the disparity between their indexes. The matter is entirely different if one attempts to explain the differential relative prices among consumer goods as against those among wholesale goods. We may attempt to account for the supply aspects of the gaps between the two price indexes in terms of the differential rates of productivity increase; but the same is not true for the demand aspect. It will be extremely difficult to establish a systematic explanation of the demand factors responsible for such gaps.

that overall productivity in retailing and distribution, affecting prices of consumer goods and services, has, in actuality, been lagging behind that in the manufacturing industry whose outputs assume a large weight in the wholesale price index.

A no less significant factor to be considered in connection with the explanation of wholesale-retail price gaps is that many major public service industries, such as the electrical power supply and the National Railways, have, in recent years, been suffering diseconomies of scale, and the resultant rising costs in these industries have induced a concomitant inflation of relative prices in the service sectors at large. Also, labor costs in small- and medium-size businesses have been rising rapidly because of the labor shortage, and we may presume that this has led to the increase in prices of consumer goods supplied by those businesses.

Changes in relative prices induce corresponding changes in money prices in the real world; and one would expect either a fall in money prices of the goods produced in the high-productivity sector or a rise in money prices of the goods made in the low-productivity sector—or a combination of the two. There are several points here that ought to be clarified concerning the relationship between productivity increase, on the one hand, and wages, money supply, and price level on the other.[6]

(1) Under full employment, if the average rate of money-wage increase is proportional to the average rate of productivity increase for the whole economy, a stable price level as well as maintenance of full employment can be expected.[7] This situation assumes, however, that each year there is sufficient net investment to increase productivity and that the marginal efficiency of capital is greater than the going rate of interest. If this is so, total profits will increase each year (if not, new investment needed to raise productivity will be reduced to zero). If all the additional output brought about by productivity increase is absorbed by higher wages, while the economy continues to operate under full employment, the situation implies that: the money supply is increasing; price inflation is being generated; labor's share of the National Income is improving; and fixed-income earners are suffering a decline in their real income.

(2) Provided that these income-redistribution effects are absent, a proportional increase in the money-wage rate and average productivity

[6] See F. Machlup, "Another View of Cost-Push and Demand-Pull Inflation," *Review of Economics and Statistics* (May 1960).

[7] The assertion that the average rate of increase in money wages equals the average rate of productivity increase in the whole economy implies that labor's relative share of the National Income remains constant. We are not suggesting a value judgment that from the standpoint of price-stabilization policy it is most appropriate to perpetuate the constancy of labor's relative share. The thesis that equality between average wage and productivity increases assures price stability is not free of qualifications. Generally speaking, many restrictive assumptions are required before we can draw inferences from a given production function or a consumption function.

can be consistent with a stable price level and full employment. But in the event that each sector allows a wage increase proportional to the productivity increase in that sector, and that (later) wages in all sectors begin to follow the highest wage rate in the highest-productivity sector, the economy is bound to generate a price-cost inflation spiral.

(3) Even if each sector allows a wage increase only (and no more than) proportional to the productivity increase, price inflation can still be generated in an economy where unemployment fails to induce a fall in wage rates and where those who become unemployed as a result of the productivity increase are assured of obtaining employment opportunities in other sectors.

(4) The argument in the above case (3) holds even if we replace "wage" with "profit"—then there will be price inflation but no accompanying rise in wages.

The foregoing analyses all point to the fact that the inability of a high-productivity industry to lower the price of its output will add to the process of general inflation, and the stabilization of "individual" prices as such will fail to insure the stabilization of the general price level. Under perfect competition, prices of goods produced in the high-productivity sectors become lower, through cost reduction, relative to the low-productivity sectors. There will be a corresponding commoditywise adjustment in absolute prices as well. If a certain market mechanism prevents the prices in the high-productivity sectors from falling, the prices of other goods will tend to rise, creating general inflationary pressure. In order, therefore, to stabilize the level of consumer prices it becomes necessary for average productivity in the consumer goods sector to increase as rapidly as the average wage rate in the same sector.

The next problem then is why wholesale prices of goods, many of which are produced in the high-productivity sectors, have been failing to fall sufficiently so as to lower retail prices—and why retail prices of goods and services, many of which are produced in the low-productivity sectors, have been rising at such an accelerated tempo, relative to wholesale prices, since 1959.

One explanation has been given by Messrs. Toshihiko Yoshino and Yoshio Suzuki.[8] Their views, representing what one might call the "Bank-of-Japan School," have been noted for their clarity and straightforwardness. According to Mr. Yoshino, for example, the excess of aggregate demand over aggregate supply that has emerged as a result of accelerated, continual expansion of effective demand in the Japanese economy over the past three years or so is the fundamental reason for the failure of wholesale prices to fall and the resultant consumer-price inflation. In the course of rapid growth, plant expansion and the rise in the level of employment have induced an increase in marginal costs of both capital and labor, which in turn has resulted

[8] T. Yoshino, ed. *op. cit.;* and Mr. Suzuki's statements appearing in Shigeto Tsuru *et al.,* "Bukka Mondai o Dō Tokuka," *Ekonomisto,* June 26, 1962.

in greater downward rigidities of wholesale prices. Particularly note-worthy has been the pronounced expansion of employment, causing an unprecedented tightening of the Japanese labor markets with an emerging critical shortage of new graduates, young workers, and en-gineers. Wages have had to increase to stimulate labor mobility in the traditional, low-productivity sectors. While the wage-gaps between the advanced and backward sectors have been closing very rapidly, the economy has been plagued by inflation of wage costs as well as con-sumer prices. These are the views held by Messrs. Yoshino and Suzuki.

If we follow this line of reasoning adopted by the Bank-of-Japan School, we view the Japanese inflation as essentially of the demand-pull variety caused by the labor-shortage bottleneck that has arisen in the course of accelerated growth, and that has helped raise wage costs and (hence) consumer goods prices.[9]

Some other economists have held an opposing view that emphasizes, instead, supply factors; they believe that the pronounced downward rigidities in the high-productivity sectors and the absorption of produc-tivity gains through higher profits and wages[10] provide a more apt

[9] Cf. T. Yoshino, ed. op. cit., p. 56, pp. 97–102, p. 119; and Shigeto Tsuru et al., op. cit., pp. 18–19, pp. 31–32. Chapters 3, 4, and 5 in the former publication con-stitute a most systematic and substantive study of recent Japanese price problems. Chapter 3, in particular, contains a lucid analysis of price behavior with respect to individual commodities as well as an analysis of the general price level. See also the aforementioned review of this book by R. Komiya, in which the reviewer ex-pounds his own views on the issue as well. Essentially the same views as Komiya's are expressed by Takafusa Nakamura in his "Bukka Jōshō Ron," Chū-ō Kōron (July 1962).

[10] When a productivity increase results in higher wage and profit rates in lieu of lower prices, the process of relative-price adjustment will tend to raise absolute prices in the low-productivity sectors. If the rate of price reduction in a high-pro-ductivity sector is not as great as the rate of productivity increase, it implies that part of the productivity gain is still being absorbed by higher wages and profits. The greater the rate of productivity increase in a given sector relative to the national, average rate of productivity increase, the higher the probability of a rise in the general price level. Schultze holds that, of the three alternative results of cost re-duction due to productivity increase in a mixed economy like that in the United States—(1) lower prices, (2) higher profits, and (3) higher wages—wage inflation is the most likely consequence. Firms are less likely to absorb productivity increase through price reduction because: (1) each firm is afraid that all other firms will interpret such price reduction as the beginning of price war and hesitates to initiate a price cut lest the stability of the oligopolistic market should be disturbed; (2) firms have not been maximizing their profits; and (3) administered pricing gener-ally is not based upon a precise analysis of demand and cost data. The higher profits alternative is also unlikely in the United States because: (1) in the long run, if not the short run, such an alternative will induce the entry of other firms into the industry; and (2) there will be greater frictions with labor unions inasmuch as the higher profits give the unions a strong motive to demand higher wages. The higher wage alternative in absorbing productivity gain is most likely because: (1) it will deter entry of new firms; and (2) the industry's "good will" will increase through higher wages, and at the same time firms will face less conflict with unions. (C. L. Schultze, "Recent Inflation in the United States," Study Paper, No. 1, Study of Employment, Growth, and Price Levels, Joint Economic Committee, U.S. Con-gress, 1959.)

explanation of the recent inflation. The conspicuous consumer-price inflation since 1959 is interpreted as a result of the fact that in the large-scale manufacturing sector, where productivity and wages have been rising faster than those in other sectors, prices have not been sufficiently reduced; at the same time, the prices in the low-productivity sectors, such as those of rent and services, have, until recently, been held at an artificially low level. This, for example, is the view held by Mr. Ryūtaro Komiya.[11] Messrs. Shigeto Tsuru and Mitsuharu Ito also belong to this "cost-push" school,[12] although their views are not identical to Komiya's.

Strict adherence to either the "cost-push" or "demand-pull" school of thought usually involves numerous difficulties, and this is true when either of these two opposing views is applied to the present Japanese inflation. Each view has its own logical coherence, and the difference between the two largely concerns the interpretation of present-day Japanese economic conditions. What are the problems involved in such interpretation?

Over the past several years, particularly during the upswings of business cycles, the levels of aggregate demand and aggregate supply in the Japanese economy are believed to have been very close to one another, with a slight excess of demand; however, it is difficult to assume that the excess aggregate demand over supply persisted in all phases of the cycles as well as in all sectors of the economy. For example, the fact that the tightening of the labor markets emphasized by the Bank-of-Japan School refers mainly to the supply of new graduates and young, skilled workers strongly suggests that the rise in excess aggregate demand has not been quite forceful enough to raise labor mobility in Japan to such an extent as to totally eliminate the long-existing wage-gaps. The Bank-of-Japan School has also been fondly describing the Japanese case as a "new demand-pull inflation"; but what is "new" and how it differs from the commonly accepted concept of demand-pull inflation are not clear. The core of the demand-pull argument lies in the notion that inflation is a phenomenon resulting from excess aggregate demand relative to aggregate supply. On the basis of this notion, then, we find it rather difficult to accept the Bank-of-Japan School's view in its totality. We are more inclined towards the view that the pronounced disparity between wholesale and consumer prices stems more from the way in which wage rates respond to productivity increase in the advanced sectors.

One difficulty associated with the approach that emphasizes the supply side of the picture is that this approach fails to explain adequately why price inflation began to accelerate itself since 1959. Komiya, for example, gives only an insufficient explanation of this problem. Expansion of effective demand, emphasized by Yoshino *et al.*,

[11] See the aforementioned book review by Komiya of T. Yoshino, ed. *op. cit.*
[12] See Shigeto Tsuru *et al.*, *op. cit.*, and Mitsuharu Ito, "Bukka Mondai no Tokikata," *Ekonomisto,* May 1, 1962.

seems to be an important factor necessary to account for this diffi-culty.[13]

In order to determine whether a given inflation is of the demand-pull or cost-push variety we must first establish what price mechanisms exist in the output and factor markets. The Bank-of-Japan School's demand-pull thesis is based upon the tacit assumption that sufficiently competitive supply-and-demand mechanisms are present in both the labor and commodities markets. Under this assumption a wage in-crease due to the rightward shifting of the demand-for-labor curve means a rise in the firm's marginal cost curve, and hence a leftward shift of the supply curve in the commodities markets. At the same time expansion of effective demand induces a shift of the demand curve in the commodities markets to the right. Consequently, both price and volume of sales increase. This is the vein of thought im-plicit in the view held by the Bank-of-Japan School.

We must note, however, that price inflation due to cost increase in the above sense does not necessarily correspond to the theory of "cost inflation." Inasmuch as Yoshino et al. do not believe in the prevalence of perfect competition in the Japanese economy but rather point out the significance of administered pricing practiced by many firms in Japan,[14] their theory should not be considered a demand-pull type.

What are the tacit assumptions underlying the approach that em-phasizes supply factors? Are we assuming that the labor markets are imperfectly competitive while a high degree of competition prevails in the commodity markets? Are we supposing, instead, that both mar-kets are characterized by imperfect competition? [15] The opposing views on the Japanese inflation are differentiated by their particular under-

[13] Komiya does not ignore demand factors, however. He writes in his aforemen-tioned review of Yoshino, ed. op. cit.: "It is true that, in the course of changes in the structure of relative prices accompanying economic growth, effective demand has continued to expand rapidly since around 1955. But . . . effective-demand ex-pansion in this process seems to have been more supportive and induced than autonomous" (pp. 94–95).

[14] The Yoshino group writes: "Of course, we cannot fully explain the recent downward rigidities in wholesale prices solely in terms of the cost increase. We must pay attention also to the sign of growing imperfections recently witnessed in many parts of the Japanese economy, e.g., a greater popularization of administered pricing. . . . But in an overall sense the degree of interfirm competition in Japan is significantly high, and the downward rigidities in wholesale prices are due mainly to the rising aggregate cost schedule throughout the Japanese industry rather than to greater market imperfections" (T. Yoshino, ed. op. cit., p. 120).

[15] Komiya emphasizes supply factors; but he does not necessarily imply that ad-ministered pricing, which is usually incorporated into the cost-inflation thesis, has become widespread in Japan. The point of his emphasis is that in Japan produc-tivity gain is prone to be absorbed by wage increase, although he is not clear as to what market mechanisms tend to induce wage increase and to prevent price reduc-tion. Since Komiya strongly suggests that the monopolistic behavior of labor unions in the advanced sectors is more responsible for inflation than is insufficient competi-tion in the general labor markets, his view should perhaps be interpreted as essen-tially a "wage-push inflation" theory.

lying assumptions about, first, a set of independent variables conditioning numerous, mutually dependent factors behind the inflation and, second, principal characteristics assigned to those independent variables.

We may reconcile the foregoing discussions on the causes of the Japanese inflation in terms of the following set of propositions: (1) productivity gains in the high-productivity sectors have been absorbed largely by wage increase rather than by price reduction; (2) money prices of goods produced in the low-productivity sectors had to rise, because the higher rate of productivity increase in the advanced sectors raised the relative prices of these goods; (3) there has been a breaking-down of the mechanism that had been sustaining the wide wage-gaps between the advanced and backward sectors resulting in higher wage costs in the traditional sectors; and (4) greater purchasing power through wage increase meant a higher level of demand for consumer goods, adding to a spiral rise in consumer prices.

What are some additional points involved in the diagnostic discussions on the Japanese inflation? Since interindustry disparities in the rates of productivity increase have been observed universally throughout other countries in different time periods, we are somewhat troubled by the thesis of Messrs. Yoshihiro Takasuka and Mitsuharu Ito that the Japanese inflation should be understood distinctly as a "productivity-gap inflation." [16] For one thing, we are not certain how "productivity-gap inflation" as such differs from "cost inflation" in the usual sense of the term. Mr. Takasuka divides (in a rather dubious way) all prices into two groups: the first group consists of prices of products produced by large corporations and the prices of investment goods; and the second group encompasses consumer goods prices and prices of outputs of small-scale businesses. Mr. Takasuka calls the first the high-price group and the second the low-price group, and tries to explain the Japanese inflation essentially as a process of the latter group catching up with the former now that the duality in the Japanese price structure has finally begun to dissolve itself.[17] The "dual structure" usually refers to the existence of wage-gaps among essentially homogeneous workers, and what is meant by the process of "dissolution of the dual structure" is the closing of such gaps. However, it is only natural that prices of heterogeneous commodities are differentiated to varying degrees depending upon particular production costs involved. We are not certain on what basis Takasuka calls certain prices "high" and others "low."

Mr. Shōichi Mizuno contends that the recent consumer-price inflation should be viewed as a process of recovery by the consumer prices

[16] Cf. Yoshihiro Takasuka, "Bukka Taikei Saihensei no Mechanism," *Tōyō Keizai Bessatsu* (Spring 1962), and "Seisan Kōzō Karamita Bukka Mondai," *Ekonomisto*, April 4, 1962; Mitsuharu Ito, "Bukka Mondai no Tokikata," *Ekonomisto*, May 1, 1962.

[17] Takasuka, *op. cit.*, pp. 78–79.

of their previously held position vis-à-vis wholesale prices—the latter having risen relative to consumer prices since a certain past time.[18] Proving this hypothesis involves the rather delicate task of demonstrating that from a time in the past to the present there have existed in the Japanese economy supply-and-demand conditions which have effectively perpetuated the constancy of relative prices. The argument sounds more speculative than empirically founded.

Lastly, Mr. Takafusa Nakamura maintains, concerning the distinction between cost- and demand-inflation, that "the relevance of the cost-inflation thesis is more or less confined to the Western-type, full-employment economy." [19] Mr. Nakamura closely correlates cost inflation with wage-push inflation; but it is rather perplexing to say that cost inflation can occur only in a fully employed economy. One wonders how Mr. Nakamura will explain the cost inflation in the United States existing side by side with a high rate of unemployment. We must remember that creeping inflation is one of the new economic problems that have often been associated with less than full-employment economies. The same critique can be directed against Mr. Mizuno's views as well.[20]

We shall now digress a little into the applicability to Japanese price problems of the Schultze thesis[21] on the mild inflation in the United States during the second half of the 1950's. The Schultze thesis is an attempt to explain inflation, occurring in an economy where aggregate supply exceeds aggregate demand, in terms of a new theory that is, strictly speaking, neither of a demand-pull nor cost-push variety. His theory begins with two premises based upon an empirical analysis of the United States economy: (1) all commodity prices and wage rates in all sectors possess the characteristic of downward rigidities; and (2) the components of demand are subject to frequent shifts. A shift in demand (e.g., from consumption goods to investment goods) in an economy where aggregate demand is less than aggregate supply will induce a corresponding shift in relative prices. For example, prices in the sector towards which demand has shifted will rise relative to those in other sectors in which demand has fallen. According to the above premise (1), however, neither wages nor prices fall in the lower demand sector; consequently, absolute prices in the higher demand sector will inevitably rise. In this manner inflation can occur even in an economy where aggregate supply surpasses aggregate demand.

This is the skeleton of the Schultze thesis. We notice that it bears certain similarities to the aforementioned cost-inflation theory of the Japanese inflation. For one thing, both theories are based upon the

---

[18] Shōichi Mizuno, *Nihon no Bukka Hendō* (Tōyō Keizai Shimpo Sha), p. 234.

[19] Takafusa Nakamura, "Bukka Jōshō Ron," *Chū-ō Kōron* (July 1962), p. 43. The same view is expressed by Shōichi Mizuno, *op. cit.*, p. 240.

[20] Many statements made by Mr. Mizuno are rather confusing. For example, in the above-mentioned *Nihon no Bukka Hendō* he explains inflation in terms of the demand-pull thesis (p. 239), as does the Bank-of-Japan School, while elsewhere he shifts his position to the wage-push line of argument (p. 240).

[21] See C. L. Schultze, *op. cit.*

notions of shifts in relative prices and the wage-price downward rigidities. Professed causes of relative-price changes and commodity groups affected by the downward rigidities are not the same in the two theories; but the theoretical frameworks of the two are essentially the same.

The Schultze thesis differs from the argument commonly heard in Japan in that the former equates changes in relative prices with shifts in the community-indifference curves rather than in the production-possibility curve, while the Japanese version emphasizes the unevenness of shifts in the production-possibility curve as a prime cause of relative-price changes. Failure of absolute prices to fall is explained by Schultze primarily in terms of downward rigidities of wages and prices in the sectors where relative prices have declined; in Japan the explanation seems to lie in wage increase coupled with constancy of absolute prices, despite the lowering of relative prices in the advanced sectors. Therefore, a "general wage inflation" in Japan will mean the approach of the general wage level to that of the high-productivity sector; and in the United States it will mean, instead, an approach of the general wage level to those in sectors where relative prices have risen. These comparative characteristics seem to indicate that Japanese price problems reflect certain aspects of the economics of accelerated growth.

APPRAISAL

How in the course of economic growth should consumer-price inflation be appraised from the policy standpoint? This is our next problem. At the very bottom of this dilemma lies a value judgment one has to make about the relative importance of wholesale prices as against consumer prices. On the one hand, there is the extreme view that rapid growth is the main target of economic policy, and price problems should either be disregarded or receive only secondary consideration. On the other hand, there is the contrary view that inflation is detrimental to the nation's economy, and price stabilization should be given top priority or at least enjoy as much regard as the objective of growth in economic policy. If the latter view be taken, the present inflation becomes an urgent problem that requires an urgent solution.

A group of economists have insisted that some consumer-price inflation is an unavoidable phenomenon in the course of rapid growth. This group includes Osamu Shimomura, Shigeto Tsuru, Takafusa Nakamura, Moto-o Kaji, Mitsuharu Ito, Yoshihiro Takasuka, and Shō-ichi Mizuno.[22] Allowing for nuances in their views, there is a consensus of opinion among these economists that insofar as we acknowledge

[22] See Osamu Shimomura, "Anzen Unten nitsuki Oshizukani," *Ekonomisto*, June 20, 1961; "9% no Seichō ni Fuan Nashi," *Ekonomisto*, October 17, 1961; "Watakushi no Egaku Nihon Keizai no Vision," *Tōyō Keizai Shimpō*, March 9, 1963. See also Shigeto Tsuru *et al., op. cit.*; Takafusa Nakamura, *op. cit.*; Shōichi Mizuno, *op. cit.*; Yoshihiro Takasuka, *op. cit.*

the built-in downward rigidities in the Japanese markets as an irreversible economic reality, we should regard consumer-price inflation as not merely inevitable but also, to some extent, "desirable," in that it helps "smooth" the process of growth. They emphasize the fact that the consumer-price inflation which has been developing during the beginning years of the Income-Doubling Plan has been largely induced by rising service costs, which in turn reflect rapid wage increase in the traditional sectors; in brief, inflation has accelerated the dissolution of the dual structure in Japan.

Any pro-inflation thesis is subject to at least two criticisms. First, inflation of consumer goods prices and service costs brings forth differential effects on consumers in terms of their income categories. Fixed-income earners, and those whose incomes fail to rise as fast as the price level, are forced to bear a disproportionate share of the burden. Any pro-inflation argument, therefore, assumes a value judgment that discounts (tacitly or otherwise) the importance of income-redistribution effects of inflation. There is a vital need for an empirical study of the incidence of inflation, similar to the recent work by S. E. Harris in the United States.[23]

Second, those who hold that the consumer-price inflation is inevitable for growth must clarify how they will solve the problem of savings in an inflationary economy. The high propensity to save among general consumers has undoubtedly contributed to Japan's postwar growth. But it is highly probable that in an economy where inflation has become a permanent and "built-in" phenomenon, consumers will lose their incentive to save, and the nation's economic growth itself will be deterred by the declining rate of saving.

Stable consumer prices (rather than wholesale prices) will then be the main concern of a price policy based upon these two anti-inflation arguments, one of which stresses the importance of equitable income distribution, and the other which stresses the importance of savings as a prerequisite of continual growth.[24]

Mr. Shimomura is perhaps the most ardent member of the pro-inflationist school. According to him, the stability of wholesale prices is the important factor in the process of growth, and, particularly from the standpoint of balance-of-payments considerations, there is little to worry about so long as wholesale prices remain stable. At present Japan is experiencing an inflation of consumer prices; but consumer prices include prices of both physical goods and services, whereas the service content of wholesale prices is nil, implying that the present inflation is largely a service-price inflation. The fact that physical goods prices are remaining constant, whereas service prices are rising, means that the value of human labor is becoming greater; interpreted in this way, consumer-price inflation is not only unavoid-

---

[23] S. E. Harris, "The Incidence of Inflation; or Who Get Hurt," Study Paper, No. 7, *Study of Employment, Growth, and Price Levels*, Joint Economic Committee, U.S. Congress, 1960.

[24] See, e.g., the previously cited articles by R. Komiya and T. Yoshino, ed. *op. cit.*

able but also desirable in the process of growth. Mr. Shimomura concludes that the present inflation provides little ground for apprehension inasmuch as it is a manifestation of rising "human value" and not a problematical increase in physical goods prices.[25]

His proposition that wholesale prices represent physical goods, while consumer prices represent both physical goods and services, is much too oversimplified.[26] In the first place, we find it difficult to accept the view that the service-price inflation, coupled with the constancy of physical goods prices, necessarily implies a rise in "human value." Prices relevant to the general consumer are those that include wholesale prices and various categories of service prices. The "value," in the Shimomura sense, of workers acting as consumers can indeed fall if their higher wages are more than offset by the loss of purchasing power due to consumer-price inflation.

The determination of service prices as against physical goods prices depends upon the relative contents of various factors used in the process of producing those outputs—and is not as simple a matter to distinguish one from the other as Mr. Shimomura suggests. The difference between goods and services is essentially one of degree in terms of their relative factor contents. For instance, services, such as haircuts and public transportation, include capital contents, while goods contain varying amounts of labor contents. It is, therefore, a gross oversimplification to hold that all outputs can be meaningfully classified into two categories of goods and services merely on the basis of their outer appearances, and that the constancy of goods prices, combined with rising service prices, necessarily means a higher valuation of human value.

In the second place, according to Shimomura, we must worry about inflation chiefly for its deteriorating effects on the nation's balance of payments; hence, we need not be troubled by inflation provided that wholesale prices remain stable. To be more precise, it is not so much wholesale prices as export prices that must be stabilized, and his argument implies that fluctuations in wholesale or export prices should cause no concern if the nation's external balance is maintained. Thus, for Shimomura, price stabilization *per se* is not an economic policy objective but rather a means of achieving balance-of-payments equilibrium.

Relative prices in the international markets depend no less upon other countries' economic conditions than upon our own. Except for rare cases of extremely low price elasticity of demand, *ceteris paribus*, the lowering of prices results in an improvement in the external balance; and other countries' successful attempts at price reduction in order to improve *their* balance-of-payments positions simultaneously

[25] See O. Shimomura, "Anzen Unten nitsuki Oshizukani," *op. cit.*, pp. 12–13; "9% no Seichō ni Fuan Nashi," *op. cit.*, pp. 20–24; "Watakushi no Egaku Nihon Keizai no Vision," *op. cit.*, pp. 36–38. See also S. Mizuno, *op. cit.*, p. 160.

[26] To do Mr. Shimomura justice, we should take up his "marginal demand-supply ratio." However, we must confine ourselves here to the price aspects of his thesis.

means a deterioration in *our* external balance. In more general terms, the nation's balance of payments is a function of its growth rate, price elasticity of demand, the pace of technological progress, and numerous other factors. Shimomura seems to disregard these external factors which affect the nation's balance-of-payments problems. He attributes the increase in Japan's per capita GNP from the present $500 to, say, a future level of $1,800 to the process of economic growth—and complains that too many people seem to confuse growth with inflation.[27] This is a rather confusing mode of thought. Increase in per capita GNP may be a symptom of economic growth, but it has little to do with inflation as such. The occurrence of inflation is just as likely in an $1,800 economy as in a $500 economy. The fact that per capita GNP increases from $500 to $1,800 does not in itself guarantee freedom from inflation problems. The relevant question is what happens to consumer prices as per capita GNP rises from $500 to $1,800.

In the third place, the stability of wholesale prices in Japan is primarily due to the fact that the rate of increase in productivity in the manufacturing industry has been approximately equal to the rate of wage increase in that industry. Shimomura contends that wage inflation is not a problem so long as goods prices expressed at the wholesale level remain stable; but it is likely that even wholesale prices will begin to rise in the future, through either administered or competitive pricing, as a result of the further tightening of the labor markets together with the more aggressive demands of labor unions for higher wages. In other words, there is no assurance—notwithstanding Shimomura's optimism—that the coexistence of stable wholesale prices and rising consumer prices will last much longer. In the process of growth some increase in service costs and wages may be inevitable; but we are not certain whether we can interpret, as Shimomura does, wage increase to be indicative of rising "human value," even if that wage increase proceeds faster than labor-productivity increase. No less important is the fact that consumer-price inflation is bound to exert pressure for further wage increase.

Of those who emphasize the importance of stable consumer prices, there are two groups: one that is concerned with the adverse effects of consumer-price inflation but nevertheless recognizes its virtue in the Japanese context as a catalyst (if not cause) of the dissolution of the dual structure in the economy; and the other that attributes the recent inflation to unwarrantedly rapid growth and advocates slower growth so as to prevent the price increase from exceeding 1 to 2 per cent per annum. Toshihiko Yoshino, Yoshio Suzuki (both of the Bank of Japan) and Kiyoshi Tsuchiya represent the second group.[28]

[27] See, for example, O. Shimomura, "9% no Seichō ni Fuan Nashi," *op. cit.,* pp. 21–22, and "Watakushi no Egaku Nihon Keizai no Vision," *op. cit.,* p. 38.

[28] Cf. Mr. Suzuki's statements appearing in T. Yoshino, ed. *op. cit.,* and S. Tsuru *et al., op. cit.* For Mr. Tsuchiya's view, see K. Tsuchiya, "Kōdō Seicho ka no Keizai Seisaku no Kihonteki Shikaku," *Kigyō Keizai Bunseki* (Iwanami Shoten, 1962), and his remarks in K. Tsuchiya *et al.,* "Dokomade Tsuzuku Neagarizo," *Bungei Shunjū* (May 1962).

If we assume that the disparity between wholesale and consumer prices is inevitable, the only way to obtain stable consumer prices is to reduce wholesale prices. Inasmuch as a considerable proportion of investment funds to large manufacturing corporations has been supplied by commercial banks in Japan, such yearly reduction in wholesale prices would mean a proportional increase in the real interest burden of the firms—for the same reason that N. Kaldor[29] has used in the reverse situation.[30] This is one of the complications involved in the choice between stable prices and rapid growth. Price policy must be formulated in the context of the national economy. But whatever virtues inflation might have, it seems to be an inexcusable policy error for the government to tolerate a consumer-price inflation which has raced at the galloping pace of 6 to 7 per cent annually since 1959.

PRESCRIPTION

In search of a price policy to cope with the Japanese inflation, economists have offered numerous suggestions and recommendations, some of which are contained in recently published works.[31] These recommendations range from individual-commodity price policy to monetary-fiscal and industrial policies. We lack sufficient space to comment on all of these recommendations, but we note that many of them, rather than promoting the proper functioning of the price mechanism, embody a strong flavor of protectionism vis-à-vis small- and medium-size businesses. Representative views and opinions underlying these policy recommendations have been discussed in the preceding sections of this paper. As we have shown, there is a school of thought that expresses the extreme view that rapid growth is the prime goal of economic policy, and that consumer-price inflation should cause little apprehension provided wholesale prices remain stable. There are also those who regard the inflation as a grave issue; among them, the Bank-of-Japan School emphasizes the importance of a deflationary policy which embodies orthodox fiscal and monetary measures.[32] Those who interpret the Japanese inflation to be essentially of cost-push variety propose (in addition to fiscal and monetary policy):

(1) a more effective anti-monopoly policy and the repeal of government price-support programs in order to foster the price mechanism;

[29] The Kaldor thesis, in its simplest form, holds that at a given level of money interest rate, price increase means a decline in the real interest rates; hence, the firm's investment motive tends to increase. And a mild inflation in which wage rates rise faster than the price level is good for the firms as well as for the workers (particularly from the growth-policy standpoint), assuming that savings do not fall relative to a decline in the real interest rate. (See N. Kaldor, "Economic Growth and the Problem of Inflation," *Economica* [August and November 1959].)

[30] See the aforementioned book review by Komiya of T. Yoshino, ed. *op. cit.*, p. 95.

[31] E.g., T. Yoshino, ed. *op. cit.*, pp. 179–184; and Sōgō Seisaku Kenkyū Kai, *Bukka Seisaku e no Teigen* (August 1963), especially pp. 9–20.

[32] T. Yoshino, ed. *op. cit.*, p. 83; S. Tsuru *et al.*, *op. cit.*, p. 36; and Sōgō Seisaku Kenkyū Kai, *op. cit.*

(2) a workable labor policy to suppress excessive wage-increase demands by labor unions;

(3) an industrial policy directed towards modernization of commercial sectors and increased productivity in the service industry.[33]

The most important problem in price policy seems to be how to create conditions conducive to the lowering of prices in the high-productivity sectors. No effective price policy can be formulated without considering all the mechanisms affecting price determination. Monetary, fiscal, industrial, and foreign-trade policies must all be organized into a coherent whole, directed towards the objective of price stabilization, while paying sufficient attention to the duality problems, inasmuch as the dual structure is closely related to the Japanese inflation. Viewed in this way, the cost-push school seems to have a wider vision of price problems.

[33] See R. Komiya, "Keizai Seichō to Bukka Mondai" and "Zoku-Keizai Seichō to Bukka," *op. cit.*

PART II

The Balance of Payments

4

Hisao Kanamori:

Economic Growth and the Balance of Payments*

Rapid Growth and the External Balance

In postwar Japan there has been a popular view that rapid economic growth is prone to induce a deterioration in the balance of payments. For example, the authors of the New Long-Range Economic Plan (1957) held that the projected growth rate of 6.5 per cent per annum for 1956–1962 should be regarded as the maximum rate at which the Japanese economy could grow without experiencing an external imbalance.[1] Since Japanese exports are a function of the world's import demand, and Japanese imports a function of her growth rate, too rapid a growth relative to the rest of the world will result in a Japanese import surplus. This was the reasoning behind the contention of the Plan.

In reality, however, the Japanese economy has been growing at the annual rate of approximately 10 per cent, and her foreign-exchange reserve has actually increased over the past six years (see Table 4-1). Contrary to the popular view, there has been little sign of emerging external imbalance as a result of accelerated growth. What is the explanation of this apparent paradox? To answer this question, we shall first make a comparison of the projection under the New Long-Range Economic Plan (to be referred to as the Plan in the rest of this paper) and what has actually happened since 1957.

A comparison between the Plan's projection and the actual results appears in Table 4-2. We observe that: (1) Japanese exports increased much faster than projected; and (2) Japanese imports did not rise as fast as her real GNP. Namely, the behavior of both exports and imports was much more favorable to growth than the Plan had anticipated. The value of exports increased 14 per cent annually in contrast to 8 per cent for the value of imports; this was the funda-

* The author is grateful to Messrs. Masahiro Tatemoto, Tadao Uchida, and Tsunehiko Watanabe for their useful comments. The section on The Import-Saving Pattern of Industrial Growth was added to the original draft as a result of suggestions by Messrs. Uchida and Watanabe.

[1] Economic Planning Agency, *Shin Chōki Keizai Keikaku ni Kansuru Keizai Shingikai Tōshin*, November 25, 1957, p. 16.

TABLE 4-1

JAPAN'S REAL GNP GROWTH RATES AND BALANCE OF PAYMENTS

Fiscal year	Real GNP growth rates	Balance of payments (overall balance)
	(per cent)	(millions of dollars)
1957	7.9	−109
1958	3.2	+345
1959	17.9	+387
1960	13.2	+636
1961	14.0	−436
1962[a]	4.2	+289
1957–1962	(77.0)[b]	+1,112

SOURCES: Economic Planning Agency, *National Income Statistics*, and Bank of Japan, *Foreign Exchange Statistics*.

[a] Government estimates.

[b] The 1952–1962 growth rate.

TABLE 4-2

THE NEW LONG-RANGE ECONOMIC PLAN VERSUS THE ACTUAL RECORDS: THE ANNUAL GROWTH RATES, 1956–1962[a]

	A. The plan	B. Actual records	B/A
	(per cent)	(per cent)	
Real GNP	5.8	9.9	1.71
Exports (current price)	10.5	14.0	1.33
Imports (current price)	5.0	8.0	1.60
World imports (current price)	4.5	4.8[b]	1.07

SOURCES: Ministry of Finance, *Tsūkan Tōkei*, and U.N., *Yearbook of International Trade Statistics*.

[a] Fiscal years for Japan. However, fiscal 1962 refers to government estimates as of August 1962.

[b] 1956–1961 calendar years.

mental reason why Japan could achieve simultaneously both rapid growth and a balance-of-payments equilibrium.[2]

Some of the forces responsible for Japan's apparent success were external. For example, the sustained boom in other countries favored Japanese exports. The Plan's projected annual rate of increase in world import demand was 4.5 per cent, whereas world demand in actuality increased 4.8 per cent. Labor shortages in the advanced

[2] In this paper we are concerned mainly with the trade balance and exclude capital and other non-trade transactions from our consideration. We are not implying, however, that the capital inflow was insignificant during the period. On the contrary, the capital inflow from 1957 through 1962 amounted to 1.33 billion dollars; Japan in all likelihood could not have realized her balance-of-payments equilibrium without this much foreign capital.

countries caused a rise in the level of their import demand for labor-intensive products.[3] Inasmuch as Japanese exports comprise numerous labor-intensive durables as well as nondurables that enjoy a comparative cost advantage, the shift in the import demand of the advanced countries led to an increase in Japanese exports of these products.

Another external factor was a trend in the import price that fell 15 per cent from 1956 to 1961. In part, this was due to the Suez-induced import-price inflation in 1956–1957; but, more importantly, the prices of industrial raw materials and foods (which constitute a large proportion of the Japanese imports) showed a secular, declining trend during the period. Consequently, the value of Japanese imports did not rise as fast as their volume. The value of total Japanese imports in 1961 would have been 15 per cent greater, assuming that 1961 import prices were as high as those in 1956. The cumulative total of foreign exchange Japan could "save" from 1956 through 1961, thanks to falling import prices, amounted to as much as 2.5 billion dollars. From these observations it seems evident that in the absence of import-price reduction it would have been impossible for Japan to cumulate a large reserve of foreign exchange while growing at an accelerated pace.

In addition to these external forces favorably affecting the Japanese balance of payments, were there not internal forces as well that sustained her international balance? The search for such forces operating within the domestic economy is the main concern of this paper.[4]

In retrospect we feel that the assumption of the Plan that rapid growth necessarily induces a balance-of-payments deterioration was an oversimplification. It may be that, depending upon a particular pattern of growth, accelerated growth itself can have a positive effect on the nation's external balance; and we have reason to suspect that such was the case of Japanese growth since 1956. We mention four characteristics of Japanese growth that presumably have had close bearing on the balance-of-payments problems.

(1) Real output increased faster than wages.
(2) Growth was unbalanced in that the output increase was most conspicuous in the export sectors of the manufacturing industry.
(3) It was an innovation-oriented growth in that many fast-growing export sectors were those producing "new" products, the world demand for which was rapidly increasing.
(4) The pattern of growth was such that the Japanese economy became less dependent upon a foreign supply of industrial raw materials.

[3] Of those manufactured goods imported by the United States and Western Europe whose values increased more than 50 per cent from 1957 to 1960, 17 out of 24 items imported by the United States and 16 out of 26 items imported by Western European countries were "light" manufactured goods (*Keizai Hakusho*, fiscal 1962, p. 307).
[4] See P. A. Samuelson, "Tsuyoi Yen, Yowai Dollar," *Nihon Keizai Shimbun*, December 8, 1962. Samuelson holds that the real explanation for the favorable balance of payments of Japan, West Germany, Italy, France, and Holland is found in the rapid growth of these countries rather than in external forces.

The rest of the paper will examine these four points.

OUTPUT AND THE WAGE LAG

Deceptively simple as it might sound, Japanese growth was, to a large extent, due to an extraordinarily rapid increase in labor productivity coupled with a lag in the rate of wage increase.[5] Table 4-3 compares the rates of growth in industrial labor productivity and

TABLE 4-3

VARIOUS INDEXES CONCERNING WAGE COSTS AND THE BALANCE OF PAYMENTS[a]

Country	Industrial production	Employment	Labor productivity[b]	Wages	Wage cost[c]	Import volume	Export volume	Export volume Import volume	Export prices
Japan	280	154	182	148	81	225	324	146	98
Italy	181	112	162	137	85	229	280	122	86
U.S.A.	117	96	122	128	105	137	121	88	108
France	170	106	160	169	106	175	193	110	132[d]
Norway	144	105	137	151	110	157	163	104	103
Holland	159	112	142	159	112	193	187	97	100
Sweden	130	106	122	140	115	183	170	93	102
W. Germany	183	137	134	165	123	294	256	87	101
Denmark	138	119	116	150	129	190	161	85	101
U.K.	129	109	118	156	132	140	128	92	110

SOURCES: U.N., *Yearbook of World Statistics* and *Yearbook of International Trade Statistics*.
a 1960 indices with 1953 as 100.
b Industrial production ÷ employment.
c Wages ÷ labor productivity.
d 94 when adjusted for a change in the exchange rate.

money wages in ten major industrial countries from 1953 to 1960. The wage lag was most conspicuous in Japan and Italy. Labor productivity and wages rose at an approximately equal pace in the United States and France. In Norway, Holland, and Sweden, wages increased slightly faster than productivity. Lastly, wage increase was noticeably faster than productivity increase in West Germany, Denmark, and Great Britain.

When productivity increases faster than wages, it can affect the balance of payments in two ways. In the first place, it will promote exports through reduction of wage costs in exported commodities.[6] Figure 4-1 relates export volumes with wage costs in various countries

[5] The fixed exchange rate is believed to have worked in favor of the balance of payments. Under the flexible-rate system, an export surplus due to the domestic wage lag will induce a change in the exchange rate so that the country's exports will diminish.

[6] A tendency toward international equalization of export prices is indicated in Table 4-3; the export-price disparities are minor relative to differential wage costs among different countries. The wage cost is believed to be a better index of the international competitive position of a country than the export price. For this point, see F. A. Lutz, *International Payments and Monetary Policy in the World Today* (Wicksell Lectures, 1961).

and shows a significantly high, negative correlation between the two.[7] We must make a reservation, however, for the rate of export expansion is affected not only by wage costs but by the volume of output as well; for example, in the case of West Germany the volume of exports, together with total production, expanded rapidly despite a high rate of wage-cost increase.

In the second place, rapid increase in productivity relative to wages means that import demand rises relatively slowly because money income is not increasing as fast as real output, and this, in turn, affects the balance of payments. In West Germany a rapid output expansion

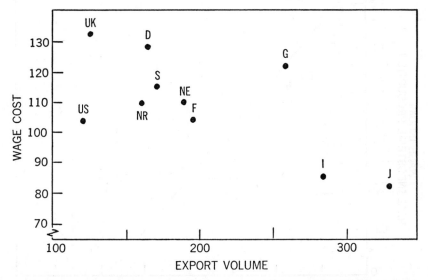

Fig. 4-1. Wage cost and export volume, 1960: major countries (1953 = 100). D, Denmark; F, France; G, West Germany; I, Italy; J, Japan; NE, Netherlands; NR, Norway; S, Sweden; UK, Great Britain; US, U.S.A. Sources: see Table 4-3.

provided an increasing volume of exportable goods; but, due to the wage-cost increase, her imports as well as exports rose at an accelerated rate. As a result, her balance of payments actually worsened during 1953–1960 relative to the Japanese experience. Changes in the wage cost thus can influence a nation's external balance both through exports and imports.

Figure 4-2 shows a correlation between the wage-productivity ratio and the export-import ratio. The time period and the countries included are the same as in Figure 4-1. These two "ratios" seem to indicate a higher degree of negative correlation than that between the wage cost and export volume in Figure 4-1. These two figures seem to

[7] In the case of France the wage-cost reduction on exports was presumably reinforced by two major devaluations (20 per cent in 1957 and 17.6 per cent in 1958) of the French franc.

support our previous assumptions concerning the export and import effects of the wage lag on the balance of payments.

In Japan an excess supply of labor accounted in part for the wage lag. But perhaps the more strategic reason was that labor productivity could rise extraordinarily fast due to a series of technological innovations in the course of accelerated growth. As a matter of fact, wages rose just as fast in Japan as in most other countries; but it was the labor-productivity increase in Japan that showed an exceptionally high

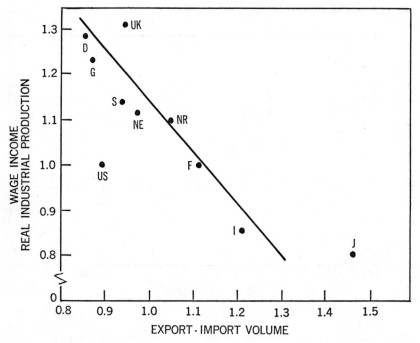

Fig. 4-2. Wage-income lag and the balance of payments, 1960 (1953 = 100). The letters stand for the same countries as in Fig. 4-1. Sources: see Table 4-3.

rate relative to other countries. Great Britain and Denmark are countries in which a low rate of productivity increase was associated with high wage cost, whereas the high-productivity countries such as Italy and France showed relative stability in wage cost. It seems from these observations that the low wage cost in Japan was primarily due to the high rate of productivity increase, and the excess supply of labor as such played only a secondary role.

Not only labor costs but also costs of raw materials were sizeably reduced through technological innovations. Table 4-4 shows that the extent of reduction in the latter from the first half of fiscal 1957 through the second half of fiscal 1961 was approximately equal to that in the former. Decline in raw-materials costs was due no less to the lowering of raw-materials prices than to the conspicuous rise in industrial production efficiency.[8] Capital costs increased during the period, but thanks to the fall in both labor and raw-material costs, total production cost could be considerably reduced. In short, Japan's growth,

TABLE 4-4

REDUCTION IN MANUFACTURING COSTS

(Indexes for the second half of fiscal 1961 with the first half of fiscal 1957 as 100)	
Raw-materials cost	84
Wage cost	86
Capital cost	120
Other cost	118
Various taxes	95
Total money cost	92
Net profit	92

SOURCE: Atsushi Nakamura, "Kōgyō Seihin Kakaku no Cost Yōin Bunseki," *Keizai Geppō* (November 1962).

sustained by a series of technological innovations, favorably affected her external balance through the rapid, continual improvement in labor productivity and production efficiency, which helped expand her exports while restraining the country's import demand.

UNBALANCED GROWTH

The wage cost is, of course, merely one of many factors affecting the balance of payments. Judging from Figure 4-2, it seems that some forces other than the wage cost exerted a favorable effect on Japan's external balance. We shall now consider the unbalanced pattern of Japanese growth as one of those additional factors.

In Table 4-5 we compare the growth rates of GNP and industrial production from 1950 to 1960 in seven major industrial-goods-exporting countries. As one would have anticipated, industrial output universally rose faster than the GNP; but in most countries the degree of disparity between the two variables was essentially the same. Therefore, it might not be unreasonable for us to assume that disproportionately rapid growth of industrial production relative to the GNP, as such, does not explain the improvement in the balance of payments of those countries. However, industrial output rose at exceptionally high rates relative to the GNP in Japan, West Germany, and Italy. Since this is true particularly with respect to Japan, we are inclined

[8] Production efficiency (i.e., raw-materials productivity) increased 29 per cent in Japan from 1955 to the second half of 1961. See Atsushi Nakamura, "Kōgyō Seihin Kakaku no Cost Yōin Bunseki," *Keizai Geppō* (Economic Planning Agency, November 1962).

towards the view that Japan's unbalanced growth had some definite effect on her balance of payments.[9]

TABLE 4-5

PATTERNS OF UNBALANCED GROWTH, 1950–1960
(per cent)

Item	A. The average annual rate of increase in GNP	B. The average annual rate of increase in industrial production	B/A
Japan	9.5	18.1	8.6
Italy	5.9	9.0	3.1
W. Germany	7.6	10.1	2.5
France	4.3	6.5	2.2
Belgium	2.9	4.1	1.2
U.K.	2.7	3.5	0.8
U.S.A.	3.3	3.6	0.3
The new long-range economic plan, 1956–1962	6.5	7.2	0.7

SOURCE: U.N., *World Economic Survey*, 1961, p. 63.

How can industrial production-centered growth affect the balance of payments? Inasmuch as 90 per cent of Japanese exports consist of industrial products, the disproportionately fast growth of the industrial sector meant a sufficient supply of exportable goods. Increase in the GNP induces a rise in the level of import demand, but in the case of Japan it seems that unbalanced growth resulted in a more favorable external balance than a more balanced pattern of growth would have, because, in general, the positive export effect of accelerated expansion in industrial output was much greater than the negative import effect of economic growth upon her balance of payments. We are not implying, of course, that the unbalanced growth of the industrial sector always exerted a consistent, positive effect upon Japanese exports. Rather, we are arguing that the rapid expansion of industrial output meant, by and large, an excess of supply over domestic demand, thus generating a considerable amount of export pressure. Japanese exports are known to fluctuate susceptibly relative to changes in foreign demand; but at times, Japanese exports fluctuated independently of trends in overseas demand, indicating that those fluctuations were primarily due to changes in the export capacity of Japan.

Figure 4-3 compares the volume of Japanese exports and of world import demand during 1954–1962. The disparity between the two

[9] Unbalanced growth of the kind under consideration was not anticipated in the New Long-Range Economic Plan. The Plan assumed that industrial production would increase only moderately faster than the GNP (see Table 4-5).

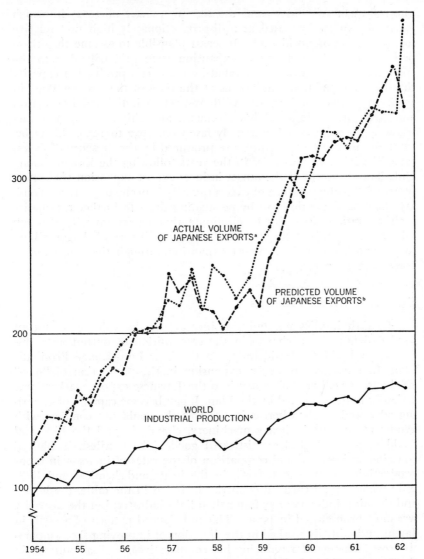

Fig. 4-3. World import demand and Japanese exports. a. The volume index of Japanese exports exclusive of those to the Communist bloc (seasonally adjusted), 1960 = 100. b. The prediction equation is: $\log Y = 2.053\log X + 0.11$, $r^2 = 94.2$. X is the world trade index, and Y the volume of Japanese exports (exclusive of those to the Communist bloc). c. The volume index of world exports of industrial products (seasonally adjusted), 1953 = 100. Source: *Chōsa Geppō*, January 1963, p. 148.

volumes was in part attributable to price changes (and many other factors), and certainly cannot be explained solely on the basis of Japan's export capacity. Nevertheless, we observe in Figure 4-3 that despite a fairly high degree of covariance between the two variables as a whole, there were periods (e.g., the second half of 1954–the beginning of 1956, 1958–1959, and the second quarter of 1962) in which Japanese exports increased at a disproportionately high rate relative to the volume of world trade. It seems plausible to assume that these periods of accelerated export expansion were primarily due to the emerging export pressure generated by the excess production capacity that followed the domestic booms at the time of the Korean War, in 1956, 1957, 1960, and 1961.[10] With respect to individual items, iron and steel, ammonium sulphate, cement, and ships are commodities whose exports increased extremely fast from 1952 to 1956, chiefly because of mounting export pressure produced by the presence of excess capacities in those industries in the years following the Korean boom. Unbalanced growth at the outset induces export expansion via export pressure. But the presence of excess capacity is prone to exert a secondary effect on domestic firms by persuading them to further rationalize their operations in order to eliminate that excess capacity through sales promotion. Such an attempt, however, will very likely contribute to yet another round of export expansion through the comparative-cost-advantage effect.

Exporting "New" Products

Growth implies not only an increase in the volume of output produced but also a change in the composition of output, and this fact was taken into consideration in the New Long-Range Economic Plan. In retrospect, however, expansion in the production of "new" products, as well as their entry into the Japanese export markets, was seriously underestimated by the Plan. Japan became capable of exporting advanced goods, whereas in the past she could not compete with Western countries in heavy machinery, chemicals, and the like, and could export only less sophisticated goods (like textiles). Table 4-6 contains an international comparison of the rates of increase in labor productivity from 1950 to 1960 in the heavy-and-chemical and light industries.[11] In all thirteen countries included in the table, the heavy-and-chemical industry grew faster than light industry; but the disparity was most pronounced in Japan. This unbalanced pattern of growth in Japan undoubtedly worked in the direction of improving the comparative-cost advantage (or reducing her comparative-cost disadvantage) in the heavy-and-chemical industry. Of course, high labor productivity *per se* does not necessarily imply a low comparative cost in money terms (e.g., high money wages can more than offset high labor productivity). But in reality the interindustry disparity in the rates of change in money wages is usually small, and (consequently) the interindustry difference in the change in real cost is often reflected in the

[10] For an econometric study on this point, see Yasuhiko Ikeuchi, *et al.*, *Yushutsu-nyū Hendō Yōin no Bunseki*, Series No. 10 (Economic Planning Agency, 1962), chapter 2.

[11] For industrial classification and the methods of calculating labor productivity, see notes to Table 4-6.

TABLE 4-6

ANNUAL RATES OF LABOR-PRODUCTIVITY INCREASE, 1950–1960
(per cent)

Country	A. Heavy-and-chemical industry	B. Light industry	A/B Productivity difference
Japan	13.4	7.6	5.8
Italy	9.6	5.3	4.3
Australia	5.3	2.6	2.7
Norway	5.3	3.1	2.2
Finland	4.1	2.2	1.9
Sweden	4.0	2.4	1.6
U.S.A.	4.3	3.1	1.2
U.K.	2.8	1.8	1.0
W. Germany	4.5	3.7	0.8
Canada	2.9	2.1	0.8
Holland	4.2	3.9	0.3
New Zealand	3.4	3.2	0.2
Belgium	3.1	3.0	0.1

SOURCE: Adapted from U.N., *World Economic Survey*, 1961, p. 68. Figures for Japan were separately calculated from the National Census. The heavy-and-chemical industry refers to the arithmetic average of average annual rates in chemicals, non-metallic minerals, metallics and machinery. The light industry refers to the arithmetic average of average annual rates in foods, textiles, clothing, wood products, paper, printing, leather, and rubber.

money cost.[12] Since world import demand for products of the heavy-and-chemical industry has been increasing, Japan's focus of growth on that industry definitely gave an advantage to her exports.

Even the Plan had anticipated certain changes in the composition of Japanese exports; for example, it predicted a relative decline in textiles and a relatively high rate of increase in metallic and chemical products. The extent of compositional change that actually took place, however, was much more extensive than the Plan's prediction, as is shown in Table 4-7.

Another noteworthy aspect of the compositional change was that a large number of "new" products that had never before been exported began to appear in the Japanese export statistics each year. Table 4-8 gives the expanding magnitude of these new commodities in total Japanese exports from 1951 through 1961. If we classify those commodities, each of whose weight in total Japanese exports reached 0.2 per cent since 1953, as new export items, there were 24 such items by 1961, amounting to $535.9 million in value. A decade ago the majority of them were negligible as export items. The value of new items accounted for 13 per cent of total exports in 1961; and as much as 18 per cent of the increase in the value of total exports over the past ten years was due to these new products. Transistor radios, tape re-

[12] For an empirical testing of this point, see Hisao Kanamori, "Nihon no Yushutsu Kōzō to Hikaku Seisan Hi," *Keizai Hyōron* (March 1963).

TABLE 4-7

COMMODITY-EXPORTS EXPANSION (AVERAGE ANNUAL RATE)
(per cent)

Item	Projections in the plan	Actual records, fiscal 1956–1961
Total	10.5	10.9
Foods and beverages	5.2	9.9
Nonmetallic mineral products	7.6	7.6
Textiles	9.0	5.5
Machinery	11.1	15.1
Metals and metallic products	11.2	14.1
Drugs and chemical products	13.7	14.7
Others	15.2	16.7

TABLE 4-8

GROWTH OF NEW-COMMODITY EXPORTS
(millions of dollars)

Item	1951	1953	1957	1959	1961
(1) Total export value	1,354.5	1,274.8	2,858.0	3,456.5	4,235.6
(2) Traditional exports	1,339.0	1,253.4	2,726.1	3,163.5	3,699.7
(3) New exports[a]	15.5	21.4	131.9	293.0	535.9
(4) Ratio of new exports to total exports	1.1	1.7	4.6	8.5	12.7
(5) Rate of contribution to increase in total exports since 1951			7.7	13.2	18.1

SOURCE: Ministry of Finance, *Tsūkan Tōkei*.

[a] Major items are drugs, synthetic textiles, construction equipment, bearings, radios, automobiles, tape recorders, manufacturing machines, transistor radios, motorcycles. For details, see *Keizai Hakusho*, fiscal 1962, p. 311.

corders, automobiles, and synthetic textiles are some representative examples of these new exports. The unexpected entry of products of technological innovation was one of the main reasons why the Plan's projection turned out to be an underestimate of actual export expansion. In economic planning, export projection is prone to be made on the basis of "old" commodities; and it is exceedingly difficult to predict the future appearance of new export items, particularly those which are not even produced in the home market at the time of planning. The fact that the annual rate of increase in the exports of traditional items from 1957 to 1961 was 8 per cent, which is lower than that in the GNP, strongly suggests that without the expansion of new commodity exports Japan would have experienced some serious balance-of-payments difficulties.

THE IMPORT-SAVING PATTERN OF INDUSTRIAL GROWTH

We now consider the pattern of industrial growth that tended to reduce the degree of Japan's dependency upon imported, industrial raw materials. Table 4-9 compares the Japanese industrial production index with the imported raw-materials consumption index from 1957 through 1960. We observe in the table that the imported raw-materials consumption per unit of industrial output in 1954 was 1.7 times as much as that in 1960. The third column shows a declining trend in the rate of imported materials consumption throughout the period. We may cite two reasons for this trend: first, during the period under consideration those industries whose import dependency is small (e.g., machinery, chemicals, synthetic textiles) grew at an accelerated rate, whereas those industries that heavily depend upon imported materials (e.g., cotton textiles, leather, rubber) expanded at a moderate pace; second, technological progress reduced the rate of raw-materials consumption per unit of output. Coal and iron ores in the steel industry are cases in point.

TABLE 4-9

INDUSTRIAL PRODUCTION AND ITS DEPENDENCY
UPON IMPORTED RAW MATERIALS

Fiscal year	A. Industrial production index	B. Imported raw-materials consumption index	A/B
1954	25.7	44.7	174
1955	26.1	45.0	173
1956	37.8	57.6	152
1957	52.6	67.1	128
1958	56.5	59.1	105
1959	72.6	79.0	109
1960	100.0	100.0	100
1961	129.0	118.2	92

SOURCE: Ministry of International Trade and Industry, *Seisan Dōtai Tōkei*.

We must note, however, that despite the fall in the degree of dependency upon imported, industrial raw materials, there was no corresponding decline in the nation's average propensity to import. Table 4-10 (column 1) shows that the ratio of imports to the GNP stayed at 11–12 per cent during 1953–1961 (fiscal). Much of the stability in the ratio was due to falling import prices; if we calculate the import ratio in terms of 1953 prices, the resulting "real" import ratio shows a rather sharp, upward-rising trend. We may cite the following reasons for the stability of the average propensity to import: (1) given the

TABLE 4-10

THE RATIO OF IMPORTS TO GNP[a]
(per cent)

Fiscal year	(1) "Nominal" ratio	(2) "Real" ratio[b]
1953	12.7	12.7
1954	11.7	12.5
1955	10.9	11.5
1956	12.9	13.8
1957	15.3	15.9
1958	10.9	12.8
1959	10.8	13.7
1960	11.6	15.5
1961	12.3	17.6

SOURCES: Economic Planning Agency, *Kokumin Shotoku Tōkei*, and Ministry of Finance, *Tsūkan Tōkei*.

[a] Imports (customs statistics) ÷ GNP.

[b] Import ratio in 1953 prices calculated on the basis of Ministry of Finance's import price index. Real GNP figures used for calculation are from the Economic Planning Agency's data.

increased weight of industrial production in the Japanese economy, the absolute value of raw-materials imports had to rise; (2) the weight of petroleum in domestic energy consumption increased conspicuously; and (3) the volume of imported finished goods and machines increased each year. These points are illustrated in Table 4-11. We observe that the weights of petroleum, machinery, and finished goods imports in the GNP have actually been increasing. The weight of raw-materials imports does not show a declining trend. We must conclude, therefore, that the degree of self-sufficiency of the Japanese economy has not been increasing over the past decade. But nevertheless, the maintenance of the Japanese external balance would have been far more difficult had the pattern of Japanese industrial growth been of the imported-raw-materials-using (rather than -saving) type or of the neutral type, which would have caused a relatively higher degree of import demand for industrial materials. In this sense we may argue, then, that the particular pattern of industrial expansion in Japan helped sustain accelerated growth of the whole economy without critical external disequilibrium.

CONCLUSION

Rapid increase in productivity relative to money wages, an unbalanced pattern of industrial growth, entry of new products into the Japanese exports, and the imported-raw-materials-saving type industrial expansion all point to the fact that economic growth meant not just a quantitative increase in the nation's output but rather a rapid,

TABLE 4-11

THE RATIO OF RAW-MATERIALS IMPORTS (CUSTOMS STATISTICS) TO GNP
(per cent)

Item	1953	1954	1955	1956	1957	1958	1959	1960	1961
Foods and beverages[a]	3.28	3.19	2.75	2.23	2.06	1.91	1.49	1.42	1.40
Broadly defined raw materials	8.14	7.32	7.25	9.47	11.62	7.22	7.72	8.57	8.96
Crude raw materials[b]	5.94	5.37	5.26	6.68	7.01	4.59	5.06	5.45	5.69
Textiles raw materials	3.50	3.01	2.58	3.08	2.85	2.19	1.91	1.97	2.02
Metallic raw materials	0.91	0.84	0.82	1.82	2.48	0.93	1.49	1.74	2.03
Mineral fuels	1.52	1.31	1.27	1.65	2.43	1.85	1.67	1.92	1.97
Coal	0.47	0.31	0.25	0.36	0.63	0.35	0.27	0.37	0.40
Petroleum	1.01	0.97	1.00	1.25	1.76	1.48	1.38	1.52	1.53
Other raw materials[c]	0.69	0.65	0.67	1.15	2.17	0.78	0.99	1.20	1.29
Iron and steel	0.07	0.06	0.04	0.24	1.09	0.09	0.14	0.23	0.33
Nonferrous metals	0.05	0.11	0.09	0.23	0.36	0.11	0.15	0.27	0.32
Machinery	0.85	0.86	0.58	0.64	1.03	1.23	1.05	1.04	1.27
Sundry and others	0.39	0.33	0.30	0.56	0.64	0.57	0.53	0.61	0.67
Total	12.66	11.71	10.88	12.91	15.34	10.93	10.79	11.63	12.32

SOURCE: Ministry of Finance, *Gaikoku Bōeki Gaikyō*.

[a] "Foods and beverages" refers to the total of foods, beverages and tobacco.

[b] "Crude raw materials" refers to "raw materials" as classified in the above Ministry of Finance statistics minus pulp, scrap paper, and synthetic rubber.

[c] "Other raw materials" refers to the total of: (1) synthetic rubber, pulp, scrap paper; (2) animal and vegetable oil; (3) chemical elements and compounds, mineral tar, dyes, tanning and coloring materials, plastic materials; (4) filament, woven materials, finished metallic materials.

qualitative change in the nation's economic activity induced by a series
of technological innovations. According to the traditional view, increase in investment (necessary for economic growth) is prone to raise
the level of import demand and therefore to cause a deterioration in
the balance of payments. Our foregoing analysis seems to suggest that
innovation-oriented, rapid growth may actually eliminate potential
balance-of-payments difficulties rather then lending itself to such difficulties. This thesis appears valid in the light of the Japanese postwar
experience in achieving both rapid growth and external equilibrium.[13]

Comment *by Masahiro Tatemoto*

PESSIMISM AND OPTIMISM

Mr. Kanamori examines the relationship between economic
growth and the balance of payments in the light of postwar experiences of the Japanese economy. There have been two opposing views
on that relationship. The economists on the pessimistic side have held
that rapid growth is conducive to a deterioration in the balance of
payments; those on the optimistic side have argued that rapid growth
will bring about an improvement in the balance of payments because
productivity increase in the course of growth will help reduce the costs
of export goods as well as import-competing goods produced at home.
Mr. Kanamori challenges the pessimistic view that has been predominant in Japan and attempts to demonstrate the validity of the
optimistic view as a long-run proposition.

[13] Mr. Tatemoto maintains in his comment on my paper that the consistency between rapid growth and the balance-of-payments equilibrium was more apparent
than real, because external equilibrium was impossible without capital inflow, and
that the plus price effect of growth on external balance was not strong enough to
offset its minus income effect. I myself do not discount the importance of capital inflow. But I feel that Japan's rapid growth had a significant plus effect on the trade
account. Of course, rapid growth tends to create simultaneously two opposing effects on the balance of payments: a negative effect through a rise in domestic income
that raises the level of import demand; and a positive effect through price reduction
that leads to an export expansion. My view is that the Japanese case cannot be adequately accounted for solely in terms of these simple income and price effects. My
empirical evidence was admittedly insufficient; but I tried to show that a pronounced
plus effect was exerted by the dynamic technological innovations in Japan. In the
absence of such internal technological change, i.e., if Japanese growth were a simple
case of domestic output expansion unaccompanied by the waves of significant innovations, I suspect that Japan would have suffered far worse balance-of-payments
difficulties even with capital inflow. For a more complete picture, capital transactions
should be taken into consideration as well. In this paper I have concentrated on the
trade-balance aspect of the problem since international capital movement involves
a different set of rules and principles than those affecting the trade balance.

Concepts of the Balance of Payments

I am somewhat troubled by Kanamori's interpretation of the concept of balance of payments. The "balance" of payments may refer to (1) the current transactions balance (keijō shūshi) that equals the difference between exports (X) and imports (M) of both goods and services. It may instead pertain to (2) the trade balance (bōeki shūshi) that shows the difference between exports and imports of commodities only. Finally, it may be defined as (3) the total foreign-exchange transactions balance or, more colloquially, the overall balance (sōgō shūshi) that covers not only exports and imports of goods and services but also capital transactions and unilateral transfers. The last one is the most comprehensive indicator of foreign-exchange reserves held by Japan and is what has been referred to in connection with the balance-of-payments crises during the postwar period.

Mr. Kanamori begins his paper by saying that he will be concerned mainly with the trade balance (2), but later goes on to demonstrate that Japanese growth did not induce a deterioration in her balance of payments in terms of the overall balance (3). This may be permissible provided that the above three balances move, as a rule, parallel to each other. Let us examine these balances on the basis of the same Bank of Japan's *Foreign-Exchange Statistics* that Kanamori has employed in order to confirm whether the three balances do behave in such a manner.

In Table 4-12 both the trade balance and the current transactions balance show a consistent, deteriorating tendency (excluding fiscal 1957), i.e., their positive balances continue to diminish and then turn negative towards 1961. Given this observation, we become rather skeptical about Kanamori's proposition that since Japan could continue to cumulate foreign-exchange reserves while growing rapidly, the commonly held view on the incompatibility of accelerated growth with the balance-of-payments equilibrium does not apply to Japan. His proposition does not hold to the extent that it is based upon only a nominal, positive balance in the total foreign-exchange transactions account.

The Balance-of-Payments Equilibrium

I have called a positive foreign-exchange transactions balance "nominal," because I feel that it is an inappropriate indicator of the nation's external-equilibrium position. It was because all the compensatory transactions (mostly in the form of foreign-capital inflow) were lumped together with the export-import transactions in Kanamori's measurement of Japanese external equilibrium that it looked as though Japan was capable of growing rapidly without disturbing her balance of payments. It is more sensible for us to define the balance of pay-

TABLE 4-12

The Balance of Payments under Different Definitions
(millions of dollars)

Fiscal year	GNP growth rates (per cent)	(1) Current transactions balance	(2) Trade balance	Capital transactions balance	Errors and omissions	(3) Overall balance (total foreign-exchange transactions balance)
1957	7.9	−90	−235	−94	75	−109
1958	3.2	500	369	−35	−120	345
1959	17.9	193	155	155	39	387
1960	13.2	−70	3	677	29	636
1961	14.0	−1,003	−864	629	−62	−436

SOURCE: Economic Planning Agency, *Keizai Hakusho*, fiscal 1962, p. 42. The GNP growth rates and the overall balance are the same as those in Table 4-1. The overall balance corresponds to changes in the foreign-exchange reserves.

ments in terms of only autonomous transactions and to exclude temporary elements in trade and accommodating financial transactions.[1] A voluminous amount of foreign capital received by Japan in fiscal 1960 consisted mostly of a temporary and rather fortuitous inflow of Euro-dollars. Six hundred and seventy-seven million dollars from United States city banks and $538 million of stand-by credit Japan borrowed from the I.M.F. in fiscal 1961 were also of a temporary and accommodating nature to offset mounting deficits in the current transactions account. In short, it is rather misleading to analyze Japan's balance of payments during the period under observation solely on the basis of changes in foreign-exchange reserves held by Japan. Kanamori's paper suffers at the very outset from a misconception of external equilibrium. He should have focused his attention on the current transactions balance for a more meaningful analysis—and we might add that entirely opposite conclusions (to his) can be drawn in terms of the current balance with respect to the alleged relationship between Japan's growth and her balance of payments.

NOMINAL VERSUS REAL BALANCE

There are some other objections to Kanamori's interpretation of the balance of payments. In its common usage the balance of payments refers to a nominal money balance, and the real balance as such is almost totally meaningless except for some specific, analytic purpose. However, economic plans (or econometric models) based upon the real national income statistics typically calculate the real balances in constant prices because of the difficulty in predicting future prices. We may express the real equilibrium as

$$\left(\frac{X}{p_x}\right) \Big/ \left(\frac{M}{p_m}\right) = \left(\frac{X}{M}\right) \Big/ \left(\frac{p_x}{p_m}\right) = 1$$

Since $\frac{X}{M} = 1$ signifies the nominal (money) equilibrium, we obtain the real balance by dividing the terms of trade into it. In general, the real-balance equilibrium does not imply a money-balance equilibrium. Kanamori was correct in citing, as a favorable external change, an improvement in the terms of trade (a fall in import prices).[2] He is incorrect, however, in treating the ratio between the export and import volume indexes (i.e., the real balance) as though it represents the

---

[1] J. E. Meade, *The Balance of Payments* (Oxford, 1951), pp. 15–16.

[2] Mr. Saburō Ohkita, one of the chief planners in charge of the New Long-Range Economic Plan, himself considers the importance of the terms-of-trade effect as he writes: "In retrospect, exports increased faster than the projection, import prices fell as much as 15 per cent relative to 1957, and Japan received short- as well as long-term foreign capital in magnitudes not anticipated by the Plan. All in all, these subsequent developments made possible Japanese growth without an external disequilibrium" (Saburō Ohkita, "Keizai Seichō to Keizai Keikaku," *Keizai Seminar* [November 1960]).

money balance in Table 4-3 as well as in Figure 4-2. He also confuses in Table 4-2 the real balance according to the New Long-Range Economic Plan with the money balance.

THE INCOME EFFECTS VERSUS PRICE EFFECTS

There remain two points that ought to be mentioned. First, with respect to Figure 4-3, it seems that most of the positive deviations of actual Japanese exports from the prediction curve can adequately be explained by the price effects; but Kanamori, without sufficient justification, relies on "export pressure" coming from the supply side as the explanatory factor. Second, with respect to Kanamori's discussion on the imported-raw-materials-saving pattern of industrial growth, there seems little basis for its inclusion, inasmuch as imports other than industrial raw materials have been expanding to such an extent that the overall degree of import dependency has actually risen rather than declined.

The foregoing objections are not meant to discredit the value of Mr. Kanamori's comprehensive analysis. His paper does illuminate the possibility of a much greater positive effect of technological innovations on the balance of payments than was projected by the New Long-Range Economic Plan. I agree that the Plan's assumption that rapid growth will necessarily induce an external imbalance was an over-simplification. My only contention is that the extent of a positive price effect of industrial-production-centered growth on the balance of payments was not, in truth, as powerful as Kanamori suggests in offsetting the negative income effect associated with accelerated growth of Japan. These price and income effects jointly determine the net effect of growth on the balance of payments—and this view is shared by Hicks as well as Johnson.[3] The majority of Japanese economists have tended to discount the importance of positive price effect in the case of Japanese growth. Given the predominance of the pessimistic school of thought in Japan, Kanamori deserves our respect and congratulations because his paper has lucidly demonstrated the more positive aspects of Japanese growth.

[3] Cf. J. R. Hicks, *Essays in World Economics* (Oxford, 1959), chapter 4; H. G. Johnson, *International Trade and Economic Growth* (1958), chapter 4. See also, Masahiro Tatemoto, *Bōeki no Keiryō-teki Bunseki*, University of Osaka Social and Economic Studies Series, No. 17 (Yuhi-Kaku, 1963), chapters 1–3.

5

Masao Fakuoka:

The Balance of Payments and a Model
of Cyclical Growth

Japan's postwar growth has been constrained three times over by balance-of-payments difficulties in 1953, 1957, and 1961. The modus operandi of constraints imposed by the external disequilibrium might be summed up as follows: rigorous entrepreneurship leads to an accelerated rate of investment, and the national income increases much faster than is warranted by the nation's export capacity. As a result signs of deterioration emerge in the balance of payments. When the extent of deterioration reaches a critical point, the central bank invokes a stringent, tight-money policy. High rates of interest and slackening domestic demand discourage the firms' investment motives. The slower pace of growth helps reduce the level of imports, and the external balance becomes favorable. As the central bank curtails its deflationary policy, the level of investment begins to rise again.

The above characterization, though admittedly oversimplified, seems a reasonably accurate description of the basic mechanism that molded the pattern of postwar cyclical growth of the Japanese economy. Buoyancy of the economy, sustained by a high rate of investment, temporary and periodic halts of growth brought on by the tight-money policy, a continual rise in the level of the balance-of-payments ceiling through augmentation of export capacity—these aspects of cyclical growth are remindful of Goodwin's balloon analogy in which he compared cyclical growth with the bouncing, upward flight of a balloon on the back of stairs.[1]

In this paper we shall construct a theoretical model of the above mechanism of cyclical growth. In its broad framework our model is based upon the Hicksian trade-cycle model except that we replace the labor-supply ceiling à la Hicks with the balance-of-payments ceiling. Our attempt then is similar to what Harry Johnson has done vis-à-vis the Harrod model.[2] The frame of reference in our model, however, is largely derived from the Japanese experiences.

[1] R. M. Goodwin, "A Model of Cyclical Growth," in E. Lundberg, ed. *The Business Cycle in the Post-War World* (1955), p. 209.
[2] See H. G. Johnson, *International Trade and Economic Growth: Studies in Pure Theory* (1958), chapter V, pp. 121–129.

With respect to the period t, let $Y(t)$ stand for the national income, $C(t)$ for consumption, $I(t)$ for investment, $X(t)$ for exports, and $M(t)$ for imports. Then we derive the basic equation,[3]

$$Y(t) = C(t) + I(t) + X(t) - M(t) \tag{1}$$

As regards the variables on the right side of the equation, we propose the usual assumptions:

$$C(t) = cY(t - 1) \tag{2}$$

$$I(t) = v(Y(t - 1) - Y(t - 2)) \tag{3}$$

$$M(t) = mY(t - 1) \tag{4}$$

We assume that exports grow exogenously at a constant rate. Hence,

$$X(t) = X(0)(1 + \lambda)^t \tag{5}$$

We make the following additional assumptions concerning c, m, v, and λ.

$$0 < c < 1 \tag{a}$$

$$0 < v \tag{b}$$

$$0 < m < 1 \tag{c}$$

$$0 < \lambda < 1 \tag{d}$$

$$c > m \tag{e}$$

$$c < 1 - \lambda \tag{f}$$

The meaning of these assumptions should be self-evident. From the definition $s = 1 - c$, it should be clear that (e) implies $s + m < 1$, and (f) $s > \lambda$. From (2) $\sim$ (5), (1) becomes a nonhomogeneous, difference equation of a well-known form,

$$Y(t) - (c - m + v)Y(t - 1) + vY(t - 2) = X(0)(1 + \lambda)^t \tag{6}$$

We can write changes in income determined by (6) as,

$$Y(t) = y_1(0)\mu_1{}^t + y_2(0)\mu_2{}^t + \bar{Y}(0)(1 + \lambda)^t \tag{7}$$

The term $\bar{Y}(0) (1 + \lambda)^t$—to be referred to as $\bar{Y}(t)$ from here on—in the right side of the equation (7) increases at the same rate as exports, and its level is determined by the "super-multiplier" of the form,

$$\bar{Y}(t) = \frac{X(0)(1 + \lambda)^t}{1 - (c - m + v)(1 + \lambda)^{-1} + v(1 + \lambda)^{-2}} \tag{8}$$

$Y_1(0)$ and $Y_2(0)$ are constants depending upon the gaps between $\bar{Y}(0)$ and the base-period condition $Y(0)$; whereas μ_1 and μ_2 are the characteristic roots of the homogeneous equation,

$$y(t) - (c - m + v)y(t - 1) + vy(t - 2) = 0 \tag{9}$$

[3] We assume the absence of the government sector.

that determines the movement in the gap, $Y(t) = Y(t) - \overline{Y}(t)$. Whether the rates of $\overline{Y}(t)$ be stable or unstable depends upon the absolute values of μ_1 and μ_2 as well as the magnitude of $1 + \lambda$; what amounts to the same thing, it also is affected by the absolute value of the characteristic root of the equation,

$$r(t) - (c - m + v)(1 + \lambda)^{-1}r(t - 1) + v(1 + \lambda)^{-2}r(t - 2) = 0 \quad (10)$$

that limits the relative gap $r(t) \equiv y(t)/\overline{Y}(t)$. It is stable if $v < (1 + \lambda)^2$, and unstable if $v > (1 + \lambda)^2$. The income gap oscillates when $(1 - \sqrt{s + m})^2 < v < (1 + \sqrt{s + m})^2$, and changes monotonically when $v < (1 - \sqrt{s + m})^2$ or $v > (1 + \sqrt{s + m})^2$.[4]

So much for the minimum groundwork. Let us turn now to the main part of the argument. We shall first examine what conditions must be met so that a balance-of-payments equilibrium be realized. We express the balance-of-payments equilibrium as,

$$X(t) = M(t) \quad (11)$$

Through substitution of (4) and (5) we derive,

$$Y(t) = \frac{X(0)(1 + \lambda)^t}{m(1 + \lambda)^{-1}} \quad (12)$$

which shows that for us to achieve a balance-of-payments equilibrium, income must be $m^{-1}(1 + \lambda)$ times as much as exports, and must keep growing at the same rate (λ) as exports. Designating $Y^*(t)$ for such growth path of $Y(t)$, from (8) and (12) we know that for $\overline{Y}(t)$ to equal $Y^*(t)$, the condition,

$$1 - (c + v)(1 + \lambda)^{-1} + v(1 + \lambda)^{-2} = 0 \quad (13)$$

must be met. What is the same thing, the condition,

$$v = \frac{(1 + \lambda)(s + \lambda)}{\lambda} \quad (14)$$

ought to be fulfilled.

Given s and λ, let v^* be the value of v that fulfills the condition (14); then we can interpret v^* as an optimum investment coefficient. Consider an economy in which v is greater than v^* because of active investment motives among entrepreneurs.[5] In such an economy the $\overline{Y}$-path lies clearly above the Y^*-path. And we can show, given the above set of assumptions, that the $\overline{Y}$-path is always unstable because, under the assumptions (d) and (f), $s > \lambda^2$ and $\sqrt{s} \neq \lambda$, which imply that $(1 + \lambda)(s + \lambda)\lambda^{-1}$ is clearly larger than $(1 + \lambda)^2$. Under the same assumptions, $v > (1 + \sqrt{s})^2$; but let us for now assume, instead, that $v > (1 + \sqrt{s + m})^2$. Suppose that Y deviates upwards slightly from

[4] See J. R. Hicks, *A Contribution to the Theory of Trade Cycle* (1950), pp. 8, 182–186.

[5] For the super-multiplier to be positive, v cannot exceed $[(1 + \lambda)(s + m + \lambda)]/\lambda$.

the $\bar{Y}$-path following a certain shock.[6] Since the subsequent movement of Y is necessarily divergent in one direction, the balance-of-payments deficit continues to increase with time. Therefore, unless some measures be taken to curb the mounting deficit, the external disequilibrium will soon grow to intolerable proportions.[7]

Suppose that the central bank has invoked a stringent, tight-money policy; as a result investment activity slackens, and the value of v falls by a sizeable margin. In order to clarify the full implications of the situation, let us consider an extreme case in which v is reduced to 0, i.e., we replace the assumption (b) with[8]

$$v = 0 \tag{g}$$

By substituting (g) into (8), the new $\bar{Y}$-path becomes,

$$\tilde{Y}(t) = \frac{X(0)(1 + \lambda)^t}{1 - (c - m)(1 + \lambda)^{-1}} \tag{15}$$

Similarly, by substituting (g) into (10), we obtain a new relative-gap formula,

$$r(t) - (c - m)(1 + \lambda)^{-1} r(t - 1) = 0 \tag{16}$$

Since $0 < (c - m)(1 + \lambda)^{-1}$ from the assumptions (a), (c), (d) and (e), the Y-path must level off and move down toward the $\tilde{Y}$-path.

A comparison of (15) with (12) reveals, since $0 < c(1 + \lambda)^{-1} < 1$ from the assumptions (a) and (d), that the $\tilde{Y}$-path lies below the Y^*-path. This means that the balance-of-payments equilibrium will be restored when Y sufficiently approaches the $\tilde{Y}$-path. In subsequent periods the balance of payments will further improve as long as Y moves along with $\tilde{Y}$. The curtailment of a tight-money policy will lead to the revival of active investment by the firms; and v will resume its initial value.

If in the beginning Y deviates downwards from the $\bar{Y}$-path, it forms a low-level path similar to the $\tilde{Y}$-path through a variation of the acceleration principle, causing a rise in income and accumulation of foreign-exchange reserves. Therefore, v will tend to resume, once again, its original value. In either case, once the initial value of v be resumed, Y cuts across the Y^*-path and penetrates the disequilibrium area, thus repeating the whole process of cyclical fluctuations.

We have seen that our model, composed of three elements—(1) entrepreneurial investment incentives, (2) a monetary-policy mechanism geared toward balance-of-payments adjustments, and (3) an upward-rising trend in income sustained by expanding export capacity—can

[6] The implication of the downward deviation will be noted later. The direction of deviation is not of fundamental importance since in our model the system will always return to the cyclical-growth path.

[7] If at the outset the $\bar{Y}$-path appears beyond such a limit, we should consider the present income to be equal to that in the base period.

[8] As a first approximation, s, m, and λ are assumed to be independent of monetary policy.

generate self-enforcing, cyclical growth. Our model reveals certain interesting features of its own: first, as long as $s > \lambda$, the investment
coefficient whose value is greater than the value at which the balance-
of-payments equilibrium is achieved tends to induce a diffusion effect;
and, second, in the recessive phase, all that is required is the slowing
down of growth rates, and the absolute level of income need not necessarily go down. These properties of the model seem consistent with
Japan's postwar experiences.

A few supplementary notes are in order. Of the critiques of the
thesis that balance-of-payments disequilibrium is prone to constrain
economic growth, the most frequently heard version runs something
as follows: "6.5 per cent was said to be the safe, maximum rate of
growth for the Japanese economy; but in actuality it has been growing
at the rate of 10 per cent without confronting critical balance-of-payments difficulties. Something (therefore) must be wrong with the above
thesis." The logic of this argument is rather misdirected and scarcely
relevant to the nature of our problem. The difference between 6.5 per
cent and 10 per cent is merely a reflection of gaps between the predicted and actual values of exports as well as imports, and has little
to do with the pros and cons of our analysis of the relationship between growth and the balance of payments.

Assuming that future balance-of-payments deficits can be precisely
predicted, our real problem is to measure the extent to which growth
will be constrained by those deficits. Solution of such a problem requires a thorough, theoretical analysis of the alternative judgments
available to the government. Many views and interpretations of the
"right" growth policy with respect to the balance of payments exist;
but they are not dealt with in this paper. The main interest of this
paper has been to build a model that accounts for the pattern of
cyclical growth in Japan resulting from the particular policy-measures
adopted by the government. The author plans to conduct an analysis
of long-run investment effects on production (not touched upon in
this paper) on some other occasion.

PART III

Income Distribution and Savings

6

Kōtaro Tsujimura:
The Employment Structure and Labor Shares

In his recent, long-term time-series analyses of 10 to 12 countries, Kuznets has made the following observations:[1]

(1) The national capital formation proportion, in general, tends to increase *pari passu* with per capita income. In the United States and Great Britain, however, per capita income has continually risen while the increase in capital formation proportion ceased at an early phase of development. In Norway, Sweden, and Japan, on the other hand, the capital formation proportion began to rise only several decades after pronounced upturns in their gross as well as per capita incomes. The commonly assumed, simple, positive correlation between income level and the capital formation proportion is subject to many exceptions in the real world.

(2) The cross-sectional studies of the postwar period reveal examples of high-income countries with low capital formation proportions as well as low-income countries with high capital formation proportions; hence, we fail to observe any close relationship between the income level and the rate of savings.

(3) The marginal capital coefficients among different countries typically vary between 2 and 5, and their time series show little similarities in the patterns of change from country to country. Even their moving averages for over 20 years fail to stabilize their values.

From the above observations Kuznets is led to conclude: (1) it is difficult to prove empirically, through time-series analysis, such simple relations as $s = kY$ or $gc = s$; (2) the alleged causative relationships between per capita income, the rate of saving, and the rate of growth are, in reality, subject to so many irregular variations that it is doubtful that one can make a meaningful, long-term economic forecast on the basis of such relationships—one must consider many "other" factors as well as variable conditions surrounding the early stage of development of each country; (3) the mode and intensity of capital utilization depend upon not only economic but also social conditions, but

[1] Simon Kuznets, "Quantitative Aspects of the Economic Growth of Nations, VI; Long-Term Trends in Capital Formation Proportions," *Economic Development and Cultural Change*, Vol. 9, No. 4, part 2 (July 1961).

we are yet to discover which of these conditions are of greater importance than others.[2]

In this paper we propose to examine the employment structure as one factor which determines the particular relationships between the income level and the rate of saving, on the one hand, and between capital formation and growth, on the other.

In the process of Japan's postwar growth, the supply of capital, rather than labor, tended to set a limit to the maximum growth rate; consequently, much attention has been focused on the relationship, $gc = s$. In brief, the labor shortage did not create a bottleneck in the Japanese economy. It should be noted that since there existed an excess supply of labor at the outset of the period, the size of the "latent" labor supply in subsequent years has been larger than the rate of increase in the active labor suggests.

We shall concentrate on the proposition that the particular employment structure in Japan has contributed to capital formation primarily through the mechanism of wage determination. This is not meant to deny the fact that a rapid increase in both workers' and farmers' incomes during 1951–1960 helped sustain a high level of effective demand. A stable expansion of farm income resulting from land reform, the rice price-support program, and technological improvements in agriculture combined with a steady rise in workers' income, undoubtedly added to the strength of consumption demand and helped minimize the negative, cumulative effect of a fall in investment demand. This paper is concerned with the interaction between workers' income and the interindustry formation and utilization of capital resulting from changes, via the price mechanism, in the supply of and demand for individual consumption goods. The recently developed Paretian consumption function indicates that the price elasticity of consumer demand in Japan is much greater than suggested by the traditional, partial-equilibrium demand function.[3] But space does not permit us to delve into the demand aspect of the problem. We shall instead direct our attention to the supply side and examine the relationships between the employment structure, wage determination, and capital accumulation.

LABOR SHARES AND CAPITAL FORMATION

The constraints on the maximum growth rate have usually been identified as those of savings and investment. According to the National Income statistics, of gross national savings during 1958–1960, approximately 20 per cent was government savings, about 47 per cent capital consumption allowances and corporate retained earnings, and 34–41 per cent personal savings. Sources of personal savings consist of compensations for employees, incomes of the self-employed, personal

[2] *Ibid.*, p. 56.

[3] See Kōtaro Tsujimura, "Family Budget Data and Market Analysis," *Bulletin of the International Statistical Institute*, Vol. 38, part 2 (Tokyo, 1961), pp. 227–228.

rental income, personal interest income, and personal dividend income. A comparison between the ratio of saving to total personal disposable income and the saving ratio with respect to compensations for employees only reveals that the rate of personal saving among non-employees is much higher than that among wage-and-salary earners (see Tables 8-2 and 8-5).

Of total personal income in 1958, the ratio between wage-and-salary income and "other" personal income was 10 to 7. The rate of saving out of wage-and-salary income was 14.1 per cent as against 23.8 per cent for other personal income in the same year. The ratios of compensations for employees to the GNP for 1951–1960 (fiscal) are contained in Table 6-1. We might hold that capital accumulation in Japan would have been hampered had these ratios been higher than they actually were. In Table 6-1 (column 4) the weight of compensations for employees in total personal income shows a definite, upward trend throughout the period 1951–1960. From 1954 to 1959 the number of employed increased by 4 million (reaching a total of 44 million); whereas the number of employees increased by more than 5 million, the number of self-employed and family workers decreased by 1 million. Consequently, the weight of employees in the total number of the employed rose from 38 to 47 per cent.

In Table 6-1 we observe that the weight of employee compensations in total personal income increased conspicuously from 45 per cent in 1951 to 55 per cent in 1960; but the weight in the GNP registered only a moderate rise from 33 to 38 per cent because of the offsetting effect of the rise in the ratio of capital consumption allowances to the GNP.

The high, overall rate of savings in Japan, then, has been due to the fact that a relatively small share of the National Income has gone to employees with a low propensity to save—although their saving propensity is "high" in comparison with that in other countries. The National Income shares depend not only upon the weight of employees in the total number of employed but also upon labor shares in different industries. Since the ratio of wage-and-salary income to total value-added shows the relationship between the value productivity and the wage rate, the high rate of savings in Japan may be said to be a reflection of the low level of wages relative to productivity.

From the standpoint of utilization of output capacity, however, we cannot hold that the small weight of employee compensations is desirable for the nation's growth. Since a stable growth of compensations for employees has significantly contributed to the steady expansion of the domestic market throughout the postwar years, we must concede that Japan's accelerated growth has also been due to the absence of both a drastic decline in labor shares and excessive wage lags relative to the productivity increase. In short, during 1951–1960 (aside from the intentions of the government, corporations, and labor unions) wages, relative to productivity, presumably stayed at a level most conducive to rapid growth, being neither so high as to hinder capital

TABLE 6-1

Employee Compensation and Capital Formation Proportion

Item	Fiscal year									
	1951	1952	1953	1954	1955	1956	1957	1958	1959	1960
(1) GNP (100 billion yen)	54	61	70	75	82	93	101	104	126	147
(2) Employee compensation (100 billion yen)	18	22	22	28	31	35	39	42	48	55
(3) (2) ÷ (1) (per cent)	33	36	31	37	37	38	38	40	38	38
(4) Weight of (2) in total personal income (per cent)	45	47	49	50	49	51	52	54	54	55
(5) Weight of capital consumption allowances in GNP (per cent)	5.1	5.9	6.7	7.5	7.9	8.5	9.2	10.0	10.0	10.4
(6) Gross domestic capital formation proportion (per cent)	30.6	27.4	27.9	23.4	25.4	31.8	31.6	27.3	35.0	38.2
(7) Weight of private capital formation in (6) (per cent)	75.3	71.8	67.5	66.1	65.7	76.6	74.8	67.2	74.7	76.1

SOURCE: Economic Planning Agency, *Kokumin Shotoku Hakusho.*

accumulation nor so low as to prevent the expansion of the domestic market. One of the factors responsible for such an "optimal" wage level is the employment structure as it has affected the supply of and demand for labor in Japan.

THE EMPLOYMENT STRUCTURE

Labor shares in the Japanese manufacturing industry, as we shall see later on, are considerably lower than those in the United States. This might be regarded as an example of the familiar phenomenon that low labor shares are usually associated with "underdeveloped" countries. Let us examine some characteristics of the Japanese employment structure in comparison with other, "more advanced" countries. Table 6-2 gives the ratios of employees to total employment in all

TABLE 6-2

THE RATIO OF EMPLOYEES IN ALL INDUSTRIES

Country	Fiscal year	Employee ratio (per cent)
Japan	1960	54
U.S.A.	1960	84
U.K.	1951	88
France	1954	65
W. Germany	1959	77
Italy	1960	63

SOURCES: Sōrifu Tōkei Kyoku, *Rōdō Ryoku Chōsa*, and *Kokusei Chōsa*; I.L.O., *Yearbook of Labour Statistics*, 1958 and 1961, and U.S. Department of Labor, *Employment and Earnings*.

industries in selected countries. In 1960 the Italian ratio was 63 per cent; but the Japanese ratio in the same year was as low as 54 per cent —as late as 1960 about one-half of total employment in Japan consisted of self-employed and family workers. Even in the manufacturing industry the weight of employees in Japan is small relative to other, advanced countries. For example, the ratios of employees in the Japanese manufacturing industry, shown in Table 6-3, are lower than the ratios of employees in all industries in the United States and Great Britain.

Within the manufacturing industry, large-scale firms usually represent the modern sector of the economy; and yet we observe in Table 6-4 that the ratio of workers in firms of 500 personnel or more was 22 per cent in Japan as against 45 per cent in the United States, 41 per cent in Great Britain, and 46 per cent in West Germany. In terms of absolute numbers the total number of workers in West German firms of 500 or more is about 3 times as large as in Japan despite the fact that the population of West Germany is only slightly larger than half

TABLE 6-3

THE RATIO OF EMPLOYEES IN THE
MANUFACTURING INDUSTRY

Fiscal year	Employee ratio (per cent)
1954	72
1956	76
1958	79
1959	81

SOURCE: Sōrifu Tōkei Kyoku, *Rōdō Ryoku Chōsa.*

of the Japanese population. In Japan 50 per cent of workers in the manufacturing industry are found within firms of 50 or less. A comparison of per-worker wage with per-worker value-added in terms of firm sizes indicates that there are not only quantitative but also qualitative differences between Japan and other countries; e.g., in Western countries the wage rate in firms of 50 or less is usually 70–80 per cent of that in firms of 1,000 or more, whereas in Japan it is less than 50 per cent (see Table 6-5). In Japan, then, the ratio of em-

TABLE 6-4

THE NUMBER AND RATIO OF WORKERS IN THE MANUFACTURING INDUSTRY BY FIRM SIZE

Firm size	Japan (1954)		U.S.A. (1954)		U.K. (1949)		W. Germany (1956)	
	Number (1,000)	Ratio (%)	Number (1,000)	Ratio (%)	Number (1,000)	Ratio (%)	Number (1,000)	Ratio (%)
Total	6,196	100.0	15,651	100.0	7,421	100.0	6,639	100.0
1–9	1,430	23.1	595	3.8	359[a]	4.8	169	2.5
10–49	1,806	29.2	1,961	12.5	840[b]	11.3	721	10.9
1–49		37.8[c]		17.2[d]				11.7[e]
50–99	554	9.0	1,475	9.4	749	10.1	651	9.8
50–99		12.0[c]		9.8[d]				8.6[e]
100–499	1,062	17.1	4,549	29.1	2,421	32.6	2,050	30.8
100–499		23.5[c]		30.2[d]				28.4[e]
500–999	404	6.5	1,964	12.5	971	13.1	868	13.1
500–999		26.8[c]		42.8[d]				51.3[e]
1,000 or more	938	15.1	5,108	32.6	2,081	28.1	2,180	32.8

SOURCES: Sōrifu, *Jigyōsho Tōkei Chōsa Hōkoku,* 1954, 1961; *Census of Manufactures,* U.S.A., 1954, 1958; *Census of Production,* U.K., 1959; and *Statistische Jahrbuch,* 1954, 1959.

[a] 1–10.
[b] 11–49.
[c] for 1960.
[d] for 1958.
[e] for 1959.

TABLE 6-5

ANNUAL PER WORKER VALUES-ADDED[a] AND WAGES[b] BY FIRM SIZE
(1,000 workers or more = 100: per cent)

Firm size	Japan (1955)		U.S.A. (1954)		U.K. (1949)		W. Germany (1951–1952)[c]	
	Value-added	Wage	Value-added	Wage	Value-added	Wage	Value-added	Wage
1–9	....	....	70.7	63.0	....	....	73.9	81.7
4–9	27.6	40.0	....	....	....	....	....	....
10–49	36.8	45.7	72.3	75.6	91.4[d]	82.5[d]	71.9 }	87.8
50–99	50.9	53.5	77.4	81.9	93.8	83.7	72.8 }	
100–499	72.1	64.8	85.6	82.9	96.4	85.5	82.8 }	91.6
500–999	95.6	79.1	92.9	88.9	98.1	89.3	90.4 }	
1,000 or more	100.0	100.0	100.0	100.0	100.0	100.0	100.0	100.0

SOURCES: For Japan, M.I.T.I., *Kōgyō Tōkei Hyō*, 1954; for U.S.A., *Census of Manufactures*, 1954; for U.K., *Census of Production*, 1949; for W. Germany, *Statistische Jahrbuch*, 1954. This table was prepared by Ryōhei Magota.

[a] Value-added divided by the number of workers. But for Great Britain the numerator is the production value (i.e., gross output minus raw-materials costs, fuel costs and other production costs), and for W. Germany, the value of sales.

[b] Total wage payments divided by the number of workers.

[c] Wages for 1951, the value of sales for 1952.

[d] 11–49 workers.

ployees is conspicuously low, even in relatively modern sectors, and the modern employment markets are surrounded by extensive layers of "premodern" labor markets.

Table 6-6 illustrates the ratios of employees by sex in the United States and Japan. Assuming that the modernization of labor markets increases the ratio of employees, male or female, Table 6-6 indicates the pronounced backwardness of the female-labor markets in Japan. Following the reasoning of W. Arthur Lewis, we might maintain that the general backwardness of the Japanese labor markets has meant a high elasticity of labor supply in the modern, advanced employment markets.

Supply-and-demand conditions in the labor markets are indicated in

TABLE 6-6

RATIOS OF EMPLOYEES BY SEX: 1954
(per cent)

	Male	Female
Japan	52.3	32.7
U.S.A.	78.7	91.1

SOURCE: I.L.O., *Yearbook of Labour Statistics*, 1957.

some of the more "direct" statistics compiled by the government. According to the Ministry of Labor's *Employment Security Statistics* (*Shokugyō Antei Gyōmu Tōkei*), there were 3.6 times as many job-seekers as the number of available jobs in 1955. In subsequent years the excess supply of labor began to diminish; and the number of job-seekers and job-openings became approximately equal in 1961. In West Germany in the same year the number of job-openings was six times as large as the number of job-applicants. The above employment statistics are known to involve a considerable amount of duplication in both job-seekers and job-openings; accordingly, when the labor markets become tight the statistics tend to show an exaggerated figure of job-openings, whereas in a recession the number of job-applicants is prone to be inflated. Even allowing for these biases, however, the above statistics illustrate the pronounced excess supply of labor in Japan as compared with West Germany.

A similar observation can be made through comparison of the new-employment rate and the job-vacation rate. In accordance with the Japanese Ministry of Labor's *Monthly Labor Survey* (*Maigetsu Kinrō Tōkei*) and the United States *Monthly Labor Review,* for the period 1953–1960 the rate of new employment in Japan was approximately 2 per cent as against 3–4 per cent in the United States; the rate of job vacation in Japan was also 2 per cent relative to 3–4 per cent in the United States. The higher rates in the United States indicate a relative tightness of American labor markets.

The question of what index(es) can best reflect supply-and-demand conditions in the labor markets involves many theoretical difficulties. Our examination of several, alternative indexes seems to show, however, that the aforementioned proposition—that in Japan the backward segments of the labor markets constitute a primary source of labor supply in the advanced sectors, while the low ratio of employees is indicative of an excess supply in the general labor markets—is largely confirmed by the more direct employment statistics.

The Marginal Productivity Theory and the Low Labor Shares

We may consider the marginal productivity theory as an effective approach to the measurement of labor shares in a certain industry in one country relative to other countries. This theory, together with that of consumer behavior, is one of the foundations of modern economic theory; and the construction of econometric models, so that they be more than simple regression analyses, often necessitates an application of the marginal productivity theory.

There are several possibilities in using production functions as an approach to the above problem. Perhaps the simplest is to compare elasticities in countries A and B by way of the Cobb-Douglas production function,

$$Q = BK^{\alpha}L^{1-\alpha}$$

Professor Kazushi Ohkawa has adopted this particular approach in his recent study and has presented the argument that Japanese labor shares are low because the importation (and imitation) of foreign technology tends to make α larger in Japan than in the advanced countries.[4]

The second approach is to apply the Marschack-Andrews model.[5] Let L be the employment of labor; w the unit wage; K the capital input; r the unit capital cost; $W(w \cdot L)$ labor cost; and $R(r \cdot K)$ capital cost. Then,

$$\text{production function} \quad Q = Q(L, K) \tag{1}$$

$$\text{value-added} \quad V = S(Q) \quad \text{(goods market)} \tag{2}$$

$$\text{labor cost} \quad W = W(L) \quad \text{(labor market)} \tag{3}$$

$$\text{capital cost} \quad R = R(K) \quad \text{(capital market)} \tag{4}$$

Let P be price; then $V = PQ$. And,

production elasticity α_K, $\alpha_L = 1 - \alpha_K$
value-added elasticity with respect to price β_0
labor-cost elasticity with respect to the volume of employment β_L
capital-cost elasticity with respect to the stock of capital β_K

From the profit-maximization condition, $\pi = v - w - R$, we derive as equilibrium equations,

$$\text{labor shares} \quad \omega = \frac{W}{V} = \alpha_L \frac{\beta_0}{\beta_L} \tag{5}$$

or

$$\text{wage = productivity} \quad w = \left(P \cdot \frac{Q}{L} \right) \alpha_L \frac{\beta_0}{\beta_L} \tag{6}$$

$$\text{wage = marginal productivity} \quad w = \left(P \cdot \frac{\partial Q}{\partial L} \right) \frac{\beta_0}{\beta_L} \tag{7}$$

By incorporating the monopoly ratios of Kalecki into the above equations, we can show the possibilities of differential labor shares under the assumption of ordinary production functions. As is well known, β_0 equals 1 if the goods market is perfectly competitive and becomes less than 1 under a monopolistic market. Similarly, β_L equals 1 under a competitive labor market and is less than 1 if the market is monopsonistic. It is clear from (5) that the more monopolistic and monopsonistic are the goods and labor markets, respectively, the smaller the labor shares become for a given value of α_L. Therefore, we can explain, for example, the larger labor shares in the United States

[4] Kazushi Ohkawa, *Nihon Keizai Bunseki—Seichō to Kōzō* (Shunju Sha, 1962), pp. 19–22.
[5] J. Marschack and W. H. Andrews, "Random Simultaneous Equations and the Theory of Production," *Econometrica*, Vol. 12 (1944).

manufacturing industry by proving that the degree of monopoly in Japanese goods and/or labor markets is higher than that in the United States.

We may adopt, as a third alternative approach to explain the international differences in labor shares, the CES production function[6] developed by the Stanford group. The CES production function is based upon the interindustry logarithmic regressions of the values-added and wages for about 20 countries, and it was intended to test empirically if the wage coefficient generally is less than 1. That the per-worker wage coefficient is less than 1 when the value-added productivity is treated as a dependent variable implies that the higher the wage rate is, the smaller the labor shares become, and conversely when the wage rate is lower. Therefore, the CES production function is capable of explaining international disparities in labor shares, provided that the constant elasticity of substitution is less than 1.

Unlike the Cobb-Douglas production function approach, which requires an elaborate explanation, the CES production function enables us to explain the smaller labor shares in the Japanese manufacturing industry relative to the United States simply by showing that the production function in Japan differs from that in the United States. We can conceive of yet other approaches, but they will not be touched upon in this paper. As Henri Poincaré once pointed out, there may be an infinite number of hypotheses one can formulate to explain a given empirical fact. Our task is to discover which hypothesis can provide the most systematic and effective explanation of the phenomena under observation.

The aforementioned proposition of Ohkawa, that the small labor shares in Japan are due to the large value of α in the Cobb-Douglas production function for Japan, may explain a wide range of phenomena if properly supplemented with additional explanatory variables. Without such supplementary variables, however, such a proposition becomes a mere tautology—unless the relatively large value of α in Japan is proven by some means independent of the data on the small Japanese labor shares. In other words, we must clarify the method by which we can quantitatively measure how, in the process of technological advancement, α_K in Japan with respect to a specific industry catches up with and surpasses that in the United States.

All-industry labor shares in Japan are lower than those in the United States. In terms of the firm sizes within Japan, however, shares tend to be larger among small firms (see Figure 6-1). The curves are reversed at the minimum as well as maximum firm sizes. The curves turn downward in Figure 6-1, as they approach the smallest firm size, for the technical reason that the wage portion of the income of self-employed among the smallest firms is not included in the statistics of

[6] H. B. Chenery, K. Arrow, B. Minhas, R. M. Solow, "Capital-Labor Substitution and Economic Efficiency," *Review of Economics and Statistics*, Vol. 43, No. 3 (August 1961). The "CES" production function stands for "constant-elasticity-of-substitution" production function.

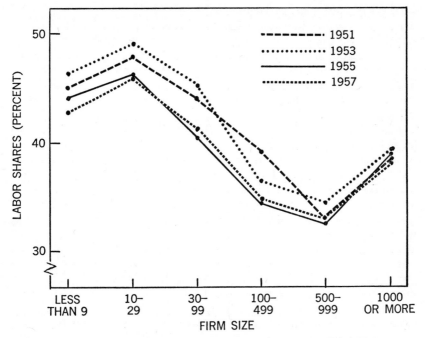

Fig. 6-1. Labor shares and firm sizes. Source: M.I.T.I., *Kōgyō Tōkei Hyō*.

total cash compensations; the downward turns will presumably dis-
appear after proper adjustments. It does not seem easy to give a systematic explanation of these size differences in Japan on the basis of
the international disparities in the value of α_K.

The degree-of-monopoly approach, mentioned above, will lead us
to conclude, by implication, that Yawata Steel and the big five auto-
makers in Japan are more monopolistic than U.S. Steel and the big
three auto-producers in the United States. In view of the intensity of
administered pricing in both countries, it seems difficult, if not impossible, to accept such a conclusion. With respect to domestic size differences, the greatest difficulty is how to explain the upturn of labor shares
at the level of largest-size firms.

The often-heard statement that "Japanese labor markets are strongly
monopsonistic" sounds plausible at first hearing. The aforementioned
labor-cost function (equation 3) is based upon the labor-supply function that characterizes labor's response to the firms' job offers. Insofar
as the Marschack-Andrews specifications are concerned, the labor-cost
function contains a policy implication that, since a high degree of
monopsony implies that one firm can control the whole labor market
and that an increase in the firm's demand for labor will induce wage
inflation, the government may be compelled to regulate the volume of
employment in order to prevent such wage inflation. But according
to the *Business Firms Statistical Survey* (*Jigyōsho Tōkei Chōsa*), there

were 3.3 million firms in all industries included, and 530,000 firms in the manufacturing industry alone as of July 1954; there is, therefore, very little we can expect of β_L in explaining Japanese labor shares. Furthermore, a recent empirical study[7] shows that the labor-supply curve (which coincides with the response curve under perfect monopsony) is not as upward-rising relative to the wage rate as has been commonly believed. This finding casts another doubt upon the validity of the β_L approach.

The third approach, based upon the CES production function,[8] has (in my view) led to one of the most fruitful works that has appeared in recent years. From the numerical values of its three parameters (substitution, shares, and output effect) we may be able to forecast future trends in labor shares as they change in the process of modernization of the economy. For example, if we assume that large labor shares in a high-wage country result from the elasticity of capital-labor substitution being less than 1, we can expect a future rise in Japanese labor shares, together with an increase in the wage level. Explanation of the differential labor shares by firm size shown in Figure 6-1 (especially the inverse relationship between the wage rate and labor shares) will perhaps be no less difficult with the CES production-function than with the other two approaches; but the disaggregation of industries will hopefully provide an effective solution. Of the three approaches, the CES approach seems most attractive.

And yet I hesitate to take up the CES function, not only because of the conclusion of the recent Review of Economic Studies symposium[9] that the CES production function, like the Friedman-Modigliani permanent-income hypothesis, is exceedingly difficult either to prove or disprove, but also because of my doubts as to the applicability of the function to "underdeveloped" countries characterized by disguised unemployment, low-level employment, excess labor supply, and the like, inasmuch as the function attempts to explain labor shares on the basis of presupposed equilibrium conditions of a competitive market that are hardly interchangeable with the above characteristics of underdevelopment.

THE DOUGLAS INQUIRY AND THE GERSCHENKRON-LEWIS MODEL

One of the motives that led Douglas to develop his production function was the wish for an empirical answer to the question: "Does the wage rate really equal the marginal product?" The neoclassical marginal productivity theory assumes full employment as one of its premises, whereas in the presence of unemployment there is no guarantee that the wage rate in the real world necessarily equals the mar-

---

[7] Iwao Ozaki and Keiichirō Obi, "Keizai Hatten to Shūgyō Kōzō," *Keizai Gaku Nempō*, No. 6 (Keio University Economic Association, 1963).

[8] See footnote 6.

[9] "Symposium on Production Functions and Economic Growth," *Review of Economic Studies* (June 1962).

ginal value product of the employed labor force; furthermore, it is theoretically possible for the wage rate to approach zero, i.e., to approach the marginal productivity of the unemployed (or social marginal labor productivity). It is well known, however, that Douglas and his associates found that the exponent of the production function closely matched the labor shares in all areas studied, except South Africa, thus tentatively proving the general validity of the marginal productivity theory.[10]

To the extent that the neoclassical thesis on the equality between the wage rate and marginal productivity, and its assumption of full employment at equilibrium, are inseparable, Douglas's proposal for an empirical testing of the theory was a legitimate one. While Douglas made an attempt, before Keynes, to relate the unemployment problem to the marginal productivity theory, he did not inquire into the causes of unemployment. Of particular interest in connection with his empirical proof of the marginal productivity theory (except for South Africa) is the fact that he was concerned with cyclical unemployment in advanced countries but not with structural unemployment in underdeveloped countries.

W. Arthur Lewis's unlimited-supply-of-labor theory,[11] with reference to underdeveloped countries, is not unrelated to the Douglas inquiry for it assumes a form of critique of the neoclassical system. Lewis has argued that in an economy of excess population, marginal productivity in agriculture and other indigenous industries can be zero or even negative; therefore, the wage rate is determined at a subsistence level. Even wages paid within the modern sectors are set not by the marginal productivity in those sectors but rather in terms of the subsistence wage rate outside the modern sectors. In the Lewis model wages in the advanced sectors are exogenously determined at a level slightly above the subsistence wage rate; then, firms adjust employment so that wage = marginal product. The Lewis model differs from the neoclassical system to the extent that in the former wage and employment are not simultaneously determined.

While Lewis has given attention to the unlimited supplies of unskilled labor in underdeveloped countries, Gerschenkron has taken note of the critical shortage of skilled workers in modern factories in underdeveloped areas of the world where there is "borrowed technology" from the advanced countries, and has pointed out the possible need in an economically backward country for more labor-saving production techniques than would be required in developed countries.[12]

Let us relate the borrowed-technology and skilled-labor-shortage

[10] P. H. Douglas, *The Theory of Wages* (1947), and "Are There Laws of Production?" *American Economic Review* (March 1948).

[11] W. A. Lewis, "Economic Development with Unlimited Supplies of Labour," *The Manchester School of Economic and Social Studies*, Vol. 22, No. 2 (May 1954).

[12] Alexander Gerschenkron, "Economic Backwardness in Historical Perspective" in B. F. Hoselitz, ed. *The Progress of Underdeveloped Areas* (Chicago University Press, 1952).

theses to the Lewis model. The conventional skilled-versus-unskilled classification of labor inadequately describes the adaptability problems of a modern industrial labor force, because adaptability implies not only specific skills and know-how but also general intelligence, trainability of workers, and social adjustability to group work. Viewed in this comprehensive manner, we can expect a wide range of qualitative variations in the kinds of workers available in underdeveloped countries, from the extremely unskilled category à la Lewis to the extremely skilled group à la Gerschenkron. In a state of severe backwardness, there may be a very uneven distribution of labor qualities, with an infinitesimal supply of modern, skilled workers on the one hand, and an abundant supply of unskilled workers throughout the indigenous industries on the other hand; but as the country moves onto higher stages of development, the number of potentially adaptable workers steadily increases, and the distribution of labor qualities becomes more even. In an extremely advanced country the unskilled-labor pool in the indigenous industries almost completely disappears, and the majority of workers consists of those whose qualifications are above the minimum adaptability requirements for modern production; consequently, with the intensification of demand for labor in such an economy, the distribution of labor skills becomes less and less conspicuous.

Despite the radical and swift changes that have recently taken place in her labor conditions, we may contend that present-day Japan has reached only a semi-advanced stage of development; with a sizeable labor-pool still existing in her indigenous industries and with a large number of potentially adaptable workers, there is a very notable range of qualitative variations in labor skills. In the language of Lewis, marginal wages in the indigenous sectors constitute a bottom line above which the structure of wages in the modern sectors is determined in accordance with the differential skills of workers,[13] as illustrated by the interindustry or interfirm disparities that persist in Japan.

From 1949 to 1955, cash income per farm family increased 2.4 times. The corresponding rates of increase in wages among different-size manufacturing firms, shown in Table 6-7, may be interpreted as the results of an upward shift in the aforementioned bottom line, thanks to a rise of income in the agricultural sector. The relatively low rates of wage increase among medium-size firms may indicate that those firms are less susceptible to the wage-push impact coming from the agricultural sector than, say, the smaller firms. The relatively high rate of wage increase among large firms is most likely due to the collective bargaining power of labor unions operating at the level of those firms. In terms of the adaptability criteria, the qualities of industrial

---

[13] While discussing wage levels in the traditional sectors, we must remember that conditions become radically different depending upon whether the agricultural sector consists largely of self-employed farmers or relies upon the extensive employment of migratory farm laborers.

TABLE 6-7

WAGE INCREASE IN THE MANUFACTURING
INDUSTRY, 1949–1955

Scale	Wage increase (per cent)
1,000 or more	2.4
500–999	2.4
100–499	2.0
30–99	2.0
10–29	2.2
Less than 9	2.2

SOURCE: Ministry of Labor, *Maigetsu Kinrō Tōkei.*

workers at large firms are subject to a wide range of variations, but unionization makes them a noncompeting group.

We have noted earlier that labor shares become larger among small firms. It is clear, therefore, that the wage rate at large firms increases less than proportionately with the rate of increase in value-added productivity. Following the Lewisian line of reasoning, wages in modern, large-scale firms should be set at a level slightly above small-firm wages, and, at that level of wages, large firms adjust the volume of employment so that wage = marginal productivity.

If this be the case, why have we failed to achieve interfirm equalization of labor shares? Why are Japanese labor shares lower than in the advanced countries? The borrowed-technology thesis of Gerschenkron may perhaps provide an answer.

Let us first view these questions from various other standpoints. The CES-production-function approach attempts to explain the falling tendency in labor shares from advanced to underdeveloped countries in terms of the propensity for the elasticity of substitution to be less than 1; but this approach assumes not only competition in goods as well as labor markets, with respect to each industry, but also that the profit-maximization equilibrium condition is being met by producers. On the other hand, under the Cobb-Douglas-production-function approach, the elasticity of substitution equals 1, implying a constancy of labor shares regardless of the relative prices of labor and capital; therefore, we fail to explain the phenomenon of differentiated labor shares in the real world. The limitation of the CES approach becomes apparent if we try to apply it to an analysis of interindustry relations within a country; namely, it is capable of explaining international differences in the wage-productivity relationship with respect to a given industry, but it does not explain interindustry wage gaps in a single country.

Table 6-8 shows that even in the United States interindustry wage rates are significantly differentiated. Of 18 industries listed in Table

TABLE 6-8

INTERINDUSTRY WAGE DISPARITIES IN THE UNITED STATES AND JAPAN

Industry	U.S.A.		Japan	
	Rank	Index	Rank	Index
Foods	13	73.8	14	45.2
Textiles	16	57.3	16	40.6
Clothing and personal items	18	52.7	18	33.6
Woods and wood products	15	58.6	16	40.6
Furniture	14	68.9	15	44.0
Paper, paper products	10	81.9	6	75.5
Printing, publication	6	88.3	8	70.6
Chemicals	4	90.3	4	84.9
Coal, petroleum products	1	100.0	3	86.6
Rubber products	9	84.2	10	61.5
Leather and leather goods	17	56.4	13	52.8
Glass and ceramics	12	77.2	11	60.4
Primary metals	5	89.4	1	100.0
Metallic products	8	84.5	12	58.3
Machinery	3	91.4	7	7.22
Electrical equipment	11	80.7	5	76.3
Transport equipment	2	95.3	2	92.0
Precision instruments	7	86.2	9	66.7

SOURCES: For U.S.A., *Census of Manufactures*, 1954; for Japan, *Kōgyō Tōkei Hyō*, 1954.

6-8, annual wages in the highest-wage industry (primary metals) and the lowest-wage industry (clothing and personal items) in Japan are 256,100 yen and 86,000 yen, respectively; the ratio between the two is approximately 3 to 1. The corresponding annual wages for the United States are $5,105 (petroleum and coal products) and $2,690 (clothing and personal items); their ratio is approximately 2 to 1. These figures show that the difference between the two countries' interindustry wage gaps is merely one of degree. A comparison of industry ranks in Figure 6-2 indicates a high degree of rank correlation among 18 industries in the two countries.

From the above observations we may draw two inferences: (1) interindustry wage disparities seem universal among different countries; and (2) rank patterns of interindustry wage differences seem similar from one country to another.

The presupposition of the CES approach, that each industry is at equilibrium, such that wage equals marginal productivity, implies, in terms of neoclassical reasoning, that full-employment equilibrium is approximated in each labor market of a given industry because, under the neoclassical assumption, wage and employment are simultaneously determined.

The case of the United States seems to suggest that labor is not homogeneous from industry to industry, and the distribution of differentiated wage rates corresponds to the adaptability differences

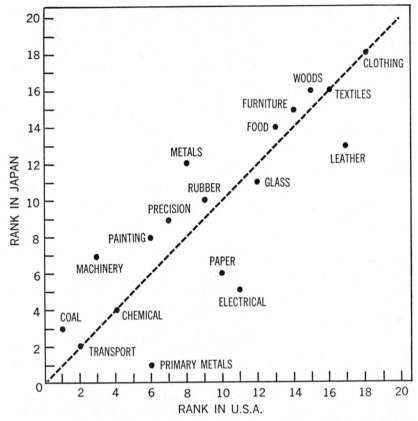

Fig. 6-2. Rank correlation between interindustry wage disparities in the United States and Japan. Source: Table 6-8.

among workers, with the workers in a given industry forming a relatively noncompeting group vis-à-vis those in other industries.

For the moment, let us suppose that in a given country each industry has its own separate labor market. The question is whether each of those separate labor markets is in a state of equilibrium with respect to supply of and demand for labor. Under the assumption that a separate Cobb-Douglas production function exists in each industry and that each industrywise labor market in the advanced country is in the neighborhood of equilibrium, except for frictional unemployment, the labor share in a given industry equals the exponent α of the production function applicable to that industry. In an underdeveloped country, provided that a labor-intensive method of production is employed, even if the wage level is low relative to the unit cost of capital, the labor share in a given industry can move up, given an equilibrium condition in the labor market, to equal α in the corresponding industry in an advanced country. In this case the minimum wage will be set (as suggested by Lewis) in accordance with the marginal income level of the self-employed, family workers, and the like in indigenous industries, and with that minimum wage as a takeoff point the structure of wages will be upwardly adjusted, from the low-wage-industry to the high-wage-industry labor markets, in terms of the differential skills and adaptabilities of the workers.

But as we have already seen, in reality labor shares are smaller in underdeveloped countries than in advanced countries; and this should not be the case, under the present assumptions, if employment responds to a given wage rate along the Cobb-Douglas production function. We feel that this apparent paradox might be dissolved by the Gerschenkron "borrowed-technology" thesis.

Technological development in the advanced countries, allowing for complications due to the confrontation of labor unions, depends upon relative prices of labor and capital;[14] this is consistent with the Cobb-Douglas assumption that, in the course of economic development, technological progress expressed as an upward shift of the production function (when plotted on a logarithmic chart) has only a neutral effect. In the advanced countries, changes in relative prices of production factors induce technological development which is followed by a neoclassical adjustment in factor-proportions while full-employment equilibrium is approximated in each labor market with respect to a given industry. In the case of semi-advanced or underdeveloped countries, however, it is doubtful whether we can maintain that the choice of technology, as well as goods to be produced, will depend upon relative factor prices determined in accordance with the factor endowments in that country. The underdeveloped countries, because of their critical manpower shortage in science and technology, typically import finished machines and equipment directly from advanced countries, in lieu of taking the painstaking steps to design and build machines that are consistent with relative factor prices at home. Direct importation of foreign technology is often preferred because it is simpler and more economical to purchase finished machines from abroad than to develop from the very beginning a whole complex of science and technology in the domestic economy.

There is yet another important reason for the popularity of borrowed technology. Advanced technology in developed countries is prone to exert a powerful influence upon the kinds of goods to be produced and upon the consumption patterns not only in those countries but, through international trade, in the underdeveloped countries as well. Consequently, whole industries in underdeveloped countries are bound to be subjected, through complementarity effects of commodities, to the influence of "foreign technology," and the probability of developing a unique home industry, taking full advantage of domestic factor endowments, tends to be reduced. In this manner, production methods and factor proportions in underdeveloped coun-

[14] See S. Melman, *Dynamic Factors in Industrial Productivity* (New York, 1956).

tries are led to resemble those in advanced countries by the direct demonstration effect through production, and the indirect effect through consumption.

As borrowed technology conditions the variety of production facilities in underdeveloped countries, factor proportions in the direct process of production become increasingly inflexible, and it is only in the indirect phases of production that factor proportions remain adjustable to the persisting relative factor prices. Therefore, the isoquant applicable to a firm in an underdeveloped country runs through the vicinity of the optimal point of a firm in an advanced country but is more steeply sloped than that facing the latter firm. The point of tangency between the isoquant and the factor-price line in an underdeveloped country determines the labor-capital proportions in the usual manner. We may call the production function implied by the isoquants in the underdeveloped country a "quasi-production function," whose elasticity of substitution is presumably less than that of the original Cobb-Douglas function.

When the wage rate relative to capital costs in Japan is lower than that, say, of the United States, production in Japan fails to become as labor-intensive as it would be under the assumption that factor proportions are determined by the "original" (as against quasi-) production function; therefore, labor shares in Japan become smaller than those in the United States. In other words, the equilibrium volume of employment (of labor) in Japan will be smaller than when the same factor prices prevail in the advanced country. In short, borrowed technology induces an unbalance between employment and relative factor prices and hence prevents the realization of the neoclassical full-employment equilibrium. The impact of borrowed technology is, by definition, felt most acutely in the modern sectors of underdeveloped countries. It is these sectors that exhibit all the manifestations of underdevelopment, historically unknown to the advanced countries, such as the so-called structural unemployment which results from the borrowed-technology-induced unbalance between employment and relative factor prices.

As we have noted earlier, the interindustry wage ranks in Japan are similar to those in the United States except that the range between the highest and the lowest wages is wider in Japan. This may be due to the greater, relative scarcity of adaptable workers in Japan. On the other hand, given the essential homogeneity of capital relative to labor, there is usually a tendency towards equalization of capital costs within any one given country. Therefore, the fact that Japanese interindustry wage gaps are greater than those in the United States implies that the relative prices of labor and capital in Japanese high-wage (as against low-wage) industries are closer to those in the United States. Namely, in connection with the borrowed-technology effect, the higher the wage level in a given Japanese industry, the less of the aforementioned disequilibrium will there be in the associated employment market.

The next section will examine Japanese interindustry disparities in labor shares (in comparison with those in the United States) and their relationship with structural unemployment.[15]

STRUCTURAL UNEMPLOYMENT AND LABOR SHARES

Let us determine how well we can explain international differences in labor shares in terms of the volume of structural unemployment (or the excess of labor supply), relative to demand, in the modern employment markets. Figure 6-3 equates labor shares out of gross

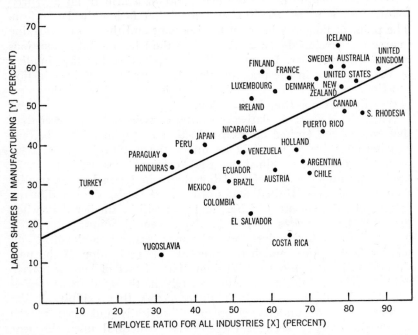

Fig. 6-3. Correlation between the employee ratio (X) and the labor share (Y). $Y = 14.85 + 0.447X$ ($\pm$ 0.102), $r = 0.624$. Source: Table 6-9.

values-added in the manufacturing industry with the ratios of employees in all industries for 32 countries whose data, taken from the U.N. statistics, are believed comparable (see also Table 6-9). The employee ratio is treated as an index of modernization in the employment market of a given country. It is assumed that the lower the ratio of employees, the more structural unemployment exists, and conversely when the ratio is high. The coefficient of correlation between labor shares and employee ratios is significant at the level of 1 per cent, indicating an inverse relationship between the volume of structural unemployment and labor shares.

[15] For related studies, see Tōkei Kenkyū Kai, ed. *Seisansei no Hendō to sono Eikyō* (Nihon Seisansei Honbu, 1958), and Yasuhiko Torii, "Nōka no Shūgyō Kōzō to Nōgyō Seisan Ryoku" (unpublished).

TABLE 6-9

EMPLOYEE RATIOS AND LABOR SHARES IN VARIOUS COUNTRIES: AROUND 1955
(per cent)

Country	(1) Employee ratio	(2) Labor shares	Country	(1) Employee ratio	(2) Labor shares
Argentina	70.1	36.5	Ireland	56.1	52.4
Australia	79.8	58.1	Japan	43.6	39.4
Austria	61.9	35.0	Luxembourg	62.6	53.0
Brazil	50.6	31.9	Mexico	45.9	30.9
Canada	81.6	49.5	Holland	68.4	38.1
Chile	71.4	34.4	N. Zealand	79.9	53.3
Colombia	52.5	28.0	Nicaragua	55.1	40.6
Costa Rica	66.5	18.1	Paraguay	33.0	38.3
Denmark	73.8	56.3	Peru	41.7	38.6
Ecuador	52.8	36.7	Puerto Rico	74.7	44.2
El Salvador	55.6	22.5	Sweden	76.8	58.0
S. Rhodesia	85.9	49.8	Turkey	13.9	30.0
Finland	58.1	58.2	U.K.	87.8	55.8
France	66.1	56.6	U.S.A.	82.1	53.9
Honduras	35.2	33.7	Venezuela	54.0	37.6
Iceland	79.3	63.8	Yugoslavia	31.6	13.3

SOURCES: For (1), I.L.O., *Yearbook of Labour Statistics*; for (2), U.N., *Patterns of Industrial Growth, 1938–1958*, New York, 1960.

From the regression coefficient (see Figure 6-3) we observe a general tendency for a 10 per cent increase in the employee ratio to induce a 3–5 per cent increase in labor shares. We must note, however, that only about 40 per cent of variations in labor shares can be accounted for in terms of employee ratios. Unexplained variations in labor shares are obviously due to numerous factors that can affect labor shares, such as: industrial structure in manufacturing; the presence or absence of minimum-wage laws; the collective-bargaining power of labor unions as well as the degree of their centralization; capital-ownership pattern; social security programs; intensity of racial discrimination; absence or presence of an international movement of labor; agricultural organization, and so on. It is interesting to observe that, without removing the effects of all these factors, Figure 6-3 still shows an inverse relationship between structural unemployment and labor shares.

In Table 6-10, which compares labor shares in various manufacturing industries in the United States and Japan, we notice that shares in Japan are consistently lower than those in the United States. This observation is to be expected from Figure 6-3, inasmuch as we learned earlier that the Japanese employee ratio (1958) is 46 per cent as against 82 per cent for the United States (1950). The consistently low level of Japanese shares does not preclude the possibility of certain inter-industry similarities between the two countries. Assuming the presence of the Cobb-Douglas production function and the full-employment equilibrium in both countries, we know that, by measuring the United

TABLE 6-10

LABOR SHARES IN SELECTED MANUFACTURING INDUSTRIES:
JAPAN AND THE UNITED STATES (1954)

Industry	(1) Japan	(2) U.S.A.	(3) (1) ÷ (2)
	(per cent)	(per cent)	
Foods	27.6	46.3	0.60
Textiles	39.2	63.9	0.61
Clothing, personal items	44.2	62.2	0.71
Woods, wood products	46.2	60.6	0.76
Furniture	53.4	60.9	0.88
Paper, paper products	37.3	48.4	0.77
Printing, publication	36.6	57.9	0.63
Chemicals	29.7	36.1	0.82
Coal, petroleum products	25.6	42.7	0.60
Rubber products	29.1	55.6	0.52
Leather, leather goods	43.3	62.7	0.69
Glass, ceramics	34.8	50.7	0.69
Primary metals	45.5	54.4	0.84
Metallic goods	46.5	57.9	0.80
Machinery	50.4	58.3	0.86
Electrical equipment	38.7	53.4	0.72
Transport equipment	55.2	59.6	0.93
Precision instruments	52.6	56.4	0.93
Others	45.5	59.4	0.76
Average	39.3	53.9	0.73

SOURCES: For Japan, *Kōgyō Tōkei Hyō*; for the United States, *Census of Manufactures*.

States labor shares on one axis and Japanese shares on the other, all the coordinates will appear on a 45-degree line. We are curious to test if similar regularities are observable in the real world. Let x be labor shares in the United States industries and z the corresponding labor shares in Japan; the regression is found to be

$$z = -5.56 + 0.847x, \quad r = 0.693 \tag{8}$$

Correlation is significant at the level of 1 per cent. We must explore to what extent we can explain the less-than-1 regression coefficient in (8) in terms of excess supply of labor in the employment market. The previously used employee ratios for "all industries" cannot be treated as an index of interindustry disparities in the employment markets. However, from the extremely low ratios of female (as against male) employees in Japan, shown in Table 6-11, we may hold that the excess supply of labor in the Japanese employment markets is particularly pronounced in the case of female workers. The ratios of female workers vary from industry to industry (see Table 6-12). It is evident that excess labor supply is closely associated with those industries that employ a large proportion of female workers, and that the ratio of female employees can therefore be used as a proxy variable to express the extent of excess supply.

TABLE 6-11

THE EMPLOYEE RATIOS: MALE AND FEMALE[a]
(per cent)

Fiscal year	Male	Female	Total
1948	44.6	24.5	36.8
1949	43.2	21.4	34.4
1950	43.8	22.5	35.4
1951	45.6	26.0	37.8
1952	46.0	26.2	38.1
1953	46.5	25.7	38.1
1954	47.2	26.4	38.8
1955	47.5	27.6	39.3
1956	50.0	29.9	41.7
1957	48.3	31.6	43.8
1958	53.8	34.1	45.8
1959	55.5	34.8	47.2
1960	57.2	36.9	49.0

SOURCE: Sōrifu, *Rōdō Ryoku Chōsa.*
[a] The ratio of employees to the total number of the employed.
Employees refer to those older than 14 for 1948–1952, and those
older than 15 for 1953 on.

TABLE 6-12

RATIOS OF FEMALE WORKERS IN JAPANESE INDUSTRIES

Industry	Ratio of female workers (per cent)
Foods	33.9
Textiles	71.4
Clothing, personal items	69.1
Woods, wood products	20.6
Furniture	12.9
Paper, paper products	31.2
Printing, publication	19.1
Chemicals	24.3
Coal, petroleum products	19.6
Rubber products	49.4
Leather, leather goods	23.3
Glass, ceramics	27.7
Primary metals	9.0
Metallic goods	19.3
Machinery	10.5
Electrical equipment	27.3
Transport equipment	8.7
Precision instruments	28.1
Others	43.9

SOURCE: *Kōgyō Tōkei Hyō,* 1954.

Let us see if we can explain labor shares solely in terms of supply-demand conditions in the employment markets. Designating z for labor shares in various industries in Japan and y for the ratios of female employees in the corresponding industries, the regression equation becomes

$$z = 45.1 - 0.139y, \quad r = 0.279 \tag{9}$$

The regression coefficient turns out to be negative, while the correlation is insignificant. It is evident that labor shares cannot be explained solely by the extent of excess supply in the employment markets. On the other hand, if we incorporate the proxy variable (y) representing the ratio of female employees in (8), the regression becomes

$$z = -5.57 + \underset{(0.179)}{0.964x} - \underset{(0.073)}{0.223y}, \quad r = 0.820 \tag{10}$$

which shows a higher degree of correlation than (8); the regression coefficient of y is significantly negative. The value of the constant in (10) is almost identical with that in (8), indicating the stability of the regression. By adding the index of excess supply, the coefficient of x in (10) increases only insignificantly to 0.964; this strongly suggests that production functions in corresponding industries in the United States and Japan are essentially the same. The fact that the coefficient of x deviates significantly from zero implies that interindustry differences in labor shares in both the United States and Japan can be accounted for by the differences in the exponents α of production functions. The negative value of the constant might be interpreted as a result of the general influence exerted by the difference in labor shares between the two countries due to the volume of structural unemployment, inclusive of both male and female workers.

On the basis of the foregoing findings, we feel reasonably certain that our central hypothesis—that low labor shares are largely induced by "borrowed technology" via the structural unemployment effect—can meet a more thorough and rigorous, empirical test than has been attempted in this paper. Our conclusion is that labor shares in Japan remained lower than in Western countries during 1951–1960 chiefly because of the presence of structural unemployment in the country; but the Japanese economy could grow at an accelerated rate because structural unemployment was not so massive as to seriously hinder, through prevention of domestic-market expansion, the formation and utilization of capital.

The employee ratio in Japan has been rapidly increasing in recent years (see Table 6-11) and is anticipated to reach the level of Western countries (80 per cent) within the next 20 years. More likely than not, there will be a corresponding rise in labor shares affecting the patterns of capital formation and utilization in Japan. Taking these facts into consideration seems a prerequisite of a sound economic policy for the future.

Comment I *by Susumu Koizumi*

Tsujimura's paper treats the employment structure as one cause of the high rate of saving in Japan, and examines the relationship between the employment structure and the labor shares. Although the paper is full of interesting and imaginative ideas, several points need clarification.

After enumerating the difficulties associated with several existing hypotheses concerning international disparities in the labor shares, Tsujimura formulates his own hypothesis, predominantly based upon the Lewis model of unlimited supplies of labor and the Gerschenkron "borrowed-technology" thesis. The Lewis model comprises an indigenous sector in which the marginal productivity of workers is extremely small and the wage rate equals the subsistence need or the average product of the workers, and a modern sector in which wages are determined in terms of the indigenous-sector wage rate and the volume of employment is determined by the principles of the marginal-productivity theory. This model can explain the process of increase in the ratio of profits to the national income as capital accumulates in the modern sector, but it cannot explain the particular level of labor shares in the modern sector. The model has little to say about the difference in labor shares between the underdeveloped countries to which the model applies, and the advanced, capitalist countries to which the neoclassical assumptions are relevant. If technology and market conditions are the same in different countries, then labor-share differences depend upon the properties of production functions or the elasticity of substitution.

Turning to "borrowed technology," Tsujimura supplies his own interpretation of the Gerschenkron thesis. When a technique to produce a certain good is developed in an advanced country, it is supposed that there exist a large number of "potential" techniques for production of essentially the same good. A system of isoquants based upon these potential production processes is called the original production function. In the advanced country, only those production processes which suit the relative factor prices in that country will be selected and brought to the stage of actual innovation. But the underdeveloped country borrows the production techniques developed in the advanced country (as they are), in lieu of developing those more in accordance with its domestic, relative factor prices, because of the lack of trained manpower, shortage of technological-development funds, fixity of domestic consumption patterns, and the like. Consequently, the production function relevant to the underdeveloped country (which Tsujimura calls the quasi-production function) tends to have a lower elasticity of substitution than the original production function in the advanced country. Under these circumstances the labor shares in the underdeveloped country (where wages are lower) will obviously be smaller than in the advanced country, provided all other market conditions are equal.

The above hypothesis presents two difficulties. The first is how to reconcile the Tsujimura hypothesis with the explanation based upon the CES production function. He seems to think that the CES approach is applicable only to those market conditions specifically assumed for statistical studies based upon that approach. This, however, is an overly restrictive interpretation of the CES function. It seems more appropriate to consider the function to have a set of its own properties that are independent of market conditions, such as the degree of monopsony in labor markets or the presence (or absence) of structural unemployment. There is little difference between Tsujimura's quasi-production function and the CES function because the latter refers to a system of isoquants derived from a set of alternative production processes that have been developed to the point of actual adaptation; and to explain the international disparities in labor shares by assuming that the elasticity of substitution of the CES function is less than 1, in lieu of assuming that the elasticity of substitution of the Tsujimura quasi-function is less than 1, is merely to state the same thing in different words.

Tsujimura regards structural unemployment as a result of borrowed technology, but, as Eckaus has pointed out,[1] structural unemployment is caused by the low elasticity of substitution of the production function. Tsujimura's quasi-production function, therefore, is little different from the CES function which also has a low elasticity of substitution. Perhaps the best way in which one can interpret the Tsujimura hypothesis is to say that it is not intended to replace the CES hypothesis but is meant rather to explain the background factors which tend to make the CES elasticity of substitution less than 1. Viewed in this manner, his hypothesis retains its value and should not be discarded as a mere tautology.

The second difficulty refers to Tsujimura's attempt to explain low labor shares as a consequence of the specific properties of the employment structure; it is not clear, however, whether his model really contains such properties. As we have noted earlier, the Lewis model does not explain the labor shares in the modern sector, and the shares are determined, more strategically, by the production function. However, in explaining the international disparities in labor shares in terms of the less-than-unitary elasticity of substitution of relevant production functions, what matters is the international differences in relative factor prices, and not whether there be structural unemployment or that the employment structure be of the kind assumed by the Lewis model.

When the modern sectors of underdeveloped countries, to which

[1] R. S. Eckaus, "The Factor-Proportions Problem in Underdeveloped Areas," *The American Economic Review* (September 1955).

the Lewis model refers, are compared with those of the advanced countries for which the neoclassical assumptions hold, it is true that, since near-subsistence wages are paid in the former and much higher wages paid in the latter, the labor shares are bound to be lower in the former than in the latter, provided that the elasticity of substitution is less than 1; therefore, viewed in terms of the end results, disguised unemployment appears to be causing the low labor shares. But the low labor shares in underdeveloped countries are more accurately a reflection of low wages due to an excess supply of labor relative to capital, and are not related to the particular employment structure, as such, under which excess supply of labor is absorbed by the indigenous sectors. To be more precise, in view of the fact that the indigenous sectors, through the average (rather than marginal) principle, tend to prevent the lowering of modern-sector wages below a certain level, and (hence) an unrestrained decline in labor shares, it seems erroneous to argue that the employment structure is the cause of low labor shares.

The preceding difficulties naturally affect the empirical testing of Tsujimura's hypothesis. Tsujimura conducts a correlation analysis with respect to employee ratios and labor shares; but, in the absence of causative links between the employment structure and labor shares, the significance of such correlation analysis is questionable. One may adopt an interpretation of causation as follows: low employee ratio → structural unemployment → low wages → low labor shares. But this is not consistent with the Lewis model. The central characteristic of the Lewisian employment structure is that the excess supply of labor (and similarly the low employee ratio) in the modern sector does not necessarily induce an unrestrained fall in wages. If we compare underdeveloped countries, where the supply of labor relative to demand is excessive, with the advanced countries, where neoclassical full employment is approximated, a positive correlation might be expected between the employee ratio and the wage rate. However, in the case of underdeveloped or semi-developed countries in which a large volume of disguised unemployment persists, there is no necessary reason for the presence of disguised unemployment (or the low employee ratio) to be interpreted as a reflection of low wages or low labor shares in the modern sectors. Disguised unemployment is, more crucially, a function of average labor productivity or the subsistence-wage level in the indigenous sectors. This is visible in Tsujimura's scatter diagram of employee ratios and labor shares. A comparison of the two groups —one consisting of advanced, Western countries and the other of Asian and Latin American countries—shows a positive correlation between employee ratios and the labor shares; and as a result the combined sample indicates a positive correlation. However, no similar correlations are observed within each of those two groups.

A final note on the statistical aspect of Tsujimura's paper. He employs the ratios of female workers as an index of excess labor supply in various industries in connection with his analysis of interindustry, labor-share disparities in Japan and the United States. But in view of the fact that female workers are typically hired because they are paid lower wages than are male workers on a given job, the use of such an index for the alleged objective of his analysis seems unwarranted.

Comment II *by Ryūtaro Komiya*

I commend Tsujimura's paper for its ambitious attempt to explore the causes of international disparities in labor shares and for its effective application of the production function as a basic tool of analysis. Since Koizumi's comment has dealt with the theoretical aspects of the Tsujimura model, I shall confine myself to citing a few statistical problems in his paper.

Tsujimura holds that the relatively small share of employee compensations in the national income has been the prime cause of the high rate of gross savings in postwar Japan. I am rather skeptical about his contention. However, inasmuch as I have discussed the matter in detail elsewhere,[2] I shall refrain from commenting—except on the following point. Tsujimura mentions, as the reason why low labor shares induced a high rate of gross domestic savings, the fact that the rate of saving out of workers' income (to be exact, out of workers' household-income inclusive of some property income) has been lower than the average rate of saving out of "other" personal incomes. As it is, however, this reasoning is largely tautological. The rate of saving of agricultural households has been considerably lower than that of workers' households since 1956; but it is rather meaningless to argue from the preceding observation that the saving rate for the whole nation has increased because the share of farm income in the national income has declined.

In Tsujimura's model only two factors (labor and capital) are considered, and the labor share is defined as that portion of total income which is not earned by capital. There is, however, a serious inconsistency between the concept of the model and the statistical indexes of labor shares actually used in his study. The same criticism can be directed to Masao Baba's paper in chapter 7 as well. The indexes of labor shares, employed by both Tsujimura and Baba, are the ratios of total cash compensations for employees to total values-added in the Ministry of International Trade and Industry's *Census of Manufactures (Kōgyō Tōkei Hyō)*.[3] Values-added in *Census of Manufactures* (the denominator in the ratio) include the following items that are not

[2] See chapter 8 of this book, and Ryūtaro Komiya, "Sengo Nihon no Shihon Chi-Kuseki Ritsu," *Keizai Gaku Ronshū*, Vol. 29, No. 2 (July 1963).

[3] For an explanation of these statistics, see footnote 1 in chapter 7 of this book.

contained in net values-added, the variable appropriate for an income-distribution analysis:

(1) fixed asset tax, local enterprise tax, and taxes paid by corporations other than the domestic consumption tax and national corporation tax;
(2) transportation, insurance, and storage expenses;
(3) sales, advertising, entertaining, and other operating expenses;
(4) nonoperating expenses other than interest;
(5) depreciation expenses (before 1956).

On the other hand, total cash compensations for employees do not include welfare expenses, allowance for retirement compensations, and some other items that should definitely be included as part of "labor shares." As Miyohei Shinohara has pointed out, the recent, conspicuous rise in indirect expenses accompanying the steady increase in the weight of the service industry has induced a pronounced gap between the labor shares derivable from the above *Census of Manufactures* and those in the manufacturing industry calculated from the National Income statistics—so much so that the former is no longer believed to be a reliable index of income distribution.[4] It is generally agreed that the ratio of wage-salary income to the total income of the manufacturing industry in the National Income statistics is the more preferable index of labor shares.[5] Yet, even the use of this index requires care because wage-salary income comprises income of the self-employed, which is a mixture of returns on both capital and labor, and because the weight of the self-employed differs considerably from country to country. Tsujimura tends to ignore all these complications, and in Figures 6-2 and 6-3, and Table 6-9, tacitly interprets the income of the self-employed as return on capital. He maintains that the more structural unemployment there is, the lower the labor shares in the modern sector tend to be. But nowhere in his paper do we find an index of labor shares in the modern sector. With respect to the interpretation of Figure 6-3, Tsujimura maintains that a country in which the employee ratio in all industries is low tends to have a large volume of structural unemployment and (hence) low labor shares. It seems more sensible to deduce, however, that in a given country the employee ratio is low because there are many self-employed people as well as family workers, the weight of whose incomes tends to reduce that of

[4] Miyohei Shinohara, "Chingin Kettei no Kijun to 'Bunpai Ronsō'," *Jiyū* (March 1961), pp. 63–69.

[5] International comparison requires special attention to comparability of data. For example, in the case of the United States-Japan comparison, the American National Income statistics classify bad debts and special depreciations as business expenses, and employees' compensations include allowances for retirement compensations, while in Japan all these items are classified as part of corporation profits; and in the United States (but not in Japan) employees' compensations comprise various welfare expenses as well as most local corporation taxes included in corporation incomes, and so on.

wage income. In order to fulfill the objective of his paper, Tsujimura needs to solve the problem of measuring the genuine labor shares in those modern sectors (although we are sometimes not sure what we really mean by the term "modern sectors") that can be internationally compared.

7

Masao Baba:

Economic Growth, Labor Unions, and
Income Distribution*

The declining trend in labor shares has been pointed out by many economists as one of the most notable phenomena in the process of growth of the Japanese economy during the postwar period. If this is true, the phenomenon bears an important implication for the future growth and stability of the economy. If Japanese growth has been sustained by a rapid rate of investment and an ever-increasing share of capital (as against labor), it is more than likely that the economy will eventually begin to suffer from excess production capacity relative to the level of consumer demand. Perhaps with this prognosis in mind, many economists have attempted theoretical as well as empirical analyses of the causes of the falling trend in labor shares. Consequently, many aspects of the problem have been brought to light. There is, however, one important determinant of labor shares which none of the past studies has dealt with, and that is the impact of labor unions. In this paper we shall conduct some statistical testing of the impact of unions with full awareness that the problem involves numerous factors which cannot easily be subjected to quantitative measurements. On the basis of our test results we shall try to draw some conclusions on the mechanism of the declining labor shares.

FACTS ABOUT FALLING LABOR SHARES

We shall first look at some basic facts about the falling trend in labor shares. Throughout this paper our attention is focused on the manufacturing industry. From the Ministry of International Trade and Industry's *Census of Manufactures* (*Kōgyō Tōkei Hyō*), labor shares among business firms employing 30 workers or more have been calculated. Labor shares are defined as the ratio of total cash compensa-

* Most calculations on the KDC-1 computer (at Kyoto University) for this paper were executed by Chikashi Moriguchi and Misako Tsuji of the Kyoto University Institute for Economic Studies. The author is grateful for their assistance.

tions for employees to (gross) values-added.[1] For the whole manufacturing industry there has been a pronounced falling trend in the ratio: from 38.1 per cent in 1951 to 36.1 per cent in 1955 and to 33.6 per cent in 1959. Table 7-1 gives labor shares in 11 selected industries (firms employing 30 workers or more) for the ten-year period 1951–1960. Only firms hiring 30 or more workers are chosen so as to make our calculation results consistent with the data on unionization[2] (the selection of 11 industries is also based upon this consideration) and to minimize the inclusion of income of the self-employed in our data.

In Table 7-1 the majority of industries show falling tendencies in labor shares. In order to clarify the matter further we now calculate: (1) the averages for 1951–1960; (2) the differences between the 1951–1956 and the 1956–1960 averages; and linear regressions (as trend equations) for (3) the entire period, (4) 1951–1956, and (5) 1956–1960. The results are summarized in Table 7-2. In terms of the differences between the 1951–1956 and 1956–1960 averages, labor shares in all industries, except textiles and printing publication, have declined. With respect to the trend equations for the entire period, the regression coefficients for the three light industries are positive but are not significant at the 5-per-cent level. All other industries, except for petroleum and coal products, show negative regression coefficients whose estimated values are significant at the level of 5 per cent. The slopes of the equations for transportation equipment, electrical equipment, and iron-and-steel are notably steep; these three industries show a pronounced declining tendency even during 1956–1960.

Takashi Hayashi of the Ministry of Labor has recently computed labor shares in terms of firm sizes (firms employing 50 workers or more) for textiles, chemicals, machinery, electrical equipment, and transportation equipment industries on the basis of "gross" values-added.[3] Table 7-3 contains the results of his computations. Hayashi interprets the general falling trend in labor shares in the manufacturing industry to be a reflection of recent, major developments in the heavy-and-chemical industries, particularly among large-scale firms. His view, by and large, seems an acceptable one.

[1] In Census of Manufactures (Kōgyō Tōkei Hyō), "total cash compensations for employees" refers to total annual wage-payments to regular as well as temporary workers, inclusive of retirement and discharge compensations; and "gross values-added" refers to the total of the value of goods sold and other revenues (from manufacturing, repairs, sales of scraps) minus the domestic consumption tax and the cost of raw materials and other costs (e.g., fuels, electricity, and commissions). For the period after 1957 depreciation expenses relative to fixed assets were excluded, and the inventories of goods, semi-finished goods, and parts were revalued so as to make the data comparable in "gross" terms for the entire ten-year period.

[2] See footnote 16.

[3] Takashi Hayashi, "Keizai Seichō to Rōdō no Bunpairitsu," Nihon Rōdō Kyōkai Zasshi, No. 29 (August 1961), p. 36. See also Takao Sasaki, "Seizōgyō ni okeru Seisansei, Chingin oyobi Kakaku no Suii," Keizai Bunseki, No. 8 (1962). Sasaki has calculated labor shares in the entire manufacturing industry as well as in 21 separate industries, for the period 1948–1960, with respect to firms hiring 4 workers or more (30 workers or more for 1958–1960). His study also shows a secular, falling trend in shares.

TABLE 7-1

SHIFTS IN LABOR SHARES IN ELEVEN SELECTED INDUSTRIES
(per cent)

Year	Textiles	Paper, pulp	Printing, publication	Chemicals	Coal, petroleum products	Rubber products	Iron and steel	Metallic goods	Machinery	Electrical equipment	Transport equipment
1951	30.7	25.2	37.4	31.7	16.2	48.1	46.5	43.0	54.7	41.7	72.4
1952	40.9	34.1	34.5	37.2	20.5	36.0	60.3	43.9	51.0	40.9	57.0
1953	35.9	31.6	36.5	28.7	18.2	37.9	45.3	44.3	52.3	38.0	51.3
1954	37.4	36.2	33.6	29.3	24.2	28.3	51.1	42.5	48.8	37.4	55.1
1955	34.5	34.6	33.3	27.8	19.9	29.4	42.4	41.1	48.1	37.9	61.1
1956	34.8	32.4	34.6	27.8	23.5	31.1	34.1	42.8	47.0	39.1	53.7
1957	38.5	33.2	35.8	31.2	19.9	29.8	35.6	37.4	44.1	36.8	50.8
1958	39.2	34.3	30.3	29.0	21.6	32.0	46.5	40.2	40.2	27.5	35.0
1959	35.2	30.2	39.1	24.5	14.5	34.8	37.7	41.7	41.4	30.0	38.2
1960	35.6	30.2	39.0	22.6	15.6	31.9	35.4	38.2	39.1	30.5	33.0

SOURCES: For 1951–1959, M.I.T.I., *Kōgyō Tōkei Hyō*; for 1960, *Kōgyō Tōkei Hyō Sokuhō*.

TABLE 7-2

TRENDS IN INTERINDUSTRY LABOR SHARES

Industry	(1) 1951–1960 average (per cent)	(2) Difference between 1951–1956 and 1956–1960 averages (per cent)	(3) Slope of the trend equation (1951–1960)	(4) Slope of the trend equation (1951–1956)	(5) Slope of the trend equation (1956–1960)
Textiles	36.3	+0.9	+0.147 (0.34)[a]	+0.080 (0.90)	−0.17 (0.76)
Paper, pulp	32.2	−0.3	+0.119 (0.34)	+1.203 (0.85)	−0.75 (0.59)
Printing, publication	35.4	+0.7	+0.134 (0.29)	−0.603 (0.31)	+1.21 (1.1)
Chemicals	29.0	−3.5	−0.991 (0.28)	−1.346 (0.69)	−1.72 (0.73)
Coal, petroleum products	19.4	−1.5	−0.240 (0.36)	+1.160 (3.30)	−2.12 (0.70)
Rubber products	33.9	−3.3	−1.076 (0.52)	−3.269 (1.10)	+0.66 (0.58)
Iron and steel	43.5	−8.8	−1.859 (0.70)	−3.134 (1.70)	+0.47 (1.8)
Metallic goods	41.5	−2.9	−0.562 (0.17)	−0.263 (0.26)	−0.49 (0.56)
Machinery	46.7	−8.0	−1.717 (0.14)	−1.448 (0.26)	−1.85 (0.45)
Electrical equipment	36.0	−8.4	−1.395 (0.28)	−0.646 (0.32)	−2.40 (1.15)
Transport equipment	50.8	−16.4	−3.564 (0.70)	−2.211 (1.8)	−5.40 (1.50)

SOURCE: Table 7-1.
[a] Figures in parentheses are standard errors of estimate.

CAUSES OF FALLING LABOR SHARES

What are the causes of declining labor shares? Miyohei Shinohara has pointed out that to understand changes in labor shares it is necessary to analyze both fluctuations in the labor-cost ratio (the wage payment ÷ the value of output) and shifts in the income ratio (value-added ÷ the value of output).[4] Since the labor share = the labor-cost ratio ÷ the income ratio, a faster rate of increase in the income ratio than in the labor-cost ratio will clearly lower the labor share. The aforementioned Hayashi study gives the labor-cost ratios and the income ratios among firms employing 30 workers or more (the period 1951–1959 for the whole manufacturing industry; and 1951, 1955, and 1959 for separate industries). Sasaki also has recently calculated the two ratios for the period 1948–1960 among firms employing 4 workers or more (30 workers or more for 1958–1960). Both studies show that the income ratio for the entire manufacturing industry has risen, except in 1955 and 1957, whereas the labor-cost ratio has remained

[4] Miyohei Shinohara, "Kōgyō ni okeru Bunpariritsu," in Shigeto Tsuru and Kazushi Ohkawa, eds. Nihon Keizai no Bunseki (Keisō Shobō, 1953).

TABLE 7-3

Shifts in Interfirm Labor Shares in Major Industries
(per cent)

Industry	Year	Firm size (the number of workers)						
		30–49	50–99	100–199	200–299	300–499	500–999	1,000 or more
Textiles	1951	35.5	33.0	31.3	26.0		31.4	28.4
	1955	29.7	25.9	20.9	19.3	21.0	21.0	33.7
	1959	30.6	27.7	23.3	21.2	24.9	22.0	26.1
Chemicals	1951	45.6	41.8	39.0	39.6		24.9	29.3
	1955	42.2	38.1	39.6	37.4	36.1	29.9	29.4
	1959	42.5	40.5	40.8	38.7	37.8	31.7	26.0
Machinery	1951	52.7	50.3	50.1	53.7		48.0	72.9
	1955	50.9	47.1	45.6	45.3	49.4	39.9	61.6
	1959	49.1	45.5	42.2	38.4	40.0	38.9	38.0
Electrical equipment	1951	45.9	41.4	38.7	38.3		39.8	44.1
	1955	46.0	43.2	37.7	36.6	33.7	35.2	38.1
	1959	48.8	40.7	44.3	44.3	34.7	32.9	24.9
Transport equipment	1951	57.3	50.9	46.4	62.2		60.3	84.8
	1955	47.3	46.1	42.4	45.2	41.1	59.3	72.2
	1959	52.9	46.6	47.2	48.7	41.9	44.1	36.6

Source: M.I.T.I., *Kōgyō Tōkei Hyō.*

constant or has declined slightly. Hayashi contends that the rising income ratio is due to the combined effects of terms of trade and domestic prices, because during that period the import prices of raw materials decreased in contrast to the upward trend in domestic goods prices.

There are many other recent papers that have dealt with the question of declining labor shares. We may mention, as a representative sample, studies by Tadao Ishizaki,[5] Takafusa Nakamura,[6] Hirohide Tanaka,[7] and the *White Paper on Labor Conditions,* fiscal 1962.[8] The authors of these papers seem to agree that the decline in labor share may be attributed to five basic causes: three of the causes pertain to the labor-wage aspect of the problem, and the other two pertain to the capital-management aspect.

The first three causes are: (1) the pressure of excess supply of labor has tended to induce a relative decline in the rate of wage increase (Hayashi); (2) the weight of the young and of female workers in the total labor force, whose wages are relatively low, has increased

[5] Tadao Ishizaki, "Rōdō Shotoku Bunpairitsu no Teika to sono Yōin," *Keizai Geppō,* Economic Planning Agency (February 1962).

[6] Takafusa Nakamura, "Bunpairitsu no Teika to Shotoku Kōzō," *Tōyō Keizai Bessatsu* (Autumn, 1961), and "Shotoku Bunpai to Shōhi Kōzō" in M. Shinohara and T. Funahashi, eds. *Nihongata Chingin Kōzō no Kenkyū* (Rōdō Hōgaku Kenkyū Sho, 1962).

[7] Hirohide Tanaka, "Bunpairitsu Teika no Mechanism," *Rōdō Tōkei Chōsa Geppō,* Vol. 14, No. 8 (1962).

[8] Especially pp. 58–65.

(Hayashi); (3) technological progress has increased the productivity of the relatively young workers, but because of the "annual proportional-wage-increase system" their wages have not risen as fast (Ishizaki).

While (2) and (3) are closely related, point (3) needs some elucidation. Ishizaki writes:

Under the life-long employment and annual proportional-wage-increase systems predominant in large- and medium-size firms in Japan, wages for different age brackets have come to be pronouncedly differentiated relative to the productivity differences among workers of different ages; that is, the productivity-wage gap has become much greater for relatively young workers than for the relatively old. This has meant unfair wage rates for young workers. But from management's standpoint it has become advantageous to hire relatively young employees. The recent technological progress has intensified this trend, particularly in large- and medium-size manufacturing firms. The faster rise in overall productivity relative to the general wage level, then, might be identified as one of the prime causes of declining labor shares.[9]

The other two causes, pertaining to the capital side of the picture, are: (4) Japan's accelerated growth has been sustained by vigorous capital accumulation (Hayashi, Ishizaki, Sasaki, and the *White Paper on Labor Conditions*); (5) there has been a greater monopolization of the Japanese firms (Ishizaki).

Cause (4) may be subdivided into the following three elements: (a) a sizeable increase in the per-worker volume of capital; (b) a conspicuous rise in capital expenditures such as depreciations and interests; (c) effect of changes in the profit rates.

Clear trends in (a) and (b) can be identified in the available statistics, but the same is not true with (c). Hayashi's calculation, based upon the Ministry of Finance's *Annual Report of Incorporated Enterprise Statistics (Hōjin Kigyō Tōkei Nenpō)*, of total profit rates (value-added minus wages and salaries inclusive of welfare expenditures ÷ total capital used) actually indicates a slightly declining trend: from 20.0 per cent in 1953 to 18.7 per cent in 1956 and to 17.3 per cent in 1959. More detailed, industrywise surveys indicate that profit rates remained stable or rose only at a moderate pace in those industries in which labor shares fell conspicuously—for example, in electrical equipment, transportation equipment, and iron-and-steel—whereas the profit rate noticeably declined in the textiles industry where labor shares showed an upward trend. With regard to cause (5), Ishizaki's contention is not supported by sufficient data; the only evidence he gives is the trial calculation by the Japanese Management Association of the degree of monopoly in manufacturing,[10] which rose to 114.7 in 1960 from the base year of 1953.

---

[9] Tadao Ishizaki, *op. cit.*, p. 79.

[10] Let C be the finished-goods price index, D the labor requirement per unit of output, E the wage index, F the raw material requirement per unit of output, G the raw-materials price index; then, degree of monopoly $= C \div (DE + FG)$. See Nikkeiren Rōdō Keizai Kenkyūsho Shiryō, *Seisansei, Chingin, Bunpairitsu no Kokusai Hikaku* (1961), which is an extension of a similar calculation by Professor Y. Miya-

In addition to the above causes of falling labor shares, there is yet another important factor that deserves mention; that is the influence of the organizational pattern and the collective bargaining power of labor unions. Several recent studies have analyzed the impact of the unions on interindustry wage gaps, and their results show a high degree of correlation between the wage level and the extent of unionization.[11] To my knowledge, however, there have been no studies published in Japanese that examine the relationship between labor shares and unionization.[12]

With respect to the determinants of labor shares, Dobb's hypothesis that unionized workers can expect a larger share of output than nonunionized ones[13] seems to have been extensively accepted in Japan. For example, *Japanese Economic Statistics: an Exposition* (*Kaisetsu Nihon Keizai Tōkei*) issued by the Hitotsubashi University Economic Research Institute states that "in general . . . labor shares are large in large-scale, highly-unionized industries, and are small in small-scale, weakly-unionized (or nonunionized) industries";[14] and Miyohei Shinohara writes in his *Secret of Japan's Accelerated Growth* (*Kōdo Seichō no Himitsu*): "We cannot deny that strong unionism, largely absent before the war, has helped raise industrial labor shares in postwar (as against prewar) Japan." [15] We may say that both arguments are based upon the Dobb thesis that strong unionism can alter labor shares; however, the former is not substantiated by sufficient empirical data, while the latter is no more than an impressionistic view.

In connection with our inquiry into the causes of falling labor shares, we now turn to a test of the applicability of the Dobb hypothesis to Japan.

LABOR SHARES AND UNIONISM

We can conceive of many indexes for the impact of unionism. The general administrative competence of union leaders and their skill

zaki for the period 1955–1959. (Y. Miyazaki, " 'Keizai Hakusho' no Approach ni tsuite," *Keizai Seminar*, Extra Edition [1960], p. 37.)

[11] Takao Sasaki and Ryōhei Magota, "Sangyō Betsu, Kibobetsu Chingin Kakusa," in Ichiro Nakayama, ed. *Chingin Kihon Chōsa* (Tōyō Keizai Shimpo Sha, 1956), chapter 9; Rōdō Shō Chingin Chōsa Ka, ed. *Nihon no Chingin Kōzō* (Rōmu Gyōsei Kenkyū Sho, 1960), especially pp. 224–228.

[12] Akira Ono's "Rōdō Kumiai to Sangyo kan Chingin Kakusa," *Riron Keizai Gaku*, Vol. 12, No. 1 (1961), is an excellent study dealing with the effect of unionism apart from the effect of productivity increase; however, its main concern is not the same as ours. There are several significant works available in English. Paul E. Sultan, "Unionism and Wage-Income Ratios: 1929–1951," *Review of Economics and Statistics* (February 1954), was extremely useful in the preparation of our paper. After completion of the paper, I found another interesting and similar (to ours) work: Norman J. Simler, *The Impact of Unionism on Wage-Income Ratios in the Manufacturing Sector of the Economy*, University of Minnesota Studies in Economics and Business, No. 22 (1961).

[13] Maurice Dobb, *Wages*, revised ed. (Cambridge University Press, 1946).

[14] (Iwanami Shoten, 1961), p. 69.

[15] (Nihon Keizai Shimbun Sha, 1961), p. 68.

in organizing successful strikes are the least insignificant examples, inasmuch as these leadership qualities, together with the elasticity of demand for unionized labor, constitute the main content of collective bargaining power. We shall first choose, as a quantitatively measurable index, the unionization ratio.

Table 7-4 gives the interindustry unionization ratios, calculated from the Ministry of Labor's *Labor Union Basic Survey (Rōdō Kumiai Kihon Chōsa)* and the Ministry of International Trade and Industry's *Census of Manufactures (Kōgyō Tōkei Hyō)*. The unionization ratio is defined to be the ratio of the total number of union members to the total number of workers in firms employing 30 workers or more, within a given industry.[16] We observe in Table 7-4 that, except for petroleum and coal products, the ratios show a consistent, falling trend from 1951 through 1960. For a more detailed analysis we have calculated, as in the case of labor shares: (1′) averages for 1951–1960; (2′) differences between averages for 1951–1956 and for 1956–1960; (3′) regressions for the entire period; (4′) for 1951–1956; and (5′) for 1956–1960. The results are summarized in Table 7-5. A comparison between Tables 7-1 and 7-4, or between Tables 7-2 and 7-5, seems to suggest strongly that the decline in unionization has been a cause of falling labor shares.

In order to draw a more definitive conclusion, we have conducted a rank correlation analysis equating averages, average-differences, and regression coefficients of labor shares and unionization ratios in terms of their industry ranks. The results of this analysis are shown in Table 7-6. Of particular interest to us are the combinations (2′) (2) and (3′) (3), both of which bear plus signs. However, the rank correlation coefficient of the former (+0.491) is insignificant at the 5-per-cent level, and that of the latter (+0.573) is barely significant at the same percentage level. What emerges from these observations is the impression that although the falling unionization ratio must have had some influence upon the decline in labor shares, its overall impact seems to have been much weaker than generally believed.[17]

---

[16] Ideally, the number of union members should be adjusted to include only those in firms employing 30 workers or more. However, the estimated, interfirm unionization ratios in the manufacturing industry in 1960 were: 70.6 per cent for firms of 500 workers or more; 40.7 per cent for firms of 100–499; 9.7 per cent for firms of 30–99; and only 2.1 per cent for firms of 29 or less (Ministry of Labor, *Rōdōkumiai Kihon Chōsa Hōkoku Sho*, fiscal 1960, p. 34). It is safe to assume that the unionization ratios in small firms (30 or less) are negligibly small, and hence their exclusion will not seriously disturb the accuracy of our computation results. Total numbers of employees in the calculation of the above ratios, however, are from Sōrifu Tōkei-kyoku, *Rōdō Ryoku Chōsa*.

[17] In Japan the majority of labor unions (about 90 per cent) are organized on the basis of individual firms rather than industries. Therefore, our results, based upon industrywise unionization ratios, must be somewhat discounted in order to measure the real impact of unions.

There are economic as well as noneconomic reasons for the falling unionization ratio. The most important of all seems to be that in the course of accelerated growth the increase in the absolute number of newly employed has exceeded the rate of increase of union members. We must also consider another possibility that the workers in what were originally small firms remained nonunionized even after the firms, in later years, had grown much larger.

TABLE 7-4

SHIFTS IN UNIONIZATION RATIOS

(per cent)

Year	Textiles	Paper, pulp	Printing, publication	Chemicals	Coal, petroleum products	Rubber products	Iron and steel	Metallic goods	Machinery	Electrical equipment	Transport equipment
1951	64.8	57.1	69.9	83.9	55.8	80.4	75.8	68.4	59.4	89.9	91.5
1952	68.8	63.0	64.1	74.0	63.7	65.2	89.2	46.8	58.6	82.3	78.6
1953	59.6	57.8	57.6	80.2	57.8	66.4	83.0	45.1	60.4	74.7	77.4
1954	59.9	57.4	60.0	87.6	56.1	62.2	92.4	40.6	66.9	78.8	80.0
1955	58.5	52.3	60.6	82.0	62.8	62.0	89.6	42.2	58.1	81.1	78.2
1956	55.4	49.1	56.5	79.1	62.5	53.2	83.7	35.2	46.8	56.9	70.2
1957	58.3	46.6	53.9	78.1	65.1	52.0	85.2	29.1	47.8	53.6	66.7
1958	59.2	48.8	53.6	74.7	75.2	56.4	70.3	29.6	47.4	54.4	72.7
1959	53.5	46.0	53.4	74.1	72.0	48.9	61.0	26.9	43.9	44.0	67.9
1960	56.9	43.9	53.5	74.2	71.8	53.8	57.3	26.6	37.0	42.6	63.8

SOURCES: Ministry of Labor, *Rōdōkumiai Kihon Chōsa*, and M.I.T.I., *Kōgyō Tōkei Hyō*.

TABLE 7-5
Trends in Unionization Ratios

Industry	(1') 1951–1960 average (per cent)	(2') Difference between 1951–1956 and 1956–1960 averages (per cent)	(3') Slope of the trend equation (1951–1960)	(4') Slope of the trend equation (1951–1956)	(5') Slope of the trend equation (1956–1960)
Textiles	59.5	−4.5	−1.14 (0.33)[a]	−2.22 (0.65)	−0.18 (0.81)
Paper, pulp	52.5	−12.2	−1.93 (0.28)	−2.07 (0.77)	−1.10 (0.46)
Printing, publication	58.3	−7.3	−1.61 (0.30)	−2.15 (0.75)	−0.65 (0.30)
Chemicals	78.8	−5.2	−0.88 (0.46)	−0.21 (1.2)	−1.38 (0.34)
Coal, petroleum products	64.3	+9.4	+1.91 (0.43)	+0.83 (0.85)	+2.55 (1.28)
Rubber products	60.1	−12.0	−2.68 (0.53)	−4.22 (0.57)	−0.19 (1.10)
Iron and steel	78.8	−14.2	−2.76 (1.05)	+1.43 (1.40)	−7.70 (1.60)
Metallic goods	39.1	−16.9	−3.85 (0.62)	−5.27 (1.60)	−1.94 (0.62)
Machinery	52.6	−13.8	−2.66 (0.55)	−1.66 (1.50)	−1.35 (1.73)
Electrical equipment	65.8	−27.0	−5.43 (0.65)	−4.70 (1.80)	−2.82 (1.73)
Transport equipment	74.7	−11.1	−2.40 (0.43)	−3.00 (1.06)	−1.16 (6.9)

SOURCE: Table 7-4.
[a] Figures in parentheses are standard errors of estimate.

TABLE 7-6

RANK CORRELATION BETWEEN
UNIONIZATION RATIOS AND LABOR SHARES

Labor share	Unionization ratio		
	(1')	(2')	(3')
(1)	−0.064	−0.473	−0.545
(2)	−0.582	+0.491	+0.518
(3)	−0.536	+0.518	+0.573

SOURCES: Tables 7-2 and 7-5.

Let us examine another index of the impact of unionism—the frequency of work-stoppage labor conflicts, taken from the Ministry of Labor's *Labor Disputes Statistics* (*Rōdō Sōgi Tōkei Chōsa*). The "frequency of work-stoppage labor conflicts" refers to the number of strikes (exclusive of those lasting for less than four hours) and lockouts. We have totaled the number of labor conflicts in eleven industries during 1951–1960, although we must allow for some overlappings, because the frequency for a given year is counted as the sum of the number of new conflicts occurring in that year and of old conflicts carried over from the preceding year. In decreasing order, they are: 709, machinery; 508, chemicals: 494, transport equipment; 398, electrical equipment; 285, primary metals;[18] 242, textiles; 242, printing and publication; 201, metallic products; 185, paper and pulp; 70, rubber products; and 42, petroleum and coal products. Their time series indicate no systematic trends in the interindustry frequencies of labor conflicts.

The analysis of rank correlation between the above ranks and those of labor shares in Table 7-2 (reversed in decreasing order) reveals that the coefficient is −0.576 for the differences between the averages; and −0.443 for the regression slopes. The coefficient for the averages is not significant at the level of 5 per cent. Once again we are led to believe that there has been little positive relationship between unionism and labor shares. It must be noted that the above labor conflicts are not restricted to those concerning wage-allowance demands (e.g., objection to wage reduction, demand for regular wage payments, for extra rates, for discharge allowances, for retirement funds, and the like). The conflicts refer to numerous other demands in connection with the signing, revision, and effecting of management-labor agreements, discharge and reemployment rules, working hours, holiday-vacation provisions, and so forth. The demand items directly related to wages have been, on the average, approximately 60 per cent of the total.[19] We have also conducted a rank correlation analysis (similar to

[18] The frequency for iron-and-steel was essentially the same.

[19] It is highly probable that the unions make wage-increase demands on the basis of long-term real (rather than money) wage calculations. This paper, however, does not deal with shifts in "real" labor shares. Mr. S. Fujita has suggested to me the importance of examining also the "after-tax" income shares.

TABLE 7-7

SHIFTS IN INTERINDUSTRY LABOR PRODUCTIVITY[a]
(1,000 yen)

Year	Textiles	Paper, pulp	Printing, publica- tion	Chemicals	Coal, petroleum products	Rubber products	Iron and steel	Metallic goods	Machin- ery	Electrical equipment	Transport equipment
1951	281	720	401	517	1,006	271	434	307	258	337	227
1952	261	612	492	499	966	373	375	326	326	417	357
1953	301	680	535	694	1,237	417	536	409	348	493	442
1954	316	646	636	785	1,044	569	550	417	418	560	456
1955	350	674	676	878	1,375	558	672	426	418	528	411
1956	368	752	726	945	1,272	538	1,040	416	453	504	514
1957	353	766	748	884	1,587	560	973	529	545	577	601
1958	366	723	946	1,008	1,585	548	760	489	604	782	897
1959	424	866	766	1,240	2,519	508	962	503	626	696	834
1960	476	916	869	1,478	2,608	625	1,098	610	734	756	987
Slope of the trend equation:											
(1951–1960)	+20.30 (2.5)[b]	+25.42 (6.5)	+51.95 (7.2)	+95.58 (10.5)	+173.06 (31.8)	+28.72 (7.8)	+77.83 (14.1)	+28.44 (3.7)	+48.97 (3.0)	+43.61 (6.5)	+78.74 (9.5)
(1951–1956)	+20.49 (3.6)	+8.91 (12.7)	+65.09 (4.4)	+96.23 (11.0)	+67.54 (28.3)	+58.34 (13.5)	+112.42 (29.5)	+24.37 (7.0)	+37.74 (4.5)	+35.29 (13.0)	+46.03 (13.5)
(1956–1960)	+28.70 (9.1)	+42.80 (17.1)	+30.40 (28.6)	+142.20 (36.0)	+360.40 (76.6)	+12.20 (14.1)	+10.50 (46.3)	+36.20 (14.8)	+64.30 (7.4)	+62.30 (24.8)	+117.90 (27.3)

SOURCES: Tables 7-1 and 7-4, and M.I.T.I., *Kōgyō Tōkei Hyō*.

[a] Labor productivity (gross value-added ÷ the number of workers) in firms employing more than 30 workers.

[b] Figures in parentheses are standard errors of estimate.

the two above) between the rates of increase in the number of union members and labor shares—only to find the same negative result.

Productivity, Unionization Ratio, and Labor Shares

We may assume that an increase in productivity (value-added productivity), together with strong bargaining power of the unions, will, *ceteris paribus,* induce a corresponding rise in labor shares. We may further assume that those unions which operate in highly unionized industries are capable of exerting powerful pressure for wage increase whenever the profit rate increases. Then, treating labor productivity and the unionization ratio as independent variables, we can construct a labor-share function. We have calculated such functions for eleven industries, using the data in Tables 7-1 and 7-4 and the data on labor productivity (gross value-added ÷ the number of workers) for firms of 30 workers or more (see Table 7-7) computed from the M.I.T.I.'s *Census of Manufactures,* the summary of which is shown in Table 7-8.

TABLE 7-8

ESTIMATED LABOR-SHARE FUNCTIONS[a] I: 1951–1960

Industry	Coefficient of unionization ratio	Coefficient of labor productivity	Constant	S^2	$\overline{R}^2$
Textiles	0.252 (0.39)[b]	0.009 (0.026)	18.2	9.9	−0.198
Paper, pulp	−0.560 (0.82)	−0.047 (0.017)	96.05	5.99	0.388
Printing, publication	−0.411 (0.35)	−0.015 (0.011)	69.59	7.62	−0.026
Chemicals	−0.317 (0.13)	−0.014 (0.002)	66.36	2.42	0.848
Coal, petroleum	0.227 (0.20)	−0.005 (0.002)	13.11	7.14	0.334
Rubber	0.027 (0.17)	−0.047 (0.015)	55.51	7.75	0.772
Iron and steel	−0.024 (0.14)	−0.028 (0.006)	66.4	17.53	0.742
Metallic goods	−0.069 (0.07)	−0.029 (0.010)	57.14	1.91	0.643
Machinery	−0.009 (0.07)	−0.035 (0.005)	63.78	1.28	0.955
Electrical equipment	−0.014 (0.015)	−0.034 (0.006)	56.31	1.88	0.921
Transport equipment	0.167 (0.24)	−0.043 (0.008)	62.71	12.27	0.919

[a] Regression equations: labor shares and unionization ratios in percentage; and labor productivities in 1,000 yen.

[b] Figures in parentheses are standard errors of estimate.

At least two aspects of the results in Table 7-8 are noteworthy. First, all the unionization-ratio coefficients, except for one industry, are insignificant at the 5-per-cent level; and most of the coefficients bear minus signs. The coefficient for chemicals is significant but still has a negative sign. Under the assumption that strong, linear trends persist in the variables, we have recalculated Table 7-8 in terms of the first differences. The results are given in Table 7-9. The degree of significance for many coefficients has improved, but there is little noticeable increase in the extent to which unionization ratios affect labor shares. Secondly, the majority of coefficients of productivities, unlike those of unionization ratios, are significant; but they are negative, except for one industry. All of them become negative in Table 7-9. Parenthetically, our recomputation of Table 7-8 in terms of "rates of change" in the variables has also revealed essentially the same results as those in Table 7-9.

To sum up, there is little evidence that the unionization ratio can

TABLE 7-9

Estimated Labor-Share Functions[a] II (First Differences): 1951–1960

Industry	Coefficient of union- ization ratio	Coefficient of labor produc- tivity	Constant	S^2	$\overline{R}^2$
Textiles	0.483 (0.197)[b]	−0.095 (0.033)	0.030	4.088	0.805
Paper, pulp	0.350 (0.256)	−0.036 (0.012)	1.859	2.408	0.852
Printing, publication	−0.098 (0.14)	−0.038 (0.003)	1.974	1.521	0.906
Chemicals	−0.183 (0.18)	−0.029 (0.009)	1.187	6.061	0.644
Coal, petroleum	−0.069 (0.12)	−0.125 (0.002)	2.286	3.264	0.835
Rubber	0.377 (0.132)	−0.065 (0.010)	1.884	3.725	0.876
Iron and steel	0.177 (0.35)	−0.035 (0.018)	3.645	76.358	0.229
Metallic products	−0.031 (0.097)	−0.039 (0.013)	0.627	3.710	0.488
Machinery	−0.041 (0.11)	−0.038 (0.017)	0.168	2.695	0.342
Electrical equipment	0.012 (0.078)	−0.037 (0.008)	0.561	2.635	0.754
Transport equipment	0.544 (0.174)	−0.069 (0.009)	3.151	7.094	0.886

[a] Regression equations: labor share and unionization ratios in percentage; and labor productivities in 1,000 yen.

[b] Figures in parentheses are standard errors of estimate.

significantly influence labor shares; on the other hand, the rise in labor productivity seems actually to decrease labor shares.

LABOR SHARES AND INVESTMENT—CONCLUDING REMARKS

The preceding labor-share functions analysis has shown that labor productivity by and large yields a negative effect on labor shares. This, at first, seems a very peculiar finding. We must recall, however, that gross values-added were used as both the numerator for labor productivity and the denominator for labor shares. We had to rely on "gross" values in order to make our data consistent for the entire period from 1951 through 1960. Since gross values comprise depreciation and other capital expenditures, the analysis of "net" effect of productivity increase on labor shares necessitates an examination of shifts in various capital expenditures. The Mitsubishi Economic Research Institute has recently estimated the ratios between labor and capital costs in values-added from the Ministry of Finance's *Incorporated Enterprise Statistics* (*Hōjin Kigyō Tōkei*); the estimates, reproduced in Figure 7-1, indicate that the decrease in the ratio of wages, allowances, and welfare expenditures is approximately matched by the increase in various capital costs.

On the basis of the above Mitsubishi study, Takao Sasaki has stated: "The decline in labor shares during 1952–1960 assumed an important role for growth in the sense that it absorbed much of the increasing investment costs and enabled firms to reduce prices of goods as raw-material costs decreased; namely, it made possible the simultaneous achievement of investment expansion and stable prices. In view of the fact that the high rate of investment raised the degree of capital intensity, which in turn induced a continual rise in labor productivity, one might argue that the relationship between declining labor shares and increasing labor productivity was an inseparable one." [20] Sasaki's contention (particularly its second half) seems consistent with our findings from Tables 7-8 and 7-9.

In Table 7-10 we have compiled, from the M.I.T.I.'s *Census of Manufactures*, total values of fixed-asset investments[21] in eleven industries. Average annual rates of increase are given in the last row. A comparison of Table 7-10 with Table 7-2 suggests that the high rate of plant-and-equipment investment has been closely associated with the pronounced fall in labor shares—particularly with respect to the machinery and equipment industries.

The declining tendency in labor shares, of course, is the joint effect of factors operating on both the labor-wage and capital-management sides. Even if we allow for the peculiarities of the Japanese labor market and wage system, we are inclined, in the light of the preceding

---

[20] Sasaki, "Seizōgyō ni okeru Seisansei, Chingin oyobi Kakaku no Suii," *op. cit.*, pp. 59–60. See also *White Paper on Labor Conditions*, fiscal 1962, pp. 64–65.

[21] Total of annual increases (or decreases) in the values of new fixed assets acquired, used fixed assets acquired, lands purchased, and new constructions.

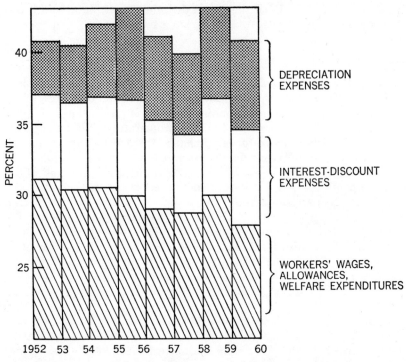

Fig. 7-1. Weights of capital and labor costs in values-added. Sources: Takao Sasaki, "Seizōgyō ni okeru Seisansei, Chingin oyobi Kakaku no Suii," *Keizai Bunseki*, no. 8, 1962, p. 23; "Seizōgyō ni okeru Chingin, Bukka, Seisansei no Suii," in Nihon Seisansei Honbu, *Seisansei to Chingin, Bukka*, 1962, p. 58. For reference, the numerical figures upon which Figure 7-1 is based are reproduced in the Supplementary Table below.

SUPPLEMENTARY TABLE

WEIGHTS OF CAPITAL AND LABOR COSTS IN VALUES-ADDED
(gross value-added[a] = 100)

Item	1952	1953	1954	1955	1956	1957	1958	1959
Depreciation expenses	3.56	4.13	5.11	5.72	5.71	5.44	6.22	6.16
Interest-discount expenses	6.21	6.15	6.46	7.00	6.18	5.86	7.52	7.03
Wages, etc.	30.96	30.28	27.74	29.04	26.48	25.76	26.29	25.05
Welfare expenditures			2.70	0.83	2.61	2.67	2.64	2.45

[a] Gross revenue minus total user-costs.

analyses, towards the view that labor shares fell primarily because the accelerated rate of expansion in plant-and-equipment investments and associated capital costs superseded the impact of labor unions. There are many other problems that must be solved before a more definitive conclusion can be drawn. For example, we must examine the weights in values-added (from the M.I.T.I.'s *Census of Manu-*

TABLE 7-10

TOTAL VALUES OF INTERINDUSTRY FIXED-ASSET INVESTMENTS
(millions of yen)

Year	Textiles	Paper, pulp	Printing, publication	Chemicals	Coal, petroleum	Rubber	Iron and steel	Metallic goods	Machinery	Electrical equipment	Transport equipment
1955	34,144	17,284	6,109	45,801	9,860	2,769	48,148	5,294	11,944	13,214	15,999
1956	63,351	31,101	7,541	103,351	13,766	5,277	40,396	8,208	17,704	18,324	29,236
1957	72,992	51,392	11,696	133,446	26,378	10,144	111,779	13,919	38,459	37,844	53,995
1958	50,625	33,974	9,135	108,792	17,726	6,403	107,276	12,378	34,493	43,298	58,039
1959	49,451	44,103	12,787	111,950	14,018	9,175	132,880	20,030	42,202	61,178	57,442
1960	75,029	81,935	15,722	199,201	33,220	15,483	260,850	32,144	85,387	97,311	105,694
Average annual rate of increase (per cent):	20.4	45.2	23.9	43.6	42.9	51.6	31.2	47.2	55.9	52.0	51.0

SOURCE: M.I.T.I, *Kōgyō Tōkei Hyō*.

factures) of such expense items as advertising, research and development, entertainment, and other indirect expenditures. As Takafusa Nakamura and Miyohei Shinohara have pointed out,[22] the weights of these "non-productive expenditures" (Nakamura) and the "tertiary industry" (Shinohara) have conspicuously increased in recent years, the consequence being a fall in the relative share of labor in the manufacturing industry. We do not have sufficient statistical data, at present, to attempt an analysis of labor shares from the capital-management side; we must await future research in order to learn more about the extent of negative effects of accelerated investment expansion, increase in non-productive expenditures, and growth of the tertiary industry upon labor shares.[23]

Comment *by Masao Fukuoka*

Baba's paper begins with an elaboration of statistical facts pertaining to the declining relative share of labor in postwar Japan, and ends with the suggestion that the rapid rate of plant-and-equipment investment and capital accumulation appears to be a plausible explanation of the phenomenon. He examines a list of customary hypotheses on the causes of falling labor shares, such as: (1) low wages due to excess supply of labor; (2) an increase in the weight of the relatively young and female workers whose wages are low; (3) unfairly low wage rates for young workers, relative to their productivities, attributable to the annual proportional-wage-increase system; (4) a rise in capital costs in the course of rapid capital accumulation; (5) monopolization of the firms—and then he proceeds to emphasize the importance of (6) the impact of unionization and collective bargaining power. However, his empirical study leads him to conclude that the rapid increase in productivity due to an accelerated rate of investments, superseding the impact of the unions, seems the most satisfactory explanation.

His conclusion is based on what he calls the "labor-share function," with labor productivity and the unionization ratio as independent variables. In theory the function is an increasing function of the two

[22] Takafusa Nakamura, "Shotoku Bumpai to Shōhi Kōzō," *op. cit.*, p. 68; M. Shinohara, " 'Shotoku Bumpai to Shōhi Kōzō' o yonde," in Shinohara and Funahashi, eds. *Nihongata Chingin Kōzō no Kenkyū,* pp. 96–97.

[23] A few words about Fukuoka's comment on this paper. As a *quid pro quo* for his "high-handed" comment, I must say that I do not believe every empirical study ought necessarily to be clad in the colorful attire of theory. I have my own theoretical counter-arguments concerning Fukuoka's remarks, but I shall postpone expounding them until another occasion. With respect to his third point, I recommend that he reread with greater care the section of this paper entitled "Labor Shares and Unionism" and footnotes therein.

variables; but after statistical analysis Baba finds that the relationship between the labor share and the unionization ratio is not significant, and that the labor share is a decreasing function of labor productivity.

I have neither space nor ability to evaluate in detail Baba's statistical methods and data. I shall instead make a brief comment on certain theoretical aspects of his paper. My overall impression is that Baba pays too little attention to recent developments in the theory of income distribution (e.g., Solow's econometric studies). To be more specific, most of his explanations are no more than "fact-findings" in the style of Japanese government agencies, and hardly incorporate some of the recent, significant works by Hicks, Meade, Solow, Kalecki, Kaldor, *et al*. Fact-finding, of course, is important. But I feel that when an academic economist attempts an explanation of labor shares in a given country, he should build his analysis upon a foundation of universal theories relevant to the subject. Baba himself quotes Dobb in the course of his discussion, indicating that he is not necessarily restricting himself to the narrow confine of a certain institutional phenomenon observed in postwar Japan.

My first point is that he should have taken a much clearer stand on the theoretical presuppositions of his model. His "labor-share function" is a function of labor productivity and the unionization ratio, implying that a certain production function is being assumed behind the relationship between shares and productivity, and a certain bilateral-monopoly situation is presumably being considered behind the shares and unionization ratios. The reader is not informed, however, whether Baba is adopting a marginal distribution theory based upon the above production function and the profit-maximizing behavior of the firms, or a certain game-theoretic model pertaining to the manner in which unions and firms counteract each other in determining their relative shares. Nor is the reader certain, in the event that the two approaches are simultaneously adopted, how they are interrelated with one another so that the particular "labor-share function" assumed by Baba is to be generated.

My second point refers to his remark that, contrary to the *a priori* notion that a rise in labor productivity raises labor shares, his empirical study has demonstrated that the opposite is true. One wonders why the "opposite" does not necessarily follow in theory. For example, Hicks has shown that, depending upon the nature of technological progress and the elasticity of substitution, an innovation-induced increase in labor productivity can, *a priori*, reduce labor shares. Similarly, Kaldor has recently indicated in his theory of distribution that an increase in the weight of investment in the national income can lower the relative share of labor. Baba should have made clear from what theory he derived his *a priori* expectation.

My third point concerns the validity of his conclusion that the fall in unionization ratios did not have any clear effect on labor shares. Since the majority of the unions in Japan are organized on the basis of individual firms, one wonders to what extent the unionization ratio

8

Ryūtaro Komiya:
The Supply of Personal Savings*

The high rate of personal savings in postwar Japan is a well-known phenomenon. An international comparison in Table 8-1 of savings in leading industrial countries for the decade of the 1950's shows that the rate of personal savings in Japan, expressed as a ratio either to the Gross Domestic Product[1] or to personal disposable income, is conspicuously higher than that in other countries. The high savings propensity in Japan cannot be viewed as a temporary phenomenon in the course of recovery and reconstruction from the war.[2] In Table 8-2, which illustrates shifts in the savings rate in Japan since 1950, for example, we notice that even after 1955, the year in which the recovery came to an approximate close, the savings ratio to the GNP and the average propensity to save, with respect to disposable income of all personal categories as well as to wage-salary earners' household income, continued to increase at a marked pace.

Throughout the postwar years, strong pressure for expansion of effective demand has latently persisted in the Japanese economy, not

* This is a revised version of the second half of my paper, "Capital Accumulation in Postwar Japan," which I read at the Zushi Conference. The first half has been published under the title, "The Rate of Capital Accumulation in Postwar Japan," in *Keizai Gaku Ronshū*, Vol. 29, No. 2 (July 1963). I have received useful suggestions from many individuals on this paper, but I am particularly grateful to Mr. Miyohei Shinohara for his painstaking and detailed comments. Whatever errors and shortcomings that remain are, of course, my own. I thankfully acknowledge receipt of financial aid for the research underlying this paper from the University of Tokyo Economic Research Fund, the Tokyo Economic Research Center, and the Central Committee for Savings Promotion.

[1] There is only a negligible difference between the Gross Domestic Product (GDP) and the Gross National Product (GNP) for postwar Japan. The two may be regarded as interchangeable.

[2] There is a school of thought, however, which holds that the high rate of saving in postwar Japan is of a transitional nature associated with the process of postwar reconstruction. For example, Miyohei Shinohara has presented a hypothesis that the ratio of family-owned liquid assets to the National Income has drastically decreased after the war, relative to the prewar ratio, and the high rate of saving in postwar Japan is in part a reflection of the households' efforts to restore their prewar standards. Whether households or other economic units in actuality adjust their savings in accordance with what they "remember" to be the prewar standards remains rather uncertain.

TABLE 8-1

INTERNATIONAL COMPARISON OF THE RATES OF PERSONAL SAVINGS: 1950–1960
(per cent)

Country	(1) Ratio of personal savings to GDP	(2) Ratio of personal savings to gross domestic savings	(3) Ratio of personal savings to total personal disposable income
Japan	10.9	37	15.2
Italy	10.7[a]	52[a]	...
Norway	10.2[a]	37[a]	9.3
Australia	9.7	29	13.2
Belgium	9.4	51	10.5
W. Germany	8.7	34	13.2
Finland	8.3	31	11.8
Denmark	7.5[a]	41[a]	9.7
Austria	6.2	37	8.7
Holland	5.8	32	10.2
New Zealand	5.7	26	8.5
Canada	5.2	23	7.6
U.S.A.	5.2	28	7.4
Sweden	4.4	21	6.6
France	4.3	23	6.1
U.K.	1.9	12	2.9
Japan (1955–60)	11.4	37	16.3

SOURCE: U.N., *Yearbook of National Accounts Statistics.* Time periods are slightly different for some countries.

[a] Includes net corporate savings.

infrequently inducing balance-of-payments difficulties and price inflations. By and large, Japan's postwar economy has been of the "classical" (as against the "Keynesian") model, characterized by the repeated imposition of stringent fiscal and monetary policies to suppress excessive demand rather than by chronic unemployment, insufficient demand, and the persistence of idle capacities. In such a situation, "saving is a virtue," and, *ceteris paribus,* the greater the supply of saving, the higher will be the rate of capital accumulation and economic growth. The rapid increase in personal savings during 1955–1961 is one of the reasons why the Japanese economy could grow at an accelerated pace without experiencing hyper-inflations or catastrophic balance-of-payments crises,[3] despite the fact that private plant-and-

---

[3] I am not ignoring the fact that accelerated growth has induced an inflation of consumer-goods prices since 1959 and a balance-of-payments crisis in 1961. It should be noted, however, that Japanese wholesale prices have remained stable, in contrast to an upward trend in wholesale prices throughout the 1950's in the majority of other industrial countries; that the several balance-of-payments "crises" Japan has experienced in the postwar period were of a cyclical nature; that her foreign-exchange reserves have actually indicated a rising, long-run trend.

TABLE 8-2

THE AVERAGE PROPENSITY TO SAVE IN JAPAN: 1950–1961
(per cent)

Fiscal year	(1) Ratio of personal savings to GNP	(2) Average propensity to save in personal sectors[a]	(3) Average propensity to save of workers' households[b]
1950	10.4	13.8	...
1951	13.2	19.1	2.0
1952	11.3	15.6	4.4
1953	7.4	10.6	5.6
1954	7.5	10.4	7.2
1955	10.1	13.9	8.9
1956	10.5	14.9	11.3
1957	10.8	15.3	11.9
1958	11.3	15.5	12.1
1959	12.4	18.3	13.4
1960	13.4	20.1	14.3
1961	13.8	21.3	15.9

[a] Ratio of personal savings to total personal disposable income. *Kokumin Shotoku Hakusho*, fiscal 1961, p. 102.

[b] Calculated from Sōrifu Tōkei-kyoku, *Kakei Chōsa Nempō* by the following formula: average propensity to save = 1 − [(consumption expenditures) + (consumption expenditures in kind)] ÷ [(real income) + (income in kind) − (non-consumption expenditures)]. Figures in this column refer to calendar years.

equipment investments have continued to expand at the extraordinary rate of 29.6 per cent per annum (the 1955–1961 average) since 1955. Therefore, an analysis of the causes of the high rate of personal savings may aid us in understanding Japan's postwar growth. In this paper we shall probe and appraise various factors that have been popularly discussed as the causes of the high propensity to save in Japan. The main conclusions may be summarized as follows:

(1) The view that the high rate of personal savings (households' average propensity to save) is due to the unequal distribution of income in Japan is erroneous. The pattern of Japanese income distribution is one of the most equal, relative to international standards.

(2) The ratio of personal property income (dividend, interest, rent) to total personal income in Japan is rather low compared with that in other countries. There are many countries in which that ratio is higher than it is in Japan, but those countries do not necessarily reveal a high rate of savings. It seems wrong to argue that the rate of personal saving in Japan is high because the share of property income in total personal income is large.

(3) The high rate of saving among the self-employed (excluding those in agriculture, forestry, and fishing) and the large share of income of the self-employed in total personal income are said to be one

of the main causes of the high, overall propensity to save in Japan. The relative importance of this factor, however, is rapidly diminishing.

(4) The high rate of growth in real personal disposable income and, in the case of wage-salary earners' household income, the rapid increase in the weight of extra income (bonuses) in their real income are believed to be one of the most significant causes of the high personal savings rate in postwar Japan.

(5) An international comparison reveals no evidence of a correlation between the ratio of social-security expenditures to the National Income and the rate of personal savings. The contention that the Japanese personal savings rate is high because of the underdevelopment of social-security programs is not supported by empirical evidence. But the relative absence of social-security expenditures may be regarded as one important factor responsible for the high level of government savings.

(6) The unique features of life-cycle patterns in income and consumption, together with the underdevelopment of consumer finance in Japan, seem important reasons for the high rate of personal savings.

THE SIZE DISTRIBUTION OF INCOME

The belief that the high rate of personal savings in Japan is due to an unusually unequal distribution of income compared with other countries seems prevalent among many economists.[4] Some emphasize inequality in the size distribution while others refer to inequality in the functional distribution of income for labor and capital. In this section we shall treat the former, the size distribution.

An international comparison of size distributions is full of pitfalls. Not only statistical limitations but also international differences in life cycles[5] of family formation, income, and consumption tend to make it an almost impossible task. Of the numerous income-distribution statistics for different countries, we may cite two examples that are based upon relatively similar survey methods: the statistics of pre-tax family-income distribution in Japan available in the *Employment Status Survey* (*Shūgyō Kōzō Kihon Chōsa Hōkoku*); and the statistics of before-tax income distribution periodically published in the *Survey of Current Business* by the United States Department of Commerce. On the basis of the findings of these two surveys, Tadao Ishizaki has recently shown that there is little difference between the income dis-

---

[4] See, e.g., Miyohei Shinohara, *Kōdo Seichō no Himitsu* (Nihon Keizai Shimbun, 1961), p. 229, and *Nihon Keizai no Seichō to Junkan* (Sōbun Sha, 1961), pp. 20–22.

[5] An economically meaningful income distribution is one based upon total lifetime incomes of individuals. But practically all available statistics show income distribution at a point in time. Although saving may perhaps be best treated as a function of income at a point in time, I feel that the problem of life cycles in income and saving should be separated from that of income distribution.

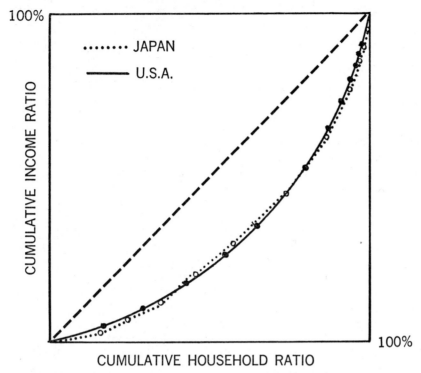

Fig. 8-1. Lorenz curves of pre-tax income distributions in Japan and the United States, 1959. Sources: Sōrifu Tōkei-kyoku, *Shūgyō Kōzō Kihon Chōsa,* and U.S. Department of Commerce, *Survey of Current Business,* July 1962, p. 16.

tributions in Japan and the United States.[6] The Lorenz curves drawn from the same sources appear in Figure 8-1. The two curves are almost identical, and whatever difference there might be is negligible. We observe, however, that towards the extreme ends of the distributions the Japanese curve displays a slightly greater equality, while towards the center it deviates slightly further from the 45-degree line than does the United States curve.[7]

In the United States the majority of people in the low-income bracket consist of the aged (for example, in 1950 68.7 per cent of heads of households earning less than $1,000 were older than fifty-five years of age, and 53.7 per cent of heads of households earning between

[6] Tadao Ishizaki, "Kaisō-betsu Shotoku Bunpu to Shotoku Saibunpai," *Nihon Rōdō Kyōkai Zasshi,* No. 29 (August 1961). Ishizaki takes the stand that Japanese income distribution is slightly more unequal than the United States distribution. I have several objections to his reasoning; those related to this paper will be mentioned later.

[7] In connection with these observations, Ishizaki writes: "The highest tenth decile comprises 29 per cent in Japan as against 30 per cent in the United States, whereas

$1,000–2,000 were older than fifty-five.[8] Many of these old people are retired and live on property income, pensions (private pensions are not classified as income), and remittances from relatives. But in Japan the majority of these elderly people tend to be absorbed in large families and are not likely to appear as independent, low-income households in the income statistics. On the other hand, incomes of unmarried youth in Japan must inevitably be low due to the annual proportional-wage-increase system, and this makes the income distribution appear unequal. There should be many other reasons why the income statistics of the two countries cannot be meaningfully compared. Insofar as pre-tax income distributions are concerned, however, there seems no evidence that the distribution is more unequal in Japan than in the United States.[9]

Chapter 9 of the U.N.'s *Economic Survey for Europe*, 1956, contains pre- and postwar income-distribution statistics for European countries; but, unlike the statistics for Japan and the United States, they were compiled as a by-product of taxation statistics, and not as independent survey results. Consequently, the statistics for many countries fail to list those incomes which fall below tax-exemption points, and the definitions of income are geared solely to income-tax purposes; in short, the comparability of survey methods and concepts seems questionable.[10] Ignoring these complications for the moment, we have compiled in Table 8-3 the income shares of the tenth decile and the fifth quintile under the assumption that the highest-income brackets

the lowest first decile accounts for 1.5 per cent in Japan in contrast to 1 per cent in the United States. The distribution in the United States seems to indicate a higher degree of equality" (*ibid.*, p. 28). I trust that he meant "a higher degree of inequality." He further writes: "In the United States there exist conspicuous income gaps between whites and Negroes. There is a large concentration of Negroes in the low-income brackets, and whites are distributed in the middle brackets and higher. The weight of whites in the low-income brackets is rather insignificant. . . . This fact is largely responsible for the unequal pattern of income distribution in the United States." The preceding statement, however, is not well founded. The American Negroes account for only 10 per cent of total population, and therefore it is impossible for the majority of whites to be found in the middle brackets or higher.

[8] See Robert Solow, "Income Inequality since the War," in *Postwar Economic Trends in the United States*, ed. by E. Freeman (1960), pp. 127–129.

[9] However, the income-redistribution effect of public finance is believed to be greater in the United States than in Japan. We must also note that the income concepts used in the *Employment Status Survey* differ from those used in the National Income statistics, and the former largely ignore those incomes which do not assume the form of cash payment. Adjustment for this point will presumably increase the share of the low-income bracket in Japan.

[10] According to Ishizaki, the U.N.'s income-distribution statistics are those of "personal incomes" as distinguished from "household incomes," to which the aforementioned statistics for Japan and the United States refer. However, in the U.N.'s statistics, the combined income of a married couple is classified as independent income, and, for several countries, incomes of children living with their parents are combined with the latter's incomes. Thus, "incomes" in the U.N. statistics are largely in the nature of household incomes, and we should perhaps not be overly concerned with differences between these statistics and those for Japan and the United States.

are most closely related with the rate of savings. We observe in the table that as far as the highest-income brackets are concerned, Japan displays a relatively equal pattern of distribution in comparison with other advanced countries. For example, the distributions in Holland and West Germany are clearly more unequal than that in Japan, and, in terms of the tenth-decile shares, those in Denmark and Great Britain are also more unequal than that in Japan. Sweden is the only country that shows a more equal distribution (1954) than Japan.[11] In terms of the ninth-decile shares, the value is notably greater for Japan than for other countries.

TABLE 8-3

Pre-Tax Income Shares of the Highest-Income Brackets
in Advanced Countries

Country	(Fiscal year)	(1) Tenth decile	(2) Fifth quintile
U.K.	(1955)	29.3	43.7
Holland	(1950)	35.0	49.0
W. Germany	(1950)	34.	48.0
Denmark	(1952)	30.7	...
Sweden	(1948)	30.3	46.6
	(1954)	27.3	42.8
U.S.A.	(1957)	...	45.6
Japan (a)	(1956)	27.0	43.0
	(1959)	29.0	46.0
(b)	(1959)	28.5	45.3

Sources: For European Countries, U.N., ECE, *Economic Survey for Europe in 1956*, ch. 9, p. 6, Table 3; for the United States, *Survey of Current Business* (July 1962), p. 16; for Japan, (a) from *Shūgyō Kōzō Kihon Chōsa* and (b) from *Rōdō Ryoku Rinji Chōsa*.

On the other hand, the share of the lowest-income bracket is somewhat smaller in Japan than in European countries. This bracket, however, presents the most serious difficulties, conceptual as well as methodological, in international comparison (e.g., definitions of unemployed, part-time employees, family workers, and the like differ from country to country).

Finally, there can be little doubt that there is greater inequality of income distributions in underdeveloped countries than in Japan. For example, according to the income-distribution statistics quoted by Kuznets,[12] the share of the fifth quintile is 50 per cent in Ceylon,

[11] The 1954 figures for Sweden are based upon unadjusted taxation statistics and are not comparable to the 1948 figures. When adjusted, the Swedish distribution becomes more equal. See U.N., *Economic Survey for Europe*, 1956.

[12] Simon Kuznets, "Economic Growth and Income Inequality," *American Economic Review* (March 1955), p. 21.

55 per cent in India, and 56 per cent in Puerto Rico. Many African countries that have long been colonies of the European nations show much greater disparities: in Southern Rhodesia the non-African population, accounting for only 5 per cent of the total, earns 57 per cent of total income; in Kenya 2.9 per cent of the total population claims 51 per cent of total income; and the corresponding figures for Northern Rhodesia are 1.4 per cent and 45 per cent, respectively.[13]

In the light of the preceding comparisons it is difficult to prove empirically that Japanese income distribution is more unequal than those in other countries. On the contrary, the Japanese distribution seems one of the most equal in the entire world, and relatively equal even in comparison with those of the advanced countries.[14]

We are not certain how the distribution of income influences savings. Underdeveloped countries display a pronounced inequality in their distributions of income, but the ratio of savings to the GNP in those countries usually amounts to only 4 to 7 per cent. In the United States and European countries there has been a tendency towards a more egalitarian distribution of income from the prewar to the postwar periods,[15] and yet the average propensity to save in these countries has not shown a falling trend.[16] In three countries in which

---

[13] According to I. B. Kravis, those countries in which the degree of inequality in income distribution is approximately the same as in the United States are Great Britain, Japan, Canada; those with more unequal distributions are Italy, Puerto Rico, Ceylon, El Salvador; and those with more equal distributions are Denmark and Holland (I. B. Kravis, "International Differences in the Distribution of Income," *Review of Economics and Statistics,* Vol. 42, No. 4 [November 1960], p. 409). Harry Oshima has also demonstrated the equality in Japanese income distribution in comparison with the United States, the Malayan Federation, Ceylon, and the Philippines (Harry Oshima, "The International Comparison of Size Distribution of Family Incomes with Special Reference to Asia," *Review of Economics and Statistics,* Vol. 44, No. 4 [November 1962], pp. 439–445).

[14] As a conclusion of his international comparison of distributions of income, Ishizaki maintains that although there is no significant disparity in the distribution of income between Japan and other advanced countries, the main difference is that the distributions in advanced countries became notably more egalitarian from the prewar to the postwar period, and some tendency towards equalization has continued during the postwar years, whereas in Japan there was a conspicuous equalization right after the war but since then the trend has been reversed (Ishizaki, *op. cit.,* pp. 28–29). However, in view of the fact that there has been a fundamental change in the Japanese labor markets since 1959, with a rapid closing of wage gaps that had kept widening prior to that year, it seems that Ishizaki's inequalization trend applies only to the period up to 1959. Thorough empirical research on this point is yet to be conducted. It is noteworthy that in 1959, the year in which there was a conspicuous inequalization, Japanese distribution was still relatively equal to other countries.

[15] U.N., *Economic Survey for Europe,* 1956, ch. 9, and Robert M. Solow, *op. cit.,* pp. 108–116.

[16] Average propensities to save (out of disposable income) in 1938, calculated from U.N., *National Income Statistics, 1938–1948,* were 6.7 per cent, Australia; 4.5 per cent, Canada; 7.1 per cent, France; 5.2 per cent, Holland; 3.2 per cent, Great Britain; 1.4 per cent, the United States. Great Britain and France are the only countries in which the values have become lower since the war. We must, of course, allow for the effect of the depression on the 1938 prices; but the ratios of net savings to Net

the distribution assumes a pattern which is neither extremely unequal nor exceedingly egalitarian, the average propensities to save are as follows: in Japan the propensity is between 10 and 14 per cent, depending upon the data; in the United States it is from 1 to 5 per cent;[17] and in Great Britain it is negative.[18] In his recent study, Hisao Kanamori has indicated that Japanese city-workers' households, regardless of their income brackets, save consistently more than their counterparts in the United States,[19] and that if the distribution of their incomes were the same as that of their American counterparts, the rate of savings of Japanese city-workers' households would be higher than it is today. Kanamori concludes that insofar as workers' households are concerned, one cannot argue that the distributive inequality is the cause of the high rate of saving in Japan.[20]

From the preceding analyses it is clear that the high Japanese

---

National Products in the accompanying table do not reveal any indication of a declining tendency in the average propensity to save.

THE RATE OF NET SAVINGS BEFORE AND AFTER THE WAR[a]
(per cent)

Country	Prewar		Postwar (1950–1960)
U.K.	3.9	(1921–1938)	8.2
W. Germany	7.0	(1928–1938)	18.7
Italy	8.0	(1921–1940)	12.3
Denmark	8.4	(1921–1939)	12.3
Norway	9.4	(1920–1939)	19.0
U.S.A.	7.2	(1919–1938)	9.9
Canada	5.2	(1921–1940)	12.2
Australia	9.2	(1920–1938)	21.5

SOURCE: R. Komiya, "Sengo Nihon no Shihon Chikuseki Ritsu," *Keizai Gaku Ronshū*, Vol. 29, No. 2 (July 1963), Table 4.
[a] The ratio of Net Investment (= Net Saving) to Net National Product.

[17] The sample-survey data of the Michigan Survey Research Center and the Wharton School quoted in I. Friend and Stanley Schor, "Who Saves?," *Review of Economics and Statistics*, Vol. 41, No. 2, part 2 (May 1959), p. 217.

[18] See U.N., *World Economic Survey*, 1960, p. 28, footnote 14.

[19] We must note, however, that the level of income of Japanese city-workers' households is high relative to agricultural households and households other than those of city-workers; in Japan, city-workers' households belong to a comparatively wealthy class.

[20] Hisao Kanamori, "Nihon no Chochiku Ritsu wa Naniyue Takai Ka," *Keizai Geppō* (November 1961), pp. 90–92. He writes: "The distribution of all incomes in Japan appears more unequal than that in other advanced countries, but the overall inequality is largely generated by households of the self-employed. Inequality is not pronounced if we take the distribution of income of city-workers' households." It is not clear, however, what evidence there is in support of the first half of his statement.

propensity to save cannot be explained in terms of inequality in the distribution of income.

THE PROPERTY-INCOME RATIO

According to another view the Japanese average propensity to save is high because the shares of property income and the income of the self-employed are large in Japan. For example, we come across the thesis in the U.N.'s *World Economic Survey*, 1960, that the ratio of the sum of property income and the income of the self-employed to total personal income, and the rate of growth in real disposable income, are the two most effective variables in explaining international differences in the average propensity to save.[21] It is, however,

TABLE 8-4

RATIOS OF PROPERTY INCOME AND INCOME OF THE SELF-EMPLOYED
TO PERSONAL INCOME: 1950–1960
(per cent)

Country	(1) Ratio of property income	(2) Ratio of income of the self-employed	(3) Average propensity to save with respect to personal disposable income (figures in parentheses are ranks)		(4) Ratio of prewar (1938) property incomes
U.S.A.	12.4	13.4	7.4	(8)	16.9
Switzerland	11.2[a]	19.3[a]			22.5
Belgium	10.9	25.0	11.3[b]	(4)	20.0
U.K.	10.0	9.6	2.9	(11)	...
Canada	9.7	15.9	7.6	(7)	14.2
New Zealand	9.2	26.9	8.5	(6)	10.4[c]
Australia	8.8	23.6	13.2	(2)	15.0
Japan	5.9	38.9	16.2	(1)	21.0[d]
France	5.9[a]	26.5[e]	6.1	(10)	...
Finland	5.6	34.3	11.8[e]	(3)	14.5[e,d]
Norway	3.8[f]	17.2[f]	9.3[g]	(5)	11.4
Sweden	2.5	15.5	6.6	(9)	...

SOURCES: For (1), (2), and (3), U.N., *Yearbook of National Accounts Statistics;* for (4), Simon Kuznets, "Quantitative Aspects of the Economic Growth of Nations," *Economic Development and Cultural Change*, Vol. 7, No. 3, Part 2 (April 1959), pp. 78–80.
[a] Ratio to the National Income.
[b] 1950–1959.
[c] Does not include personal dividend income.
[d] Does not include interest on government bonds.
[e] 1954–1960.
[f] 1951–1960.
[g] 1950–1959, according to U.N., *World Economic Survey*, 1960.

rather misleading to combine property income and the income of the self-employed; the two should be treated separately.

[21] U.N., *World Economic Survey*, 1960, pp. 27–28.

Table 8-4 gives the ratios of net property income, consisting of rent, interest, dividend, and the like, received by individuals to personal income in selected countries.[22] The ratio in Japan increased rapidly from 3.1 per cent in 1950 to 8.1 per cent in 1960. Even if we take the values for 1955–1960, the property-income ratio was lower in Japan than in the United States, Switzerland, Belgium, and Canada. Furthermore, there is no visible correlation between the ranks of property-income ratios and average propensities to save. A comparison of prewar and postwar figures in Table 8-4 shows that the property-income ratios were much larger before the war, and yet there is no indication that the decline in the ratio during the postwar period has significantly affected the rate of saving.[23] In the case of Japan, her prewar ratio was above 20 per cent, one of the highest in the world, but the ratio has drastically decreased after the war due to the agricultural reforms and the Zaibatsu dissolution.[24] Notwithstanding the postwar decline in the ratio, however, the Japanese average propensity to save (out of personal income) has been much higher after the war than it was during the second half of the 1920's.

The foregoing examples are sufficient to illustrate that the property-income ratio does not effectively explain international differences in the average propensity to save.

THE ROLE OF THE SELF-EMPLOYED

For several reasons the self-employed are apt to save more than are other categories of consumers: it is often necessary for them to finance part of their investment by their own savings; their income is subject to irregular fluctuations, and their "transient-income" ratio à la Milton Friedman tends to be high; they have a greater need than workers to prepare for illness and retirement. Table 8-4 shows that the ratio of income of the self-employed to total personal income in Japan is very high, suggesting that the saving of the self-employed is largely responsible for the high rate of saving for all personal sectors in the country.

The fact that the self-employed play an important role in the supply of savings has been pointed out by Friend and Kravis,[25] and their study has provided the hint which enabled Miyohei Shinohara to discover that in Japan the average propensity to save of the self-employed is conspicuously high.[26] According to the Shinohara study, as

[22] To be exact, we must deduct from personal income imputed rent and imputed interest (all of which, by definition, are spent on consumption) so as to derive income paid only in cash. There is, however, no such data available.

[23] See footnote 16.

[24] These changes in the factorial distribution of income must have had some significant equalization effect upon the size distribution of income.

[25] Irwin Friend and I. B. Kravis, "Entrepreneurial Income, Saving and Investment," *American Economic Review*, Vol. 47, No. 3 (June 1957).

[26] Miyohei Shinohara, *Shōhi Kansū* (Tokyo, 1958), pp. 219–220, and "The Structure of Saving and the Consumption Function in Postwar Japan," *Journal of Political Economy* (December 1959).

well as the similar work by Hiroshi Kawaguchi, the rate of saving among households of the self-employed with respect to their pre-tax income has been above 30 per cent even during the post–1955 period. As is discussed in the Appendix to this chapter, however, the statistics in the *Family Savings Survey* for fiscal 1959 (*Chochiku Dōkō Chōsa Hōkoku*) and in other sources do not indicate that the rate has been as high as estimated by the two authors. The best guess seems to be that the average propensity to save of households of the self-employed is between 20 and 25 per cent, and that of "corporation managers" (company executives, high-ranking government officials, and the like) is in the neighborhood of 20 per cent.

It is rather startling that the self-employed people in Japan, with their typical annual income of only 400,000 yen, are saving as much as 20 per cent (or more) of their pre-tax income. It seems safe to assume that the high rate of saving of the self-employed, as well as the large weight of their income in total personal income, is not insignificantly responsible for the high, overall propensity to save in Japan.

The importance of the above factor, however, is steadily diminishing. For example, the share of income of the self-employed (inclusive of agriculture, forestry, and fishing) in the National Income was 50 per cent in fiscal 1950, but it continued to decrease in subsequent years, reaching 30.3 per cent in fiscal 1960. The extent of decline in

TABLE 8-5

AVERAGE PROPENSITY TO SAVE OF AGRICULTURAL HOUSEHOLDS,
URBAN WAGE-SALARY EARNERS' HOUSEHOLDS, AND OTHER HOUSEHOLDS[a]
(per cent)

			Other households		
	(1)	(2) Urban wage-salary earners' households	(3) The Shinohara estimates	(4) The Kawaguchi estimates	(5) The entire personal sector
Fiscal year	Agricultural households				
1951	10.3	1.8	52.0	56.3	17.7
1952	7.9	4.0	47.3	43.1	14.6
1953	6.0	5.0	27.6	23.7	9.9
1954	3.4	6.3	26.0	25.2	9.8
1955	9.7	7.9	24.1	30.6	13.1
1956	3.6	10.1	33.2	32.1	14.2
1957	6.2	10.9	...	32.7	14.6
1958	7.3	11.2	...	33.1	14.9
1959	8.7	12.4	...	...	...
1960	10.8	13.3	...	...	...

SOURCES: (1) Nōrin Shō, *Nōka Keizai Chōsa Hōkoku;* (2) Sōrifu Tōkei-kyoku, *Kakei Shōsa Hōkoku;* (3) Shinohara, *The Growth and Cycles in the Japanese Economy,* p. 207; (4) H. Kawaguchi, *Chochiku no Kōzō Bunseki,* 1960, p. 49; (5) *Kokumin Shotoku Hakusho.*
[a] With respect to pre-tax income.

the share of the self-employed exclusive of agriculture, forestry, and fishing, however, is believed to have been less drastic.

The pronounced fall in the weight of the self-employed, and the steady rise in the rate of savings of workers' households—these are two outstanding trends observed during the 1950's (see column 2 in Table 8-5, and column 3 in Table 8-2).

Before closing our discussion of the relationships between saving and the distribution of income, we may state in summary that even if the often-heard claim that the share of labor in Japan is small were true, we fail to discover any definitive factors in the distribution of personal income which can explain the high level of personal savings, except for the large weight of income of the self-employed, exclusive of agriculture and forestry. As we have seen earlier, the property-income ratio in Japan is relatively small while the rate of saving of city-workers is high in comparison with those in other countries.[27]

THE GROWTH RATE AND THE EXTRA-INCOME RATIO

In addition to the ratio of the sum of property income and income of the self-employed to personal income, the U.N.'s *World Economic Survey*, 1960, cites the rate of growth in real disposable income as another important factor which accounts for international differences in the average propensity to save. There are countries like France and Holland in which the rate of growth in per capita real disposable income is high, while the average propensity to save is low; there are also countries like Belgium and Denmark in which the rate of saving is high despite the low growth rate. Nonetheless, a survey of countries such as Japan, West Germany, and Austria (particularly after 1955) strongly suggests that the high rate of saving in these countries is closely related to their rapid economic growth. Continual increase in real income may easily induce a rise in the rate of saving. In the case of Japan after 1955, income has risen faster each year than was generally anticipated, and each year the high rate of growth has been considered as a temporary phenomenon.[28] In such a situation the increased portion of income is not regarded by the consumers as part of their "permanent income" à la Friedman, and therefore their saving is prone to increase. In this sense we may hold

[27] With regard to net corporate savings, the author is skeptical of the view that the rate of accumulation is high in Japan because of low labor shares. For an elaboration on this point, see Komiya, "Sengo Nihon no Shihon Chikuseki Ritsu," *op. cit.*, pp. 32–34.

[28] Japanese economic policy makers, as well as economists, have repeatedly maintained that Japan's accelerated growth is merely a short-term phenomenon. Projected growth rates under different Economic Plans (5 per cent under the Economic Recovery Plan; 6.5 per cent under the New Long-Range Economic Plan; and 7.2 per cent under the Income-Doubling Plan) were all severely criticized as overly optimistic. Even among general consumers a tone of pessimism was prevalent concerning the future of the Japanese economy.

that the higher-than-anticipated growth rate raised the level of saving, which in turn helped accelerate economic growth. Since 1955 the rapid rise in the level of income has been accompanied by a pronounced increase in the extra-income ratio, principally among workers' households. Shinohara has held that the recent increase in temporary and extra income should be interpreted as one cause of the rising rate of saving by city-workers.[29]

It is a unique custom of Japanese corporations to pay employees regular bonuses, as a profit-sharing system, at the end of each year or quarter. Before the war, bonuses were restricted to white-collar workers with an emphasis on supervisory personnel, but during the postwar period the system has been extended to cover all workers in large corporations as well as the increasing number of workers in small- and medium-size firms. Consequently, the ratio of bonuses to workers' annual income, together with their saving, has risen rapidly. Figure 8-2 illustrates the relationship between saving and extra income in real

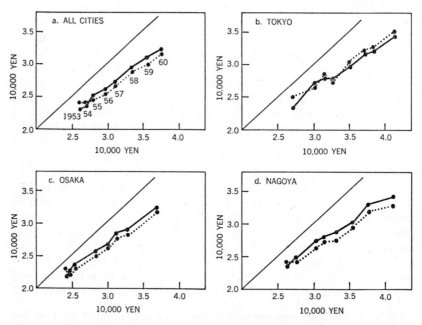

Fig. 8-2. Extra income and saving of wage-salary earners' households: 1953–1960. The horizontal axis measures real disposable income. The vertical axis measures real consumption expenditures for the dotted lines, and the nonextra-income portion of real income for the broad lines. Source: Sōrifu Tōkei-kyoku, *Kakei Chōsa Nempō*.

disposable income. "Extra income" here is defined as bonuses, overtime allowances, extra-work allowances, and other income paid only in a given month—but it consists largely of bonuses. Figure 8-2 and

[29] M. Shinohara, *Kōdo Seichō no Himitsu*, p. 222,

similar figures for 24 cities in Japan indicate that while the extra-income ratio has continuously risen since 1955, there is a close relationship between the amount of total extra income earned by workers and the amount of their saving in a given year. The relationship between the two, however, differs from city to city: in Tokyo and Fukuoka the two match each other closely, whereas in Nagoya and many other cities savings exceed extra incomes by approximately constant amounts. On the other hand, in Chiba and Obihiro savings are below extra incomes. Table 8-6 gives figures upon which a and b in Figure 8-2 are based.

TABLE 8-6

EXTRA INCOME AND SAVING OF WAGE-SALARY EARNERS' HOUSEHOLDS

Fiscal year	(1) Real disposable income[a] (yen)	(2) Real extra-income[a] (yen)	(3) Ratio of (2) to (3) (per cent)	(4) Real saving[a] (yen)	(5) Ratio of (4) to (1) (per cent)
All cities:					
1953	26,294	3,208	12.2	2,312	8.8
1954	26,796	3,054	11.4	2,863	10.7
1955	28,096	3,006	10.7	3,450	12.3
1956	29,687	3,681	12.4	4,368	14.7
1957	31,216	4,245	13.6	4,780	15.3
1958	33,424	4,479	13.4	5,144	15.4
1959	35,405	5,098	14.4	5,824	16.5
1960	37,793	6,047	16.0	6,604	17.5
Tokyo:					
1953	27,018	3,728	13.8	2,065	7.6
1954	29,657	3,677	12.4	3,111	10.5
1955	31,343	3,542	11.3	3,398	10.8
1956	32,275	4,454	13.8	4,459	13.8
1957	35,234	5,250	14.9	5,203	14.8
1958	36,945	5,246	14.2	4,963	13.4
1959	38,339	5,866	15.3	5,683	14.8
1960	41,245	7,053	17.1	6,675	16.2

SOURCE: Sōrifu Tōkei-kyoku, Kakei Chōsa Nempō.
[a] In 1955 prices.

The above statistical facts do not imply that literally all extra income is saved by workers. According to monthly statistics of the Family Income and Expenditure Survey (Kakei Chōsa), in those months with little extra income it is only the extremely low-income households whose saving becomes negative, and in those months with a large extra income (e.g., December and June) expenditures show a sizeable increase. It is also inappropriate to regard extra income to be in the nature of Friedmanian "transient income," and the rest of income as "permanent income." For one thing the bonus in Japan is a rather fixed and anticipated element in the total annual income of workers. The so-called Life-Long Employment and Annual Proportional-Wage-Increase Systems in Japan tend to stabilize the employment relationship as well as wage levels, and it is probable that the annual income of Japanese workers fluctuates far less than it does in the United States and other countries. Therefore, we cannot argue that the rate of saving for workers' households is high in Japan because the "transient-income" ratio is large. The recent rise in workers' saving should perhaps be best interpreted as a reflection of the expanding lag in the level of consumption relative to income, for in the course of Japan's accelerated growth the extra-income ratio has increased at a persistently rapid pace along with a faster-than-anticipated increase in real income.

THE LIFE CYCLE OF INCOME AND SAVING

The pattern of the life cycle of income and saving differs from country to country. There seems to be some evidence that the unique properties of this life cycle, as well as several demographic characteristics of postwar Japan, have encouraged the high rate of personal saving in the country.

(1) Miyohei Shinohara believes, on the basis of Colin Clark's thesis that saving is accumulated by the young and depleted by the old, that the small ratio of aged in the Japanese population is one reason for the high rate of saving.[30] On the other hand, Hisao Kanamori holds that, in the light of data in the *Family Savings Survey*, fiscal 1959 (*Chochiku Dōkō Chōsa Hōkoku*), households of the aged show a higher propensity to save than those of the young even after income-size differences between the two age groups are removed. In Figure 8-3, prepared by Kanamori, the dots indicate the relationship between income and saving of workers' households, regardless of the ages of household-heads; and the x's illustrate the relationship between income and saving when workers' households are arranged in terms of age brackets. Kanamori concludes that the large proportion of the relatively young in the age composition does not constitute an explanation of the high rate of saving; on the contrary, "if the ratio of the old were larger, the rate of saving would be higher in Japan." [31]

(2) The conspicuously high rate of saving among the old seems unique to Japan, and is presumably a result of the Annual Proportional-Wage-Increase System. In Table 8-7, which compares wage gaps in terms of age brackets in Japan and West Germany, the relatively high income of the old in Japan is clearly indicated. The pattern of income distribution in terms of age brackets for West Germany (as shown in Table 8-7) represents those of European countries and the United States. While there exist some notable differences in the dis-

[30] *Ibid.*, p. 228. The contention of *World Economic Survey*, 1960, is that the second half of Clark's thesis is applicable to Great Britain and France (p. 29).

[31] Hisao Kanamori, *op. cit.*, p. 93. The *Family Savings Survey* does not distinguish marital status of household heads. The saving rate of unmarried youth is perhaps somewhat higher than for the married. See footnote 51.

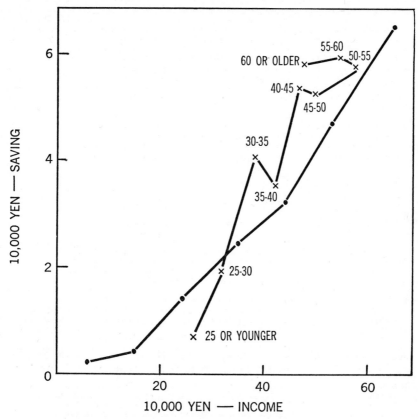

Fig. 8-3. Savings by income and age brackets (1959, all wage-salary earners).
Source: Economic Planning Agency, *Keizai Geppō*, November 1961, p. 93.

tribution of income in terms of age between Japan and Western countries, we should expect far less differences in "consumption needs" in
terms of consumers' age brackets.[32] Therefore, since consumption
needs decline with age, the households of the aged, whose level of
income remains high, are bound to save more.[33] But we must note
that, in Japan, those who are older than 65 or 70 (whose European
and American counterparts usually live on negative savings) are
typically absorbed into their children's households, thus presumably

[32] However, the economic burden placed upon Japanese parents by children's education, marriage, and post-marriage assistance, is clearly heavier than that upon
European and American parents.

[33] Kanamori writes: "The high rate of saving among the old in Japan seems to
support the hypothesis that the traditional ethics as to the virtue of parsimony are
influencing Japanese saving behavior." I am inclined to attach greater importance,
not to "ethics," but to the purely economic factor of income versus consumption
needs. I presume that the aged in Western countries would save more if the level
of their income were higher.

TABLE 8-7

MALE WORKERS' WAGE DIFFERENCES BY AGE[a]

Age	W. Germany	Japan
Blue-collar workers:		
30 or younger	100.0	100.0
30–40	105.2	153.7
40–45	104.2 ⎫	
45–50	102.5 ⎬	179.5
50–55	100.4 ⎧	
55–60	97.9 ⎬	147.5
60 or older	94.4 ⎭	
White-collar workers:		
25 or younger	100.0	100.0
25–35	178.0	181.2
35–45	210.1	260.6 (35–40 years old)
45–55	225.9	307.6 (40–50 years old)
55 or older	220.9	271.1 (50 or older)

SOURCE: *Rōdō Hakusho*, 1960, p. 168.

[a] Wage indexes by age. For blue-collar workers, wages of those younger than 30 as 100; for white-collar workers, wages of those younger than 25 as 100.

contributing to society's saving by lessening social overhead expenditures which the maintenance of independent households would necessitate.[34]

(3) The state of consumer finance and housing mortgages in Japan is closely related to the preceding observations. Even if the income level of the young is low, easy access to consumer finance, housing mortgages, and other debt instruments tends to encourage their consumption; their saving may easily become negative with a lowering effect on the overall rate of personal savings.[35] In Japan the system of consumer finance is still in a state of underdevelopment, and the amount of mortgage loans on houses, other than a limited amount from the Housing Loans Fund of the government, has been close to zero. Consequently, a sizeable saving accumulation usually precedes the purchase of consumer durables and houses in Japan.

In addition to those differences which we have observed in the life cycle of income and saving in Japan from those in Western countries, there may perhaps be some other differences that have determined the high rate of saving in Japan.[36]

[34] For this point, see footnote 39.

[35] It is curious that in Great Britain even households in the middle income distribution show negative savings. In Japan it is generally impossible for a household to maintain negative saving except for a relatively short period.

[36] For the properties of the life cycle which seem actually to lower the savings rate, see footnote 39.

TABLE 8-8

THE RATIO OF SOCIAL-SECURITY EXPENDITURES TO THE NATIONAL INCOME
AND THE AVERAGE PROPENSITY TO SAVE

Country	(1) Ratio of social-security payments to National Income. (1957)	(2) Ratio of government transfer pay- ments to house- holds to GDP[a] (1950–1960)	(3) Average propensity to save. (1950–1960) Figures in paren- theses are ranks.
W. Germany	20.0	12.2	13.2 (2)
France	17.9	11.1	6.1 (14)
Austria	16.5	11.8	8.7 (9)
Belgium	14.8	9.6	11.3 (5)
New Zealand	12.8	8.4	8.5 (10)
Sweden	12.5	7.0	6.6 (13)
Denmark	11.6	6.9	9.7 (7)
Finland	11.6	6.7	11.8 (4)
Holland	11.4	8.2	10.2 (6)
U.K.	11.4	6.0	2.9 (15)
Norway	9.9	6.2	9.3 (8)
Australia	8.8	5.1	13.2 (2)
Canada	8.5	6.5	7.6 (11)
U.S.A.	5.7	4.2	7.4 (12)
Japan	5.3	3.4	16.2 (1)

SOURCES: (1) Kōsei Shō, *Kōsei Hakusho*, 1961, p. 455; (2) and (3) R. Komiya, "Sengo Nihon no Shihon Chikuseki Ritsu," *op. cit.*, tables 10 and 12.

[a] Government transfer payments to households in this column consist mostly of social-insurance and social-security payments; also included are some nonsocial-security items such as scholarships, research fellowships, retirement compensations for government employees, and the like.

SOCIAL SECURITY

According to another frequently encountered theory, the rate of saving in Japan is high because, in the absence of an extensive social-security system, people are motivated to save by a sense of apprehension about illness, post-retirement needs, and other contingencies.[37] But in the light of the relationships between the ratio of social-security expenditures to the National Income and the average propensity to save in different countries (see Table 8-8), this thesis does not seem well founded.

The above conclusion may be subjected to the following argument. First, Table 8-8 does not take into account "other" factors; we may discover a more definitive relationship between social security and

[37] E.g., M. Shinohara, *Kōdo Seichō no Himitsu*, p. 228; H. Kanamori, *op. cit.*, p. 94.

the rate of saving if all other factors are made equal. Aside from whether this is true, Table 8-8 does show that the influence of social security is not so strong as to eliminate the effects of all other factors. Second, it may be argued that the real extent of social security programs and the degree of insecurity experienced by the general consumer can hardly be measured by simple ratios of social-security cost to the National Income or to the GDP; therefore, the results in Table 8-8 are inconclusive. This is a sensible proposition; but it is econometrically impossible to either prove or disprove such a proposition.

Hisao Kanamori cites the following points in support of the thesis that insufficient social security is one cause of the high rate of saving in Japan: (1) the rate of saving in the middle low-income bracket in Japan is notably high relative to that in the United States; and (2) according to the Bank of Japan's *Public Opinion Survey on Savings*, July 1961 (*Chochiku ni Kansuru Yoron Chōsa*), a large proportion of interviewees gave as the purpose of their saving (a) "to provide for illness and other contingencies" (a reply concentrated among those in the middle low-income bracket) and (b) "for security after retirement." [38] Kanamori's proof, however, is not necessarily conclusive, because the rate of saving in Japan is high, not just in the middle low-income group, but throughout the income brackets. Furthermore, analysis of the low-income sectors involves numerous comparability problems, such as the definitions of income, the unemployed, households of the aged, irregular-income earners, and the like, so that it is extremely difficult to make a meaningful, international comparison of the bracket. A more relevant question to ask is why the rate of saving in the low-income sector approaches zero but fails to be negative in Japan, in contrast to the usual negative savings in the corresponding sectors in the United States and Great Britain. We must await further research to learn whether this phenomenon is related to social security. [39]

In any circumstance it is not easy to apply an econometric method to test the impact of social security on saving. However, if some major changes in the social security system take place within a relatively short period of time, we might be able to conduct a meaningful correlation analysis in order to draw a somewhat definitive conclusion as to the influence of social security on saving. My own impression is that social security affects saving, not so much through the consumers' sense of "insecurity" under a particular social security system in a given

---

[38] *Ibid.*, pp. 94–95.

[39] "To provide for security after retirement" seems a rather weak motive for saving in Japan, from a sociological viewpoint. Unlike the United States and some European countries, it has traditionally been held in Japan that the best way to prepare for a secure life after retirement is not to save but to bear a sufficient number of children, or to raise adopted children, who will look after the retired parents. For an extremely interesting description of this and related customs, see R. P. Dore, *City Life in Japan: A Study of a Tokyo Ward* (London, 1958), chapters 3, 4, and 6.

country, as via its effects on fiscal burdens and government saving or on the tax system to finance its programs, which in turn influences personal savings.[40]

OTHER CAUSES

The following "other" hypotheses are harder to prove or disprove econometrically than those which we have examined in the preceding sections.

The Pigou Effect

War and inflation have caused extensive destruction and the disappearance of assets owned by consumers, as well as a drastic decline in property value or real income of many individuals. Given the fall of the asset-income ratio after the war, it is conceivable that the rate of saving in Japan has been high because of consumers' efforts to restore the optimal asset-income ratio realized before the war. This hypothesis allegedly applies to liquid assets as well as to houses and other physical assets. An empirical testing of this idea is exceedingly difficult because one must somehow assume an optimal asset-income ratio for each individual consumer or group of consumers.[41]

The Traditional View on the Virtue of Parsimony

The rate of saving in Japan has been high not only after the war but during the prewar years as well; (therefore) many people contend that the traditional emphasis on a frugal life is one major explanation of the phenomenon.[42] Granted that such a view deserves careful study, especially from the standpoint of the sociology of religion, an attempt to treat it as a direct explanatory variable for an economic phenomenon is a sign of irresponsibility and defeatism. According to the available National Income statistics for the Meiji era, the ratio of Net National Saving to the NNP is estimated to have been only 3.8 per cent during the last two decades of the nineteenth century, strongly suggesting that the rate of saving was not as high then as in later periods. We also notice in Table 8-5 that the saving of city-workers prior to 1954 was much lower than after 1956–1957. Even if it were true that the spirit of parsimony circulates through Japanese blood vessels, the economist's task is to analyze how and by what economic conditions the ethos of frugality transcends itself into a high rate of saving in the real world.

[40] See R. Komiya, "Sengo Nihon no Shihon Chikuseki Ritsu," *op cit.*
[41] This point was suggested by Shinohara (*Kōdo Seichō no Himitsu*, pp. 223–225). Kanamori also holds a negative view ("Nihon no Chochiku Ritsu wa Naniyue Takai Ka," p. 93), but the proof of his negative view seems insufficient.
[42] Hisao Kanamori, *ibid.*, p. 94. Many others have held the same view.

Appendix   *The Rate of Savings of*
                 the Self-Employed

As mentioned in the text of this chapter, Miyohei Shinohara has shown that if one deducts the estimated value of savings of agricultural and urban wage-salary earners' households from total personal savings in the National Income statistics, the average propensity to save in the "residual" sector is conspicuously high. He interprets the result to be a reflection of the high propensity to save of the self-employed outside the agricultural sector. (From here on, the "self-employed," unless otherwise stated, refers to the self-employed outside the agricultural sector.)[43] Hiroshi Kawaguchi's research has shown a similar result— the propensity to save among households other than agricultural and urban wage-salary earners' tends to be strikingly high.[44] Although the Kawaguchi estimate is supposedly based upon "a careful consideration of several additional factors" [45] not found in the Shinohara study, the two estimates are essentially the same and are summarized in Table 8-5 of the main text.[46] We observe in Table 8-5 that the rate of saving among households other than agricultural and wage-salary earners' is notably high; but the rate among urban wage-salary-earners' households has been steadily rising since 1951, surpassing the rate of farm households in the years after 1956.

Recently the Statistical Bureau of the Prime Minister's Office released the *Family Savings Survey* for 1959 containing information on savings by the self-employed, corporation managers, and professionals, which was estimated through a revised and more reliable method than before. According to the report, the rate of saving by households of the self-employed is 22.5 per cent and by corporation managers 17.2 per cent (see Table 8-9). Both rates are surprisingly low relative to the Shinohara-Kawaguchi estimates.

Noting the discrepancies between the report and Table 8-5, Shinohara holds that the rate of saving by the self-employed (in the report)

[43] M. Shinohara, *Shōhi Kansū*, p. 220.

[44] Hiroshi Kawaguchi, *Chochiku Ryoku, Sono Riron to Jittai* (Zenkoku Chihō Ginkō Kyōkai, 1954), p. 186.

[45] Shinohara, *Kōdo Seichō no Himitsu*, p. 212.

[46] Interpretations of Kawaguchi and Shinohara, however, are not the same. Shinohara interprets the high rate of saving by those other than farmers and city-workers to be related to real investment (particularly inventory investment) of the self-employed. Kawaguchi calls the residual sector, to be derived by removing agricultural and workers' households, the "capitalist sector," and maintains that "inasmuch as the self-employed in Japan consist mostly of extremely small businesses, it is inconceivable, except for the postwar inflation period, that they possess such a high capacity to save as suggested by the estimate; we are led to conclude that the high rate of saving in the residual sector is primarily due to the exceedingly high propensity to save among a few in the high-income brackets" (Hiroshi Kawaguchi, *Chochiku no Kōzō Bunseki*, Zenkoku Chihō Ginkō Kyōkai, 1960, p. 52).

can easily be in the neighborhood of 30 per cent (1) by using after-tax income as the denominator in lieu of before-tax income as is done in the report (e.g., assuming that the average tax rate is 20 per cent, this adjustment will increase the rate of saving 1.25 times), and (2) by

TABLE 8-9

The Rate of Saving of Households of the Self-Employed, Corporation Managers, and Professionals[a]
(per cent)

	(1) Self-employed	(2) Corporation managers	(3) Professionals and others
Savings deposits, life insurance, portfolio, etc.	9.9	16.2	13.5
Net change in borrowing[b]	−0.5	−3.1	−0.5
Real investment[c]	4.6	4.1	16.8
Investment in production facilities	8.5	...	...
Total	22.5	17.2	29.8
Average annual income (10,000 yen)	44.8	94.8	57.2

Source: Sōrifu Tōkei-kyoku, *Chochiku Dōkō Chōsa Hōkoku*, 1959.

[a] Ratio to pre-tax income.

[b] Borrowing from financial institutions only.

[c] Housing (new construction, improvement and addition, purchase of old houses and housing equipment). Sales of houses and lands not deducted.

adding inventory investment to the saving of the self-employed.[47] To make only upward adjustments for the rate of saving in the report, however, seems rather unjustifiable. In order to make the report's estimates of savings by the self-employed truly comparable to those from the National Income statistics we must (in addition to deducting tax from the denominator): (3) add to the denominator imputed rent on lands and houses owned by the self-employed; deduct from the numerator (saving) and the denominator (income) (4) sales of lands and houses, (5) depreciation of production facilities, (6) depreciation of houses; (7) add inventory investment to saving; (8) deduct from saving interfirm credits, increase in the balance of discount bills, loans from financial institutions; and finally (9) add to saving increase in credit sales.[48] It is admittedly difficult to estimate the final result after

[47] Shinohara, *Kōdo Seichō no Himitsu*, p. 212.

[48] The London *Economist* cites as one reason for the high rate of saving in Japan the fact that small- and medium-size businesses in the country are prone to accumulate "non-autonomous" savings because they are frequently paid in long-term bills by large corporations ("Consider Japan," *Economist*, September 1, 1962, p. 816). This observation seems valid particularly with respect to the period of credit squeeze.

all these adjustments; but the downward effect of adjustments (3), (4), and (5) is likely to offset the upward effect of (1), and (2).[49]

The rate of saving by corporation managers in Table 8-9 is also rather low; but this is not too surprising because in Japan most "executive" salaries are of relatively small size, probably an indication of the fact that in contrast to other countries a high percentage of Japanese small businesses are organized as corporations. According to *Incorporated Enterprise Statistics (Hōjin Kigyō Tōkei)*, 74 per cent of all executive salaries are paid by firms with capital of 5 million yen or less, and if we include larger firms with capital of up to 50 million yen, this figure becomes 90 per cent. The average annual salary of an executive in firms with capital of 5 million yen or less is only about 280,000 yen, which is less than the average income of workers in large-scale firms with capital of 100 million to 1 billion yen. Many executives simultaneously hold several company posts; but it is evident that executive salaries in Japan, which accounted for 4.3 per cent of the National Income in fiscal 1960, largely consist of small-size incomes.

In the Kawaguchi-Shinohara estimates, what Kawaguchi calls the "capitalist sector"—the household sector excluding farmers and city-workers—comprises rentiers, the self-employed, corporation managers, professionals, and all other households. According to the *Family Income and Expenditure Survey (Kakei Chōsa)*, the average consumption level (the income level is not available in the survey) of urban wage-salary earners is higher than that for general households, implying that the majority of households other than wage-salary earners belong to the low-income brackets. From these observations it seems impossible for the average propensity to save in Kawaguchi's capitalist sector to be above 30 per cent.[50] A more realistic estimate of the average

---

[49] According to National Income statistics, the value of inventory investment by the self-employed (inclusive of agriculture and forestry) was 4.3 per cent of the income of the self-employed (used in Table 8-9) for 1959; similarly, depreciation was 8.6 per cent. Their averages for fiscal 1955–1960 were 5.3 and 7.8 per cent, respectively. The ratio of plant-and-equipment investment by the self-employed to their income was 9.1 per cent for 1959, and 8.3 per cent on the average, for fiscal 1955–1960. In view of accelerated expansion of private investment since 1955, stagnation in net investments of the self-employed is rather startling.

[50] In response to this inference, Shinohara commented at the Zushi Conference that the figures derivable from the *National Survey of Family Income and Expenditure (Zenkoku Shōhisha Jittai Chōsa Hōkoku)* for 1959 (to be exact, for September, October, and November of 1959) issued by the Statistical Bureau of the Prime Minister's Office are much higher than those of savings by the self-employed in Table 8-9. My own calculations from the national survey above are summarized in the accompanying table. We may conceive of several causes of differences between Table 8-9 and my calculations; but the most important explanation seems to be the difference in the average income level. For corporation managers and professionals, the differences in the average income match those in the average saving levels. In view of the fact that, in terms of the National Income statistics, per capita income of the self-employed (exclusive of agriculture, forestry, and fishing) for 1959 is 371,000 yen, and that the income of "households" of the self-employed comprise workers' income as well as property income, the sample in the *Family Savings Survey* seems more accurately to represent the average values. Even in terms of the *Survey of Family In-*

propensity to save of the self-employed would be approximately 20 per cent, and certainly not higher than 25 per cent.

Since personal saving in the National Income statistics is calculated as a residual item by deducting consumption from income, a considerable number of errors should be expected. The reliability of statistics on saving of the self-employed, which one derives by further deducting from the above residual item savings of farmers and workers, is highly questionable. There are some notable differences in the concept of saving employed in the *Farming Household Economy Survey* as against the *Family Income and Expenditure Survey*. There is also much uncertainty as to the extent to which the sample of wage-salary earners' households taken in those cities covered by the *Family Income and Expenditure Survey* truly represents workers in general and those living in areas other than the survey cities in particular.[51]

The reliability of the *Family Savings Survey* for 1959 is also subject to doubt. The report is based upon a sample of about 1000 households of the self-employed taken from the entire country, but only 47 of those households earned an annual income of more than 1 million yen. Inadequate coverage of high-income brackets in the household survey has been frequently pointed out. We are still in a state of striking ignorance about the composition of personal savings in the Japanese National Income statistics; for example, there has been little clarification of the occupational classifications as well as income-brackets of savers, little clarification of the kinds of saving, and so forth. Further research in this direction is sorely needed.[52]

---

come and Expenditure, the average propensity to save of the self-employed whose household income is between 400,000 and 500,000 yen is only about 20 per cent.

AVERAGE PROPENSITY TO SAVE AND AVERAGE INCOME OF THE
SELF-EMPLOYED, ETC., ACCORDING TO THE NATIONAL SURVEY
OF FAMILY INCOME AND EXPENDITURE

	Average propensity to save with respect to pre-tax income (per cent)	Average per household income (10,000 yen)
(1) Merchants, craftsmen	26.7	33.6
(2) Self-employed	45.3	64.0
(3) Corporation managers	12.8	69.8
(4) Professionals	27.2	44.5

[51] The aforementioned *Economist* article cites as another reason for the high rate of saving the fact that in Japan the majority of female workers in the textile (and other) industries, who are young and unmarried, work primarily to save enough for dowry. This is an interesting view of a foreign observer. Perhaps something similar might be said about young, unmarried male workers as well.

[52] After completing this paper I learned of a study that calculates total personal saving (1959) by aggregating the estimated values of savings in the agricultural, workers', and general households (Hiroshi Andō, "Kojin Chochiku no Shutai Betsu Sui-

Comment *by Miyohei Shinohara*

TREATMENT OF THE PROBLEM

Komiya's paper contains three sources of embarrassment on my part. First, my statements on the savings rate in *The Secret of Accelerated Growth (Kōdo Seichō no Himitsu)* are subjected to his scrutiny. Most of my statements quoted by Komiya are reprinted from my Basic Economics Series in *Nihon Keizai Shimbun* (Daily), and are not based upon the results of full-fledged research. Since the topic of saving had been relatively ignored in economists' discussions, I wrote those statements in the spirit of drawing a free sketch of whatever ideas happened to come to my attention. Although I am grateful for his having treated my casual views with all his seriousness, I feel he should have taken them for what they were.

Second, I am ever reminded how difficult it is to make an international comparison of savings and to analyze their causes. I believe that international differences in the rate of saving are multi-causal. He lightly brushes off as insignificant the relationship between the ratio of social-security expenditures to the National Income and the rate of saving; but I am not convinced. I plan to do thorough research on it on another occasion. His argument, which appears exceedingly sharp at first, is ultimately rather single-minded and lacks universal persuasiveness.

Third, I have always held a multi-causal approach to the analysis of saving. However, Komiya slants his attention only to my remark about the postwar decline in the liquid-asset ratio, and describes me as having maintained that the high rate of saving is a temporary phenomenon associated with the postwar recovery. This is embarrassing because I have mentioned the bonus effect, liquid-asset effect, social-security effect—and many other variables as well. The problem at hand is to explain why the rate of saving of workers' households has been high before as well as after the war; hence, his manner of criticism is completely off the track. As to why the rate of saving has continued to rise since 1959, I myself have stated that the bonus effect seems a relevant explanation. His doubt about people's remembrance of the prewar liquid-asset ratio is legitimate. However, the liquid-asset ratio, or the broadly-defined "Marshallian k" generally shows an upward secular trend in any country. In Japan the same ratio was still lower in 1961 than in 1935. It is, therefore, conceivable that people,

kei," *Keizai Bunseki,* No. 6 [December 1961], pp. 48–67). Andō estimates, chiefly on the basis of the *Family Savings Survey,* the rate of net saving by general households, other than farmers' and workers', to be 20.7 per cent for 1959. In his estimate, the above-mentioned "adjustment factors" (1), (2), (5), (7) and several other factors are taken into consideration. Insofar as the data in the *Family Savings Survey* are concerned, his estimate seems reasonably accurate.

aside from whether they remember the prewar ratio, try to realize the desired ratio by saving more. It seems more appropriate to speak in terms of the desired ratio, rather than the prewar ratio.

THE DISTRIBUTION OF INCOME AND THE RATE OF SAVING

Komiya insists that there is no significant relationship between the personal-property-income ratio and the rate of saving. Since I once wrote about the importance of low labor shares in accounting for the high rate of saving during the prewar period, the reader might be led to think that Komiya's criticism is directed against me. I wish to re-iterate that I argued for the possibility of a rising rate of saving out of the values-added in industry, because low labor shares in the values-added (inclusive of profits, wages, interest, rent, and other indirect expenses) would mean correspondingly high shares of profit and property income, large proportions of which tend to be saved. My problem then involved both personal and corporate savings, and hence should not be confused with the interest of Komiya's paper.

Insofar as the National Income statistics are concerned, it may be true that the personal-property-income ratio shows little correlation with the rate of personal saving. But, from the standpoint of individual recipients of income, we must remember that capital gains from securities and lands are just as much income as factor income, despite the fact that capital gains are excluded from the National Income statistics. It is more than likely, however, that capital gains have a positive effect upon the rate of savings among their recipients.

Inasmuch as Komiya's conclusions are derived from data which fail to allow for the above complication, I am not convinced when told that the Japanese income distribution (be it size or functional distribution) is as equal as those in the advanced countries. His use of the *Employment Status Survey* as a main statistical source for Japan and of taxation statistics for European countries in his international comparison of size distributions is subject to a strong bias, because capital gains are omitted from the statistics of Japanese high-income brackets whereas the taxation statistics for European countries are bound to include them.

Komiya holds that a genuine analysis of distribution necessitates consideration of life-time income, and that the life-cycle problem should be separated from the distribution problem. Since the Kuznetsian approach is severely constrained by data limitations, Komiya is led to take an alternative path, and argues that the rate of saving of the aged in Japan is high because the Annual Proportional-Wage-Increase System tends to make the slope of the Japanese wage curve steeper than those in other countries. One might as well contend that what to Komiya is a life-cycle problem can still be treated essentially as a distribution problem. As I, for one, contemplate the Japanese distribution, my attention is directed to the wide income disparity among households of the relatively old, depending upon whether one works in a large corporation or in a small business. It is well known that, in addition to their regular income, workers in large corporations are entitled to substantial amounts of other forms of real income, such as fringe benefits, welfare programs, and subsidized housing. Komiya applies the notion of constant consumption needs in explaining the high propensity to save of the aged; we should perhaps add what might be termed the relative-income hypothesis referring to the positive effect upon saving of real, relative income of those who work in large corporations, which continues to rise faster through time than the income of those who work in small businesses.

The Role of the Self-Employed

It was I who once emphasized the share of income of the self-employed as one cause of the high rate of personal saving, and Komiya criticized my view at the Zushi Conference by saying that on the basis of the *Family Savings Survey* my estimate of the rate of saving by the self-employed was grossly exaggerated. I wish to remind him that the above survey was not yet available at the time I wrote the *Consumption Function*, in which I discussed the above view. All I meant to say in that book was that from the *Family Income and Expenditure Survey* and the National Income statistics the rate of saving of the self-employed seemed conspicuously high.

Figure 8-4 gives an international comparison of relationships between the saving of the self-employed and the rate of personal saving, drawn from Komiya's data. The correlation does not appear too significant, and "other" factors have not been removed; but the figure does indicate that the two are related with one another. On this score there is no disagreement between his view and mine.

With respect to his statements in the Appendix, however, I am not certain whether after "complete" adjustments the rate of saving of the self-employed derived from the *Family Savings Survey* will change in an upward or downward direction. In terms of the *National Survey of Family Income and Expenditure,* the rates of saving (out of disposable income) are: 27.2 per cent for merchants and craftsmen; 46.0 per cent for the self-employed; and 29.2 per cent for the weighted average of the two. Komiya holds that the *Family Savings Survey* is more reliable than the *Family Income and Expenditure Survey* because the latter is slanted towards the high-income brackets; e.g., the average household income of the self-employed, according to the latter, is 640,000 yen, whereas in the National Income statistics it is only 371,000 yen. However, the number of the self-employed in commerce far exceeds that in manufacturing; and the "weighted" average income of the merchant-craftsman group and the self-employed turns out to be 368,000 yen, which is little different from the above estimate (371,000 yen) based upon the National Income statistics. Furthermore, the Economic Planning Agency's *Social Accounting Research Committee Report* indicates that the current estimate of the rate of saving by

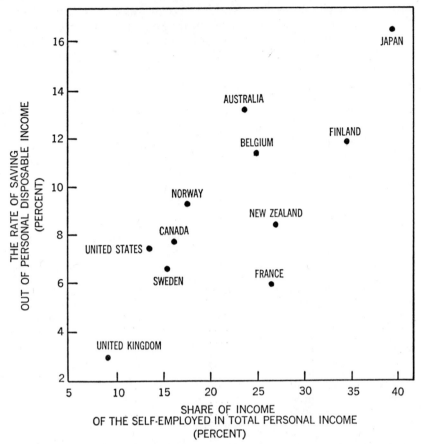

Fig. 8-4. Income and savings of the self-employed: 1950–1960. Sources: Tables 8-4 and 8-8.

the self-employed is somewhat underestimated.[1] For these reasons I cannot totally surrender to Komiya's reasoning.

Komiya focuses his attention on the fact that for the period 1955–1960 the ratio of plant-and-equipment investment by the self-employed to their income was 8.3 per cent, their depreciation-income ratio 7.8 per cent, and the rate of net investment (therefore) 0.5 per cent. However, the self-employed sector, in the computation of the above figures, comprises farm households whose depreciations (taken from the *Farming Household Economy Survey*) are extremely large because of the constant-ratio method used. On the other hand, according to the *Small- and Medium-Size Business Investment Survey Report*, plant-and-equipment investment of the self-employed (exclusive of the agricultural sector) amounted to 29.2 billion yen in fiscal 1959, and the

[1] Keizai Kikaku Chō, *Kokumin Keizai Keisan Chōsa-iinkai Hōkoku*, March 16, 1962, p. 108.

ratio of depreciation to the above investment was 18 per cent. Therefore, due to the inclusion of agriculture and the statistical illusion,
Komiya's excitement about his discovery of the low rate of net investment by the self-employed seems unjustified.

THE ROLE OF THE TRANSIENT INCOME

Both Komiya and I recognize the important role rendered by the
extra income. The extra-income hypothesis may explain why workers'
savings have risen after the war *pari passu* with the bonus-to-income
ratio, but it does not explain why the level of savings by Japanese
workers is high relative to other countries. In order to clarify the

TABLE 8-10

INTERNATIONAL COMPARISON OF THE EMPLOYEE COMPENSATIONS IN MANUFACTURING
(per cent: total cash compensations as 100)

Country	Basic wages	Overtime and other allowances	Bonuses	Nonwork allowances (paid vacation, etc.)
Japan	71.7	11.1	16.4	0.8
U.S.A.	90.5	....	1.4	8.1
U.K.	92.9	....	0.8	6.3
W. Germany	86.6	1.7	3.3	8.4
France	88.1	3.7	1.6	6.6
Italy	80.2	1.4	8.3	10.1
Austria	81.9	2.6	3.9	11.6
Belgium	91.8	....	0.7	7.5
Denmark	90.5	....	...	9.5
Greece	83.5	1.7	7.5	5.3
Turkey	63.0	15.4	7.5	14.0
Yugoslavia	77.7	4.5	8.9	8.8

SOURCE: Ryōhei Magota, "Jisshitsu Chingin no Kokusai Hikaku" in M. Shinohara
and H. Funahashi, eds. *Nihongata Chingin Kōzō no Kenkyū* (1961), p. 377.

latter, an international comparison of bonus ratios is required. As a
supplement to Komiya's analysis, Table 8-10 is presented. The Japanese
bonus ratio is unmistakably high, strongly suggesting the possibility of
further application of the permanent-income hypothesis to international comparative studies.

PART IV

Business Fluctuations and Stabilization Policy

9

Kei Mori:

Simulation Analysis of Fluctuations and Growth of the Japanese Economy: 1955–1960 *

CHARACTERISTICS OF THE SIMULATION ANALYSIS BY THE "MIXED PRIVATE-AND-PUBLIC-SECTOR MODEL"

As a part of the research project, *Econometric Analysis of the Japanese Economy,* at the Tokyo Economic Research Center, the author has constructed a "mixed private-and-public-sector model," and conducted a series of simulation analyses by the model for the period fiscal 1955–1960. In this paper we shall discuss (1) business fluctuations and (2) growth, through five cases of simulation, and comment on the structural characteristics of the Japanese economy in the light of our model analyses.

First a few words about the meaning of simulation analysis and the main characteristics of the five types of simulation discussed in this paper. Simulation refers to an attempt to clarify the mechanism of reality as it has happened or is likely to happen through systematic operations of a model, i.e., a hypothetical mechanism which is assumed to be regulating events in the real world. Simulation becomes meaningful when the following two conditions are met: first, the model sufficiently represents the real world; and, second, the handling of the model is more possible and easier than that of the real world itself.[1]

* This is a revised and expanded version of the first half of my paper read at the Zushi Conference. I have received many valuable comments on my paper from different individuals, but special thanks are due to Professors Miyohei Shinohara and Susumu Koizumi of Hitotsubashi and Osaka universities, respectively. I gratefully acknowledge my indebtedness to Professor Tado Uchida of Tokyo University for his stimulating ideas and instruction which immensely helped my preliminary study. Research for the paper has been supported financially by the Tokyo Economic Research Center.

[1] Application of simulation analysis is a very recent phenomenon. In economics, as well as in other disciplines, it still is in an early stage of development. Atlhough there are special issues of journals and a number of papers on successful cases of simulation analysis, few good, introductory works are available. The special issue of *Operations Research,* Vol. 4, No. 4 (December 1959), translated into Japanese by the Nihon Kagaku Gijutsu Renmei, may be recommended. For simulation analyses of

With respect to the "mixed model," our problem is to see, first, if an effective, econometric model can be built and, second, whether solution of the model is determinate under various circumstances. The five cases of successful simulation to be dealt with in this paper attest to the fulfillment of the second condition; but there is no foolproof method available to test if the first condition is met. We must therefore adopt a tentative, alternative method (called "simulation test") to examine the extent of disparities between the theoretical and real values of major variables in the model. The test has shown that our model performs much better than many other, similar models; hence, we assume that the first condition has also been reasonably and satisfactorily met.

All of the five simulations that follow are of the reduced form derived from the structure.[2] They cover the period from the fourth quarter of 1954 through the second half of 1962. The five types of simulation are distinguished in terms of whether real values or theoretical values calculated from the extrapolation formulas are used for exogenous variables. In all five cases, however, the predetermined, endogenous variables are the theoretical values of endogenous variables obtained through simulations.[3]

Simulation I. Real values are used for exogenous variables. As is seen in Figure 9-1, the relationship between the theoretical and real values is reasonably satisfactory. This testifies to the applicability of our mixed model to other cases.[4]

Simulation II. Of exogenous variables, real values are used for $(O)_{-1}$ (balance of machines ordered in the preceding quarter) and $(i)_{-1}$ (interest on commercial-bank loans in the preceding quarter;[5] and extrapolated values are used for the remaining variables (except for the time variable t and the dummy variable Q for seasonal varia-

---

the Japanese economy by econometric models, see Uchida and Mori, "Nihon Keizai no Simulation Bunseki," in Uchida et al., eds. Atarashii Keizai Bunseki (Sōbun Sha, 1960). For the United States economy, see J. S. Duesenberry, O. Eckstein, and G. Fromm, "A Simulation of the United States Economy in Recession," Econometrica (October 1960); and I. Adelman and F. L. Adelman, "The Dynamic Properties of the Klein-Goldberger Model," Econometrica (October 1959).

[2] The data and other materials used for construction of the model are contained in Technical Report No. 519, TCER Model V-8 no Suitei yō Data to Nidankai Saishō Nijō Suitei no Kōzō Yūdō Gata (mimeographed).

[3] All simulations begin from the fourth quarter of 1954. But the curves in the figures of this chapter begin from the fourth quarter of 1955 since they represent changes in the value, or growth rates, of the variables from the same quarter of the preceding year. Values of some endogenous variables, however, start from the immediately preceding quarter or the fourth quarter back. For the detailed steps of simulation, see Kei Mori, "Minkan-Zaisei Kongō Model ni yoru Nihon Keizai no Kōzō Bunseki: 1953–1964," Riron Keizai Gaku, Vol. 13, No. 3 (May 1963), pp. 47–48.

[4] For details, see ibid., pp. 61–62.

[5] Real values are substituted for the period from the second quarter of 1961 through the first quarter of 1962. For subsequent quarter, the author's own estimates are substituted.

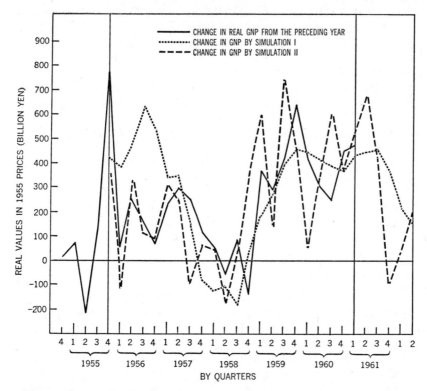

Fig. 9-1. Increase in the value of GNP (from the preceding year): real values and Simulations I and II.

tions).[6] Simulation of this type is ordinarily used for forecasting. The reason why real values are used for $(O)_{-1}$ is that there are only small gaps between real values and extrapolated values, and for the second half of the period the results are better than those from Simulation I. There are two advantages of our approach to forecasting. First, the correlation coefficients for simple extrapolated formulas for the two variables were extremely low compared with those for other formulas; this must be due to the large weight of cyclical variations, relative to trends, in the two variables. By substituting real values in simulation, cyclical variations in the two variables can be retained, which will otherwise be eliminated through simple extrapolations. The second advantage is that the data for these two variables become available about a year sooner than for the other variables; and substitution of real values can considerably increase the accuracy of predictions.

[6] The extrapolation formula is:

$$x = \alpha_0 + \alpha_1 t + \alpha_2 Q_2 + \alpha_3 Q_3 + \alpha_4 Q_4 + U$$

Extrapolated values are theoretical values calculated from the above formula.

Simulation III. Extrapolated values are substituted for all exogenous variables including $(O)_{-1}$ and $(i)_{-1}$ (but exclusive of t and Q). Simulation of this type may provide a solution to the problem of discovering the properties of the dynamic paths, under the assumption that $(O)_{-1}$ and $(i)_{-1}$ are free of cyclical variations and increase by constant amounts per quarter. We may also learn, under the third approach, how the two variables contribute to cyclical fluctuations by changing $(O)_{-1}$ and $(i)_{-1}$ independently of each other.

Simulation IV. Real values are used only for $(O)_{-1}$; extrapolated values are substituted for all other exogenous variables including $(i)_{-1}$.

Simulation V. Real values are used for $(i)_{-1}$; and extrapolated values for all other exogenous variables including $(O)_{-1}$.

Simulations IV and V are designed to estimate separate effects of deviations of $(O)_{-1}$ and $(i)_{-1}$ from extrapolated values upon changes in GNP, and are based upon Simulation III.

Analysis of Fluctuations in the Japanese Economy: Fiscal 1955–1961

There was only one recession between 1955 and 1960. The following analysis lacks generality since it covers merely one recession. But it may nevertheless shed much light on the structure of the Japanese economy and provide useful information in forecasting recessions after the second half of fiscal 1961. The strong upward trend of the Japanese economy makes it difficult to draw a clear picture of business cycles in terms of absolute values of variables. Growth rates are often used as indexes; but in this section we rely upon the value of increase in GNP from the same quarter of the preceding year (referred to below as annual difference) as an index of cyclical fluctuations (see the broad line in Figure 9-2).

Analysis of Cylical Elements by the Reduced Forms Derived from the Structure

We decompose changes in annual differences of GNP into the following four elements by the reduced forms derived from the structure of our model (see Figure 9-2):

(1) The element that depends upon temporal growth in exogenous variables other than time: i.e., $(O)_{-1}$ (balance of machines ordered in the preceding period); $(i)_{-1}$ (average rate of interest on all commercial-bank loans in the preceding period); $(L_H)_{-2}$ (housing funds in the second period back); M_W (volume index of world trade); G_F (govern-investment); T_R (government transfer payment); and S_D (the sum of government enterprise surpluses, government capital depreciations, and statistical discrepancies in the National Income statistics).

(2) The element that depends upon changes in deviations of $(O)_{-1}$ from the extrapolated values.

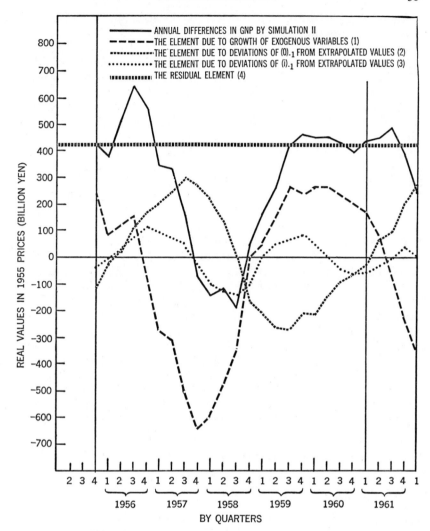

Fig. 9-2. Decomposition of changes in GNP (annual differences).

(3) The element that depends upon changes in deviations of $(i)_{-1}$ from the extrapolated values.

(4) The residual element.

Elements (1), (2), and (3) are additive;[7] and (4) is defined to be the

[7] Let B be the matrix of coefficients of endogenous variables: $B^{(-\tau)}$ matrix of coefficients of predetermined endogenous variables; Γ, matrix of coefficients of exogenous variables, y, simultaneous vector of endogenous variables; $S(y_{-\tau})$, vector of predetermined endogenous variables; x, vector of exogenous variables. Then the structural equation becomes as follows (zero vector is assumed for the error term):

$$By = B^{(-\tau)} \cdot S(y_{-\tau}) + \Gamma x$$

residual after deducting the sum of (1) through (3) from the total changes in Simulation II.

The four elements are described below:

(1) The element due to temporal growth of exogenous variables. The value of this element is fixed at 430 billion yen.[8] In other words, *ceteris paribus*, GNP increases by this amount from the same quarter of the preceding year. Since the annual average of quarterly GNP (in fiscal 1955 prices) for fiscal 1961 is 3.6 trillion yen, this element accounts for about 12 per cent of GNP.

(2) The element due to fluctuations in $(O)_{-1}$. This is the product of the coefficient that corresponds to $(O)_{-1}$ in GNP under the reduced form times the annual difference in deviation of $(O)_{-1}$ from extrapolated values, and it measures the impact effect of changes in $(O)_{-1}$. The maximum amplitude of this element has reached as high as 500 billion yen (see Figure 9-2). Its cyclical pattern does not match that of GNP and seems to lag considerably behind the latter.

(3) The element due to fluctuations in $(i)_{-1}$. The curve of this element in Figure 9-2 assumes approximately the same shape as that of the GNP curve. However, there is little resemblance in the movement of the two curves for the period fiscal 1959–1961. This is presumably due to the disturbing impact of $(O)_{-1}$ on fluctuations in $(i)_{-1}$. It is, nonetheless, too premature to conclude at this stage that the business cycle was generated by monetary policy. The amplitudes of this element were found to be much smaller than initially anticipated. Without first clarifying the mechanism of its oscillations, we cannot expect to explain business cycles in terms of this element.[9]

(4) The residual element. This is the most interesting of all elements. The amplitude of this element is as wide as, or wider than, that of

---

The reduced form derived from the structure is:

$$y = (B^{-1} \cdot B^{(-\tau)}) \cdot S(y_{-\tau}) + (B^{-1}\Gamma)x$$

The GNP formula in the reduced form is:

$$y_{\text{GNP}} = (B^{-1} \cdot B^{(-\tau)})_{\text{GNP}} \cdot S(y_{-\tau}) + (B^{-1}\Gamma)_{\text{GNP}}x = (B^{-1} \cdot B^{(-\tau)})_{\text{GNP}} \cdot S(y_{-\tau})$$
$$+ \{(B^{-1}\Gamma)_1 x_1 + (B^{-1}\Gamma)_2 x_2 + \cdots + (B^{-1}\Gamma)_K x_K\}$$

K is the number of exogenous variables. In obtaining the value of increase in GNP (annual differences), $Y_{\text{GNP}} - (Y_{\text{GNP}})_{-4} = \tilde{Y}_{\text{GNP}}$, by the above formula, the term equivalent to the sum of products of the reduced form coefficients and exogenous variables, provided extrapolated values are substituted for x, can be written as follows ($\tilde{x}$ is the value of change in x):

$$(B^{-1}\Gamma)_1 \tilde{x}_1 + \cdots + (B^{-1}\Gamma)_K \tilde{x}_K = \{(B^{-1}\Gamma)_1 a_1 + (B^{-1}\Gamma)_2 a_2 + \cdots + (B^{-1}\Gamma)_K a_K\} \times 4$$

$a_1, \ldots, a_K$ are coefficients of extrapolated values of the time variable, $x_1, \ldots, x_K$; and the term for reasonal variations disappears. In this sense they are additive.

[8] Of 430 billion yen, the sum of products of coefficients of the time variable in the extrapolated formulas and the reduced-form coefficients, alone, accounts for about 310 billion yen. The difference of 120 billion yen is due to temporal growth of the other five exogenous variables.

[9] We shall discuss this point at length later in the paper.

GNP. Understanding the contents of change in this element seems extremely important for the analysis of fluctuations in the Japanese economy.

We must note that the preceding is merely a description of the performance of the reduced forms derived from the structure, and not an analysis of the solutions of the model.

ANALYSES BY SIMULATION

The residual element (4) may be thought of as consisting of the following two parts: first, that which is due to internal fluctuations as part of a general solution when there are no deviations of $(O)_{-1}$ and $(i)_{-1}$ from their extrapolated, trend values; second, that which is due to the deviations of $(O)_{-1}$ and $(i)_{-1}$ from their extrapolated, trend values affecting changes in GNP.[10] We shall attempt to analyze these two parts through simulation.

First, we consider four "factors" assumed responsible for fluctuations in GNP. The term "factor" ought to be distinguished from "element." In the preceding section we have used the term "element" with reference to the content of direct, additive effects coming from exogenous variables calculable through simple multiplication of extrapolated values or deviations and reduced-form coefficients. "Factor," on the other hand, includes not only direct effects but also nonadditive, indirect effects coming from within the model; it refers to the effect of exogenous variables observed through comparison between the general, standard solution and particular solutions from tests designed to examine separate impacts of individual exogenous variables on the solution of the model, or to study the joint effect when the variables are allowed to operate simultaneously.

(1′) Factor due to endogenous changes observed under the temporal growth of $(O)_{-1}$, $(i)_{-1}$ and all other exogenous variables. This factor can be identified only under Simulation III, and should be of particular importance to a fast-growing economy such as Japan's. Simulation to test this factor should also provide much information on properties of endogenous cycles. Fluctuations of this factor, shown by the broad line in Figure 9-3, are of the gradually converging kind with a maximum amplitude of about 240 billion yen; after the first quarter of 1961 the curve assumes a simple, smooth growth path at the approximate rate of a 10-per-cent annual increase. Given the fact that the fluctuations of GNP around its average are in the neighborhood of 20 per cent, only up to about 6 per cent of the GNP fluctuations is due to this factor. The full cycle of this factor covers a period of three years. Inasmuch as cycles of this factor do not appear destabilizing,

[10] To be exact, the first part refers to the residual after deducting the sum products of reduced forms of trends in $(O)_{-1}$ and $(i)_{-1}$ from internal fluctuations in the residual element (4); and the second part is the residual after deducting the sum of products in reduced forms of deviations of $(O)_{-1}$ and $(i)_{-1}$ from contributions of the residual element (4) to fluctuations in GNP.

we are led to believe that the main causes of business fluctuations should be identified with movements of $(O)_{-1}$ and $(i)_{-1}$.

Factors $(2')$ and $(3')$ refer to separate effects of exogenous variables $(O)_{-1}$ and $(i)_{-1}$, and factor $(4')$ to the joint effect, through mutual interaction, of both exogenous variables. $(2')$ is obtained through comparison of results of Simulation IV with those of Simulation III, whereas $(3')$ is based upon comparison of Simulations V with III.

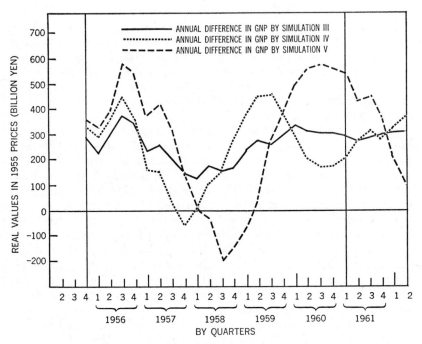

Fig. 9-3. Increase in GNP: Simulations III, IV, and V.

$(2')$ Factor due to changes in deviations of $(O)_{-1}$ from extrapolated values. This factor accounts for as much as 16 per cent of fluctuations in GNP around its average (see A in Figure 9-4). It is interesting to note that the weight of factor $(2')$ is approximately the same as that of element (2) in the preceding section. The two are different in that the latter leads the former by about three quarters, and the full cycle of the latter covers four years in the first half and five years in the second half of the period, whereas the length of the cycle of the former is four years in both halves of the period. Another important observation is that the amplitudes of factor $(2')$ and element (2) are almost identical.

$(3')$ Factor due to changes in deviations of $(i)_{-1}$ from extrapolated values. This factor accounts for 11 per cent of the average deviation of GNP; its cycle covers three years and is shorter than that of $(2')$. In the preceding section we held that business cycles were unlikely to

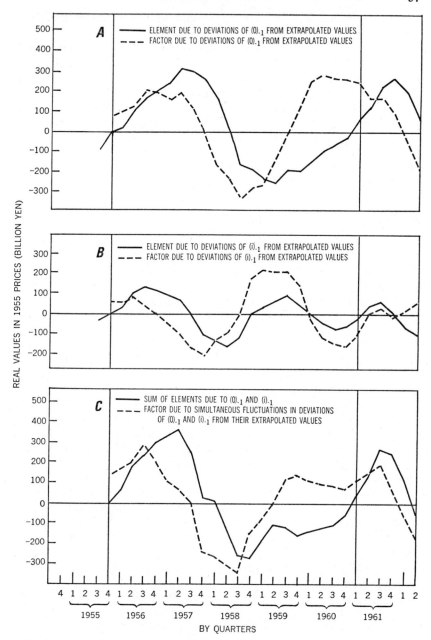

Fig. 9-4. Comparison between "elements" and "factors" by simulation analysis.

be induced by monetary policy because the weight of the element due to $(i)_{-1}$ was found to be very small. We now are led to have a second thought on that inference since the amplitude of the $(i)_{-1}$ factor turned out to be much greater than that for the $(i)_{-1}$ element. In

Figure 9-4(B) we observe that the maximum amplitude of the $(i)_{-1}$ factor reaches 400 billion yen.

(4') Factor due to simultaneous changes in deviations of $(O)_{-1}$ and $(i)_{-1}$ from their extrapolated values. This factor is derived through comparison of the results of Simulation II with those of Simulation III. A conspicuous, behavioral difference is observed in Figure 9-4(C) between this factor and the sum of the elements of $(O)_{-1}$ and $(i)_{-1}$.

Since our model is nonlinear, additivity in general cannot be expected. In the particular example of (4'), however, the simultaneous factors of $(O)_{-1}$ and $(i)_{-1}$ may be regarded as the sum of separate effects of the $(O)_{-1}$ and $(i)_{-1}$ factors. In this sense it is perhaps permissible to view our model as semilinear.

Business Cycles and Monetary Policy—the Possibility of Resonance

One encounters many theses in Japan on the relationship between business cycles and monetary policy. The majority of them focus on the causes of a recession following the imposition of a tight-money policy. Broadly speaking, there are two schools of thought. The first of these two might be termed the endogenous theory of cycles, i.e., a tight-money policy may mark a turning point in the chronology of events, but the recession itself is being induced, not by the policy, but by some internal factors. The other might be called the exogenous theory of cycles which emphasizes the direct effect of the policy itself on recession, implying that the boom may perpetuate itself in the absence of a deflationary policy.

It is the author's view that both arguments lack a sufficient, theoretical foundation. The foregoing simulation analyses seem to suggest an alternative interpretation: that there is a certain "resonance" between the economic system and monetary policy. This interpretation would reconcile (rather than repudiate) the above two schools of thought.

In physics, resonance is known to occur when the period of an oscillation matches that of another, regardless of initial conditions and cyclical patterns;[11] then the oscillation will be amplified innumerably. Provided that the lengths of both cycles are identical and that the oscillations are linear, it has been proven that the amplitude can theoretically be infinite. We may draw a useful analogy between the physics of resonance and the mechanism of business fluctuations. The amplitudes of the element and the factor due to $(Q)_{-1}$ were practically the same, while in the case of $(i)_{-1}$ the amplitude of the factor became much greater than that of the element; this is perhaps due to the "resonance" generated by the matching of the factor cycle (due to endogenous causes) with the element cycle. We are tempted to formu-

[11] For a discussion of the mechanism of resonance as applied to the economic analysis of business cycles, see R. G. D. Allen, *Mathematical Economics* (Macmillan, 1956), pp. 223–227.

late the resonance hypothesis in order to account for the unexpectedly strong impact of the $(i)_{-1}$ element on GNP fluctuations.

What is the economic meaning of resonance hypothesis? Monetary policy in postwar Japan has had pronounced effects on business cycles; in terms of the hypothesis, this was due to the "resonance" generated between the economic system and the policy (aside from whether such policy was deliberate or coincidental), which magnified the ultimate impact of the policy. Had the policy cycles been slightly different than they were, the resonance effect would have been lost with the final results as weak as those indicated in our analysis of cyclical elements.

The possibility of resonance in the course of business cycles has been suggested by J. R. Hicks and R. G. D. Allen.[12] To my knowledge, however, no one has thus far pointed out the occurrence of resonance in explaining cycles in the real world. It must be noted that the resonance could be detected only through simulation analysis, and that the more conventional analysis of the relationship between monetary policy and business cycles is apt to produce merely indeterminate results.

Digression

We now digress on two points which have so far been left unexplained.

(1) *Monetary Policy and the* $(i)_{-1}$ *Element.* In the preceding section the effect of monetary policy is identified with changes in the $(i)_{-1}$ element. This calls for an explanation. We are considering the relationship between changes in the $(i)_{-1}$ element and monetary policy centering around the discount-rate policy. Changes in the $(i)_{-1}$ element occur parallel with annual differences in the deviations of $(i)_{-1}$ from its extrapolated values. In order to facilitate our comparison of the discount rates with the $(i)_{-1}$ element, changes in the discount rate from the same quarter of the preceding year and similar changes in the deviation of $(i)_{-1}$ from the extrapolated values are plotted in Figure 9-5. Although the amplitudes of the two are different, the lengths and patterns of the cycles are strikingly similar.

The official discount rate is, of course, not the only directional indicator of monetary policy. It may still be treated as such, however, inasmuch as the loan rates do respond sensitively to the official rates.

(2) $(i)_{-1}$ *and Other Exogenous Variables.* Excluding the variables for time and seasonal variations, our model contains seven economically meaningful, exogenous variables: i.e., $(i)_{-1}$, $(O)_{-1}$, $(L_H)_{-2}$, M_W, G_F, T_R, and S_D $(= T_G + D_G + e)$. The last variable is assumed to be independent of other exogenous variables. With respect to the remaining six variables, simple correlation coefficients have been calculated

[12] J. R. Hicks, *A Contribution to the Theory of the Trade Cycle* (1950), Mathematical Appendix; and R. G. D. Allen, *op. cit.*, pp. 291–296.

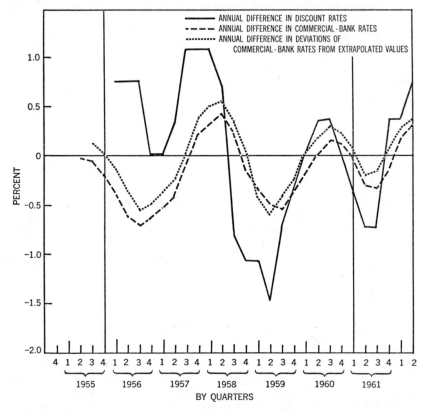

Fig. 9-5. Official discount rates and commercial-bank rates.

for the period from the fourth quarter of 1953 through the first quarter of 1960, the results of which are summarized in Table 9-1.[13] The table shows that $(L_H)_{-2}$, G_F, and T_R change independently of each other, and there seems little evidence of direct, mutual influence among these three variables. In contrast, it is difficult to isolate effects among $(i)_{-1}$, $(O)_{-1}$, and M_W since these three are mutually interdependent. It may be appropriate to assume the direction of causation among these three variables to be: $M_W \rightarrow (i)_{-1} \rightarrow (O)_{-1}$.

Since exogenous variables, by definition, are those which cannot be affected by any other economic variables, the exploration of causative relationships among them, as is done above, may be taken as contradicting the very assumptions of our model. This (legitimate) critique

[13] Our simulation model covers the period from the fourth quarter of 1953 through the first quarter of 1961, whereas simple correlation coefficients in Table 9-1 are based upon the data for the period through the first quarter of 1960. As I later recalculated the coefficients for the same period as covered by the model, the values of some coefficients became significantly different. Therefore, the following discussions should be regarded as tentative. Time limitations have compelled me to leave the table and this section as they are.

TABLE 9-1

SIMPLE CORRELATION COEFFICIENTS[a] AMONG EXOGENOUS VARIABLES

	$(i)_{-1}$	$(O)_{-1}$	$(L_H)_{-2}$	M_W	G_F	T_R
$(O)_{-1}$	-0.76[b]					
$(L_H)_{-2}$	-0.07	0.14				
M_W	-0.84[b]	0.72[b]	0.07			
G_F	-0.38	0.39	0.10	0.41		
T_R	-0.46	0.47	0.05	0.65	0.53	

[a] Based upon data for the period from the fourth quarter of 1953 through the first quarter of 1960.

[b] Significant correlations.

does not apply, however, to the relationship between M_W and $(i)_{-1}$, because in the postwar period fluctuations in M_W have typically affected the Japanese balance of payments first, and then the monetary authorities made a policy response by manipulating the official discount rates, that is, the relationship between M_W and $(i)_{-1}$ has, by and large, been determined by the government's policy decisions, rather than by endogenous economic factors. On the other hand, the relationship between $(i)_{-1}$ and $(O)_{-1}$ is problematical. $(O)_{-1}$ is ordinarily treated as endogenous, and it is strictly for the convenience of forecasting with our model that it is classified as an exogenous variable. For our purpose, the causal relationship between the two may be interpreted in the following way: monetary-policy effects are to spread from the $(i)_{-1}$ element to the $(O)_{-1}$ element, and then to the $(O)_{-1}$ factor. To the extent that this occurs in the real world, our assumption of independence between the $(O)_{-1}$ and $(i)_{-1}$ elements for forecasting is unjustified. Finally, in order to forecast while taking changes in M_W into consideration, it seems proper to proceed from the estimation of the M_W element, to that of the $(i)_{-1}$ element, based upon the anticipated government response, and to that of the $(O)_{-1}$ element.[14]

ANALYSIS OF GROWTH

The Rates of Growth in GNP

The broad line in Figure 9-6 shows the rates of change in real, quarterly GNP from the same quarter of the preceding year. Theoretical values by Simulations I, II, and III are also given in the same figure. The rates of growth display a considerable degree of fluctuation which approximately corresponds to those in the value of GNP. Except for the periods from the second half of 1957 through 1958, and from

[14] The M_W element was not estimated because of the unavailability of the data for the latter part of the period as well as the technical difficulties involved in estimation.

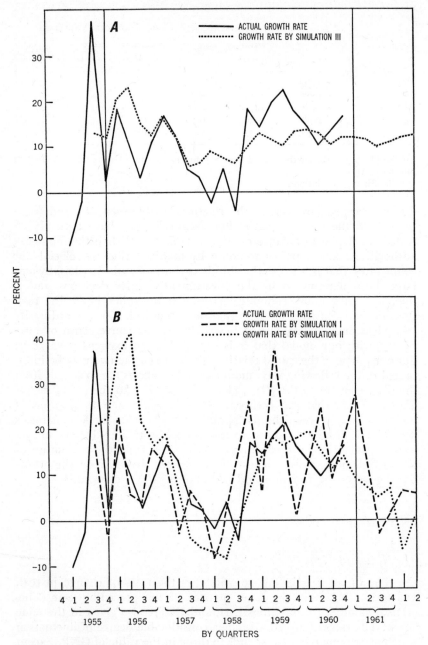

Fig. 9-6. GNP growth rates (annual differences).

the second half of 1961 through 1962, the average growth rate of 10 per cent (or higher) has been achieved. The growth rate for the endogenous factor (Simulation III) reproduces that of real GNP in a smoothened form, particularly during the second half of the period (see Figure 9-6[A]). On the other hand, in Figure 9-6(B) we notice that the theoretical values derived from Simulation I and II with respect to $(i)_{-1}$ and $(O)_{-1}$ more closely follow the growth path of real GNP, especially in the second half. These observations imply that as long as trends in the exogenous variables remain unaltered, a growth rate of about 10 per cent is assured. As we have seen earlier, however, slight changes in $(O)_{-1}$ and $(i)_{-1}$ can significantly affect the growth rate.

The Forecasting Ability of the Model

The National Income statistics for fiscal 1961[15] have not been used for the construction of our model. They are compared with the values projected by the model in order to test its forecasting ability. The predicted values in Table 9-2 are obtained through Simulation II.

TABLE 9-2

GROWTH RATES IN FISCAL 1961: REAL AND PREDICTED
(billions of yen)

	Real		Predicted	
GNP	15,214.0	(14.6%)	14,629.6	(11.3%)[a]
C	7,763.4	(8.7%)	7,696.6	(8.8%)
L_F	3,685.5	(26.9%)	3,618.1	(27.9%)
J	1,158.4	(44.9%)	1,235.5	(45.6%)
E	1,821.5	(7.3%)	1,815.0	(9.2%)
M	2,590.8	(23.5%)	2,406.2	(18.7%)
G	2,967.0	(18.3%)	2,668.9	(9.1%)

[a] The predicted value of GNP, when the real value of G_F (government investment) is substituted into the definitional formula for GNP, is 15,277.8 (16.3%), which is closer to the actual value than the one in the table.

Both growth rates and absolute values of various expenditure items are very accurately predicted. Particularly notable is the accuracy in forecasting inventory and plant-and-equipment investments, both of which could only poorly be forecasted by past econometric models.[16]

[15] Keizai Kikaku Chō, *Kokumin Shotoku Hakusho, Fiscal 1961,* released in February 1963.

[16] Few multiple-correlation coefficients of inventory-investment functions exceeded 0.6. Even when the special variables were incorporated, they failed to become higher than 0.8. The implication of these rather low coefficients for simulation tests is yet to be studied. Model III at the Tokyo Economic Research Center was nearly paralyzed when inventory-investment functions were treated as endogenous. See Kei Mori, "Nihon Keizai no Simulation Bunseki (I)," *Keizai Bunseki* (June 1960), pp. 2–17.

Forecasting errors for the two variables are less than 1 per cent. Prediction of consumption expenditures overestimates the real rate by only 0.1 per cent. Forecasting of exports is also very accurate, but the model fails to predict the extent of import expansion in fiscal 1961. The GNP as an aggregate index is underestimated by about 3 per cent; this is presumably due to a 9-per-cent underestimation of government purchase of goods and services (G). The extrapolated value was used for government investment which has a large weight in G; hence, the recent, rapid increase in government investment was only insufficiently accounted for in the model with the resultant underestimation of both G and GNP.

CHARACTERISTICS OF THE JAPANESE ECONOMIC STRUCTURE

On the basis of the foregoing analyses by our model, let us identify some characteristics of the Japanese economy with special reference to private investments.

(1) Fluctuations of GNP depend heavily upon changes in inventory investment. As against the average fluctuation in GNP of 3.6 million yen, private inventory changes, on the average, from 200 to 550 billion yen. The latter's amplitude of 750 billion yen is approximately 20 per cent of GNP; in this sense the impact of inventory investment on GNP is greater than that of plant-and-equipment investment, whose amplitude is about 500 billion yen.

(2) Inventory investment is the first difference of the inventory-stock function, whereas the independent variables in the inventory-stock function are the annual moving average of GNP_t (predetermined and endogenous) and two exogenous variables, $(O)_{-1}$ and $(i)_{-1}$. Therefore, fluctuations of inventory investment depend upon endogenously predetermined $\{(GNP^*)_{-1} - (GNP^*)_{-5}\}$ and exogenously determined $(\Delta O)_{-1}$ and $(\Delta i)_{-1}$. Consequently, for an effective explanation of fluctuations in GNP it is necessary for the movement of $\{(GNP^*)_{-1} - (GNP^*)_{-5}\}$ to closely approximate that of the real values. Since the value of GNP* extends five quarters back, the effect of events occurring near the beginning point of the period must be felt not only throughout the first half but also during the remainder of the period. Depending upon the pattern of time series of $(GNP^*)_{-4}$, $(GNP^*)_{-3}$ $(GNP^*)_{-2}$, and $(GNP^*)_{-1}$, it is conceivable that the time shape of initial values affects the entire period under projection.

(3) With regard to the plant-and-equipment investment function in our model, the coefficient of $(K_F)_{-1}$ (capital stock in the preceding quarter) deserves special attention. This coefficient as it appears in the structural equation of the model is significant and bears a plus sign. If the sign were minus, fluctuations in the endogenous sectors would most likely be radically different. In such a case $(K_F)_{-1}$ would tend to reduce the rate of economic growth and to impose a constant, downward pressure on the economy; therefore, rapid recoveries of investment booms, observed since 1959, as well as accelerated growth, would

have been impossible. There exist conflicting views about the sign of this variable;[17] but from our analyses it seems reasonably safe to assume the sign to be plus at least up to fiscal 1961. The rate of increase in P (private income other than incomes of workers and the self-employed, i.e., the sum of corporate profits, interest, and rental income) increases rapidly in the early phase of a boom, but tends to fall in the later phase, preceding other endogenous variables. P can suppress the rate of expansion in I_F (plant-and-equipment investment) to the extent that the impact of decline in P reaches I_F via P_C (corporate income). Similarly, in reduced form, the expansion of $(K_F)_{-1}$ is bound to suppress P.

(4) The reduced-form coefficients of $(K_J)_{-1}$ (the stock of inventory in the preceding quarter) and $(P_C)_{-1}$ are minus relative to GNP as well as to its various distributive and expenditure components. This illustrates the auto-contracting tendency in GNP and its components when a boom induces an expansion of these variables. Any reduction in the rates of growth of GNP or its components tends to accelerate their contractions; and conversely with respect to the downward swing of a cycle. A comparison of these results with the aforementioned explanation of inventory investment and plant-and-equipment investment reveals much of interest about the manner in which (partial) quantitative as well as qualitative relationships within the structure reappear as quantitative relationships in the reduced form.

Comment I *by Susumu Koizumi*

The most interesting part of Mori's paper is that in which he draws some inferences about the characteristics of business fluctuations in Japan through comparison of various simulation results. I shall focus my attention on that part.

Simulations that concern us are:

Simulation II. Actual values are used for the rate of interest (i) and balance of machines ordered, and extrapolated values for all other exogenous variables.

---

[17] The coefficient of the capital stock as it appears in the investment function in the theory of trade cycles is usually assumed to be minus. E.g., see M. Kalecki, "A Macrodynamic Theory of Business Cycles," *Econometrica*, Vol. 3 (1935), pp. 327–347; and N. Kaldor, "A Model of the Trade Cycle," *Economic Journal* (March 1940). Areas of controversy may be summarized as follows: first, controversy as to the validity of the theoretical assumptions involved; second, critique of the failure of excess supply to reverse the investment trend; third, disagreement as to whether the plus sign of a coefficient can imply an auto-expanding tendency of capital stock; fourth, controversy surrounding the view according to which the plus coefficient implies that increase in yearly depreciation is explained by capital stock, since plant-and-equipment investment is expressed as gross investment inclusive of depreciation. The author accepts the last view.

Simulation III. Extrapolated values are used for all exogenous variables.

Simulation IV. Actual values are used for O, and extrapolated values for all other exogenous variables.

Simulation V. Actual values are used for i, and extrapolated values for all other exogenous variables.

The main conclusions drawn from the above four simulations are:

(1) GNP fluctuations generated by Simulation III show a converging tendency toward eventual monotonic growth. The length and pattern of the cycle approximately match those of $-(i)_{-1}$.

(2) GNP fluctuations generated by Simulation II closely approximate those in the real world in terms of amplitude, position, and pattern. As the separate effects on cyclical fluctuations of O and i are tested in Simulations IV and V, the amplitudes of GNP generated in both cases are greater than that generated in Simulation I.

From these observations Mori hypothesizes that cyclical fluctuations in Japan have been induced by the resonance of fluctuations in $-(i)_{-1}$ and in the endogenous sectors of the economy. The results of Mori's simulation analyses are all interesting, but we are troubled by his manner of interpreting those results. First, we are skeptical about the nature of i and O. In general, the matrix equation of the system in reduced form is written as:

$$y_t + A_1 y_{t-1} + \cdots + A_n y_{t-n} = B z_t \qquad (1)$$

(A_1 and B are coefficient matrices; y_τ vectors of endogenous variables; and z, vectors of exogenous variables.) If the variables in the z-vector are truly exogenous, Mori's interpretations are justified. We shall drop $(O)_{-1}$ from our discussion because Mori himself maintains that this variable should be treated as endogenous; however, this leaves unsolved the problem of how A_1 and B will change if we endogenize $(O)_{-1}$.

$(i)_{-1}$ presents a difficulty. Mori also points out the possibility of this variable being affected by M_W. There is no problem if we can assume that $(i)_{-1}$ can be influenced only by M_W and not by domestic economic conditions. Mori's line of reasoning, that M_W first affects the balance of payments, which in turn, influences i, implies that the balance of payments depends only upon changes in M_W. The reality of this implication is highly questionable, since in the relatively short run fluctuations in Japanese imports induced by domestic economic conditions tend to affect the balance of payments far more than fluctuations in Japanese exports, which largely depend upon M_W. Mori's resonance hypothesis cannot be accepted so long as the independence of i from domestic economic changes remains unproven.

For the purpose of short-term forecasting it may be permissible to treat as exogenous some variables which are inherently endogenous. The distinction must be strict, however, if one is attempting to judge the characteristics of business fluctuations through simulation analysis.

Even if we suppose for the moment that i is an exogenous variable, the problem still remains. With respect to GNP fluctuations generated by Simulation III, we notice that the monotonic growth of GNP is of the kind that continues to increase by increasing amounts through time (see Figure 9-3 in Mori's paper). Trend equations for exogenous variables used in Simulation III are the first-order equations with respect to t. Therefore, if the system is stabilizing, GNP fluctuations should continue to diminish and approach a pattern of monotonic growth by a constant amount. But the results obtained by Simulation III seem to indicate that the system of difference equations is actually destabilizing, its real root being larger than 1. If this is true, the resonance hypothesis may apply to the period 1956–1961, but it is hardly applicable to Japanese business cycles in general. For example, if the initial condition is such that the influence of the real root which is larger than 1 is predominant, Mori's attempt to grasp the phenomenon of cycles in terms of the resonance effect of oscillation of the system becomes rather meaningless.

How should the simulation results be interpreted, then, if not by way of Mori's resonance hypothesis? The answer to this question requires not only sufficient knowledge of the nature of the model and the detailed steps of simulation, but also, perhaps, additional simulations. Whatever I have to say below is merely guesswork.

One popular hypothesis on business cycles in Japan holds that the system itself is destabilizing. According to this hypothesis, any upturn of economic events in Japan is prone to gather a cumulative momentum up to the point of causing a serious balance-of-payments crisis; then the upper turning point is marked by the imposition of a tight-money policy. If this hypothesis were true, Mori's Simulation III should have generated the GNP values that are over and above the upper turning points in real world; but we note in Figure 9-3 that the peaks of the cycles generated by Simulation III are lower than they are in reality. This observation at first seems to contradict the hypothesis, but we must call attention to the fact that Figure 9-3 gives fluctuations in the value of change (annual difference) in GNP. This means that even if the time series is falling (unless it approaches zero), the value of GNP can still continue to rise. Consequently, the results of Simulation III all tend to point to a positive increase in GNP. Furthermore, the difference between the peaks, noted above, can easily result from some minute disparities between real and extrapolated values of exogenous variables for the early phase of the period and does not necessarily imply the destabilizing nature of the system. In these terms, the reconciliation of the inherent-instability hypothesis with the simulation results do not seem impossible. The 10 per cent growth rate and other similarities in GNP fluctuations, produced by Simulation III, to the movement of GNP in the real world suggest some interesting problems concerning the necessity and effectiveness of monetary policy. However, we first need to examine whether the impressive similarities were, in truth, purely accidental.

Comment II *by Miyohei Shinohara*

Given my well-publicized "distaste" for econometrics, it is ironic that I have been asked to comment on this paper. If my memory is correct, I believe I made the following points at the Zushi Conference:

(1) In Mori's simulation analysis of business fluctuations $(i)_{-1}$ and $(O)_{-1}$ are given strategic roles, and the results of the analysis depend heavily upon the particular behavior of these variables. This is clear from the fact that in Simulation II real values are used for $(O)_{-1}$ and $(i)_{-1}$, whereas all other predetermined exogenous variables are assumed to increase by constant amounts per quarter. The results of this kind of analysis, I fear, may easily be biased toward the fortuitously given, but particular, roles assigned to $(O)_{-1}$ and $(i)_{-1}$.

(2) In his report at the conference Mori emphasized the importance of monetary policy as an initiator of business cycles. But it takes a certain naivety to swallow this inference of the model on monetary policy when one knows that the model contains only two monetary indices, $(i)_{-1}$ and $(L_H)_{-2}$. This difficulty presented by the model is reinforced by its failure to incorporate the mechanism of the positive balance of payments, which initiates a boom in the domestic economy through relaxation of monetary controls.

(3) At the conference, Mori's policy discussions were heavily geared toward business-cycle problems, presumably because the residual change in the value of GNP, after removing the effects of $(i)_{-1}$ and $(O)_{-1}$, closely resembles and precedes ΔGNP. We must note, however, that this observation is not perhaps unrelated to the strategic choice of, and particular assumptions about, $(i)_{-1}$ and $(O)_{-1}$. This is but another illustration of the inconclusiveness of Mori's study.

(4) His model is basically a "demand model." Factors that alter plant-and-equpiment investment demand appear only as the investment (demand) function. Business fluctuations are not understood as phenomena attributable to the interaction of changes in supply capacities resulting from plant investments and changes in effective demand. My feeling is that a model of this sort, no matter how well it may explain the past, will most likely fail in accounting for future changes, say, in aggregate supply relative to demand. There is a need for another supplementary, more broadly-framed model capable of explaining even the changes in the stages of economic growth.

The above four points, I believe, are the highlights of my remarks at the conference. In the revised version of Mori's paper, however, I notice that his monetary-policy-inducement hypothesis of recessions has been largely withdrawn and replaced by the resonance hypothesis. I am not really prepared to make additional comments on the revised paper, save the following, cursory notes.

The aforementioned fact that the residual changes precede ΔGNP may well be a reflection of lags in the movement of $(O)_{-1}$ and $(i)_{-1}$. In view of the fact that the official discount rate follows the business trend and so does the "balance" of machines ordered, it is not overly surprising to discover a lead of the residual change relative to ΔGNP in Figure 9-2. Mori is perhaps implying paradoxically that for forecasting one should pay attention not to the leading indexes but to the lagging series. I once pointed out that the inventory cycles in small- and medium-size businesses in Japan lead those in large corporations, chiefly because of the residual nature of small- and medium-size finance which functions as a cushion during recessive periods. Essentially the same may be said about the lead of the "residual change" in Figure 9-2—that is, if $(O)_{-1}$ and $(i)_{-1}$ lag, the residual change necessarily leads, and conversely when the $(O)_{-1}$ and $(i)_{-1}$ lead.

In all candor I have little to say on the resonance hypothesis. I wish merely to add a note that even if the hypothesis is theoretically sound, a realist like myself finds it hard to accept—unless the hypothesis incorporates more monetary variables and reflects more of the actual monetary mechanism in Japan than it does.

Finally, I must emphasize that I am not necessarily denying the value of "economic-engineering" models such as Mori's. The only thing I object to is the usual touch of unreality and the rather hopelessly mechanistic view of the economy, frequently associated with such models. Still I have no hesitation in commending his paper as an example of pioneering econometric research in postwar Japan.

10

Keimei Kaizuka:
The Stabilization Effect of Fiscal Policy*

INTRODUCTION

This paper attempts to appraise the stabilization effect of Japan's postwar fiscal policy within a simple framework of National Income analysis. The term "stabilization" refers to the anti-cyclical policy which purports to achieve a domestic condition conducive to the optimal economic activity of the nation. If we take GNP as an index of aggregate economic activity, the stabilization policy signifies an effort to stabilize GNP at a certain desired level or in terms of its optimum growth rate. In advanced countries such as the United States and Great Britain, the optimum rate is usually defined as a full-employment rate of growth of GNP without inflation.[1]

In the case of the Japanese economy the particular employment structure creates many difficulties in interpreting the concept of "full employment." In this paper, therefore, we shall examine how and to what extent the fiscal-policy sector has neutralized and counteracted GNP-fluctuations, i.e., we shall assume the stabilization of GNP itself to be the criterion for judging the effectiveness of fiscal policy. In reality, however, because the achievement of a balance-of-payments equilibrium, rather than stabilization of GNP, has been the most significant policy objective of the government, we must also include in our discussion an examination of the effectiveness of fiscal policy with respect to the balance of payments. The first half of this paper appraises the overall stabilization effect of fiscal policy, centering

* The author is grateful to Professors Sei Fujita, Kenjiro Ara, Susumu Koizumi, Ryūtaro Komiya, and Tsunehiko Watanabe for their useful comments and suggestions on this paper. Research for this paper has been financially supported by grants from the Tokyo Economic Research Center, the University of Tokyo Economic Research Fund, and the Central Committee for Savings Promotion.

[1] E. C. Brown has analyzed the fiscal policy of the 1930's in terms of the full-employment criterion. (E. C. Brown, "Fiscal Policy in the Thirties: a Reappraisal," *American Economic Review* [December 1956]). Works in the United States and Great Britain have not necessarily been explicit in their treatment of policy objectives. The usual procedure is to presuppose the desirability of stabilization in general, and then to analyze the built-in stabilizing factors.

around the discretionary fiscal policy; the second half deals with built-in, automatic stabilizing factors.

FISCAL POLICY AS A STABILIZER

The impact of the entire fiscal-policy sector on fluctuations in the level of GNP might be grasped in the following *ex post* form. Let Y be GNP, C consumption, I investment, G government spending, X exports, and M imports. Then,

$$Y = C + I + G + X - M \tag{1}$$

Assuming the linear consumption and import functions,

$$C = a + c(Y - R + T - V) \tag{2}$$

$$M = b + mY \tag{3}$$

provided R is government revenue, T transfer payment, and V business saving. By substituting (2) and (3) into (1), and rewriting,

$$Y = \frac{a - b - c(R - T + V) + I + G + X}{1 - c + m} \tag{4}$$

In (4), in addition to the usually exogenous I, G, and X, we treat R, T, and V as exogenous as well. In the numerator of (4), $G - c(R - T)$ represents the government sector, and $I + X - cV$ the private sector. Thus, the extent to which the government sector stabilizes GNP fluctuations can be seen by measuring how much change in $I + X - cV$ is offset by the change in $G - c(R - T)$; i.e., if $(\Delta I + \Delta X - c\Delta V)$ and $[\Delta G - c(\Delta R - \Delta T)]$ move in the opposite (same) direction, we consider fiscal policy to be stabilizing (destabilizing). Table 10-1 summarizes the data required for the above purpose. The period covered is from fiscal 1952 through fiscal 1960. The net contribution of the government sector to final demand, $G - c(R - T)$, has always borne a plus sign, indicating the positive role played by fiscal policy. The offsetting influence of fiscal policy upon fluctuations in the private sector is shown not so much by its absolute level, $xG - c(R - T)$, as by the value of its change, $\Delta G - c(\Delta R - \Delta T)$. The impact of national tax reductions is shown in columns 9 and 10 of Table 10-1.[2]

Next we follow in chronological order the shifts in the central government's discretionary policy and appraise the role played by such policy. Discretionary policy may be understood as general budgetary policy, often loosely described as "sound" or "neutral" fiscal policy, as well as concrete policy measures designed for specific objectives. In this paper we are mainly concerned with discretionary policy in the general and broad sense of the term.

[2] "Tax reduction" refers to the difference between tax revenue in a given year and the estimated tax revenue in that year, had the previous year's tax rates remained unaltered.

TABLE 10-1

THE STABILIZATION EFFECT OF FISCAL POLICY
(billions of yen)

	(1) Gross private domestic capital formation (I)	(2) Exports (X)	(3) Business saving (V)	(4) Government purchase of goods and services (G)	(5) Government revenue minus government-enterprise surpluses (R)	(6) Transfer payment (T)	(7) $\Delta I + \Delta X - c\Delta V$ (change from the previous year)	(8) $\Delta G - c(\Delta R - \Delta T)$ (change from the previous year)	(9) National tax reduction value (change from the previous year)	(10) $0.7 \times$ (9)
Fiscal year										
1952	1,204.0	830.1	591.7	1,155.5	1,300.8	179.6				
1953	1,335.2	916.4	832.9	1,410.6	1,450.4	212.8	48.8	194.6	105.1	73.5
1954	1,156.9	960.8	853.2	1,483.4	1,518.9	330.8	−148.3	63.5	4.5	3.1
1955	1,371.6	1,092.5	985.8	1,604.1	1,557.5	343.8	253.6	147.8	39.4	27.5
1956	2,263.5	1,272.3	1,390.0	1,628.2	1,794.9	350.6	788.7	−137.4	0	0
1957	2,401.6	1,385.5	1,500.5	1,822.2	2,040.2	379.2	174.0	32.4	72.0	50.4
1958	1,903.7	1,354.5	1,521.4	2,002.3	2,080.6	425.1	−543.5	185.9	26.0	18.2
1959	3,289.4	1,614.8	2,160.2	2,292.4	2,401.6	486.5	1,198.8	108.5	41.3	28.9
1960	4,267.1	1,882.0	2,760.8	2,683.0	3,039.2	562.7	824.5	−47.4	−5.0	−3.5

SOURCES: Keizai Kikaku Chō, *Kokumin Shotoku Hakusho*.

ᵃ For columns (7) and (8) the value of marginal propensity to consume (with respect to disposable income), $c = 0.7$, is used. The regression derived from the National Income statistics is: $C = 0.708 Y_d + 944.51$.

(1) Fiscal 1953. The budget for fiscal 1953 reflected the government's contention that it was not necessary to adhere strictly to the principle of a comprehensively balanced budget; special, tax-exempt national bonds for 20 billion yen and government-enterprise bonds for 16 billion yen were issued to finance public loans and investments, while a sizable tax reduction was initiated. There came a reversal of budgetary policy as excessive demand in the domestic economy led to the imposition of a tight-money policy in October. In order to prevent a further increase in government expenditures, the revised budget for the General Account cut 9.5 billion yen from public works expenses. This reduction, however, was small relative to the net increase in expenditures from the General Account of 52.2 billion yen under the revised budget. From columns 7 and 8 of Table 10-1, it is clear that the sizable national-tax reduction, together with a rise in government spending, had a considerable, destabilizing effect upon the private sector.

(2) Fiscal 1954. A "tight budget" was formulated in view of persisting balance-of-payments difficulties. The orientation of the initial budget was carried forward into the revised budget; there was little net increase in expenditures within the General Account under the revised budget because the entire 30.8 billion yen increase in expenditures was financed by savings and reductions in "other" expenditure items in the same account. The tight budget reduced the rate of increase in government purchase of goods and services; but the slackening of private economic activity under deflationary policy lowered the rate of personal (and other) tax revenue (personal tax revenue increased by merely 0.5 billion yen from the preceding year), while government transfer payments increased by 18 billion yen. Fiscal policy, by and large, was stabilizing, offsetting to some extent the decline in the private sector.

(3) Fiscal 1955. The budget was drawn within the limits of 1 trillion yen. The revised budget was based upon the need to aid local finances and to offset the deficit in the Foods Administration Account. Contrary to its professed characteristics, however, the budget *ex post* was destabilizing, because private economic activity was accelerated by the increase in government purchase of goods and services as well as by the decrease in the rate of tax revenue that resulted primarily from the corporation-tax reduction.

(4) Fiscal 1956. Unlike the previous year, no arbitrary limits were considered in determining the size of the budget. Towards the end of fiscal 1956 there was an unanticipated increase in tax revenue (mainly, an increase in the corporation-tax revenue), providing an enormous tax surplus for fiscal 1958. Increase in the government purchase of goods and services was moderate, and fiscal policy on the whole had a stabilizing influence.

(5) Fiscal 1957. In view of the growing public discontent with "sound" public finance, the government adopted a "positive-expenditure" policy combined with major tax reductions. Some members of

financial circles, however, voiced the opinion that sound fiscal policy should be continued in order to avoid "overheating" of the boom. Prices began to rise, and the budget was criticized by many observers as inflationary; but the Ministry of Finance held the view that there was no sign of major inflation in the country. The deficit in the balance of payments was regarded as a temporary phenomenon. In the initial budget the tax revenue was reduced by 72 billion yen, and expenditures within the General Account were raised by 47.8 billion yen. Appropriations for various government enterprises were also increased (e.g., a 48.5 billion yen increase for the National Railway System). Immediately following the introduction of the budget, however, a critical aggravation of the balance of payments occurred, and the government was forced to adopt a stringent monetary policy. The Ministry of Finance continued to hold that there was no urgent need for a tightening of fiscal policy but, in response to a strong recommendation from financial circles, decided to take a series of emergency measures. For example, 15 per cent of public loans and investments were suspended, and a total of 16.5 billion yen worth of public works projects initially budgeted for the General and Special Accounts and for government enterprises were also suspended. In the revised budget, however, salary improvements and the like caused a net increase of 47.1 billion yen in the General Account. Throughout fiscal 1957 the purchase of goods and services by the Central Government alone increased by 160 billion yen, and the increase in total government purchase (inclusive of local governments) reached the neighborhood of 200 billion yen. Since the tax-revenue increase (largely from corporation and indirect taxes) was voluminous, however, fiscal policy as a whole remained neutral or only moderately destabilizing.

(6) Fiscal 1958. The balance-of-payments difficulties were reflected in the budget for fiscal 1958. Fearful that the spending of the 100 billion yen surplus in the General Account carried over from fiscal 1956 would be inflationary, the government deposited 54.5 billion yen of the surplus in the Revolving Fund to be transferred back to the General Account for use only after an amelioration of the domestic economic conditions. In September, in the face of a slackening trend in the economy, the government raised public works expenditures by 5.6 billion yen and actively engaged in the purchase of surplus dairy products and textile machinery. Fiscal policy counterbalanced to a significant degree the decline in the private sector through an increase in the government purchase of goods and services (by 100 billion and 80 billion yen at the central and local levels, respectively) and a decrease in corporation-tax revenue (by 60 billion yen).

(7) Fiscal 1959. After a series of debates and discussions within the government, the principle of "sound" public finance was upheld in formulating the budget for fiscal 1959. The deposit from the previous year was withdrawn for active use as a part of the 1959 budget. Although an initial emphasis was placed upon the objective of a balanced budget, an unexpectedly large increase in the government pur-

chase of goods and services made the fiscal policy of 1959 somewhat destabilizing.

(8) Fiscal 1960. There was a split of opinion within the government as to the choice between a policy of restraints and an optimistic, positive approach to public finance. The budget, finally drawn, was designed to be neutral in its effect upon the private sector. The relative absence of tax surplus from fiscal 1958 necessitated the postponement of scheduled tax reductions. A large increase in corporation (and other) tax revenues made the fiscal policy of 1960 approximately as neutral as it was intended to be at the beginning of the year.[3]

To sum up, fiscal policy played a neutral or stabilizing role during the periods 1953–1954 and 1957–1958 when the private sector was at turning points (see Table 10-1), but with respect to other periods the precise influence of fiscal policy is rather uncertain. The foregoing survey examined to what extent the fiscal policy has had a stabilizing (or destabilizing) effect on the private sector. As we have mentioned earlier, however, such stabilization has not been the consciously considered objective of government policy. Instead, the balance-of-payments equilibrium has been the most frequently discussed goal of economic policy. We naturally require a different criterion for examining the stabilization effect with respect to the external-equilibrium objective. There exists no foolproof criterion, of course, but we shall adopt the following tentative approach: the government sector should stimulate (suppress) private economic activity when there is a surplus (a deficit) in the balance of payments.[4]

There was a surplus in the balance of payments during the following periods: the third quarter, 1952 through the second quarter, 1953; the third quarter, 1954 through the first quarter, 1956; the third quarter, 1957 through the third quarter, 1960. A balance-of-payments deficit persisted during the following periods: the third quarter, 1953 through the second quarter, 1954; the second quarter, 1956 through the second quarter, 1957; since the fourth quarter, 1960.

On the basis of the above criterion we may derive the following evaluation of government performance with respect to the external-balance objective through comparison of column 8 of Table 10-1 with balance-of-payments conditions:

(1) Fiscal 1953. Rather stimulative. The government should have practiced more restraint.

[3] Although the fiscal 1961 budget was approximately balanced, there was a tax reduction of about 65 billion yen. According to the recently released *Kokumin Shotoku Hakusho,* fiscal 1961, $\Delta I + \Delta X - c(\Delta V)$ for 1960–1961 was 1,079 billion yen, and $\Delta G - c(\Delta R - \Delta T)$ was 114.9 billion yen—indicating that fiscal policy was actually somewhat destabilizing, chiefly because of the major increase in government expenditures.

[4] This is, of course, but one alternative working rule. However, it may be said to be a formalization of the loosely-knit criterion in policy considerations with respect to the desired relationship between the balance of payments and the domestic economic condition.

(2) Fiscal 1954. Moderately stimulative. Fiscal policy moved in the right direction.

(3) Fiscal 1955. Rather stimulative. Fiscal policy again went in the right direction.

(4) Fiscal 1956. Restrictive. Correct performance in the face of an external deficit.

(5) Fiscal 1957. Fiscal policy remained neutral in the course of improvement in the external balance.

(6) Fiscal 1958–1959. Rather stimulative. Correct performance from the standpoint of external balance.

(7) Fiscal 1960. Moderately suppressive despite signs of improvement in the external balance.

Insofar as the balance-of-payments criterion is concerned, fiscal policy was "incorrect" only in 1953, and was either correct or neutral in all other periods.[5]

Three observations emerge from the foregoing analyses concerning the stabilization role of fiscal policy.

First, tax reductions of major proportions (e.g., in 1953, 1955, 1957 and 1959) by and large had a destabilizing effect in boosting private economic activity.

Second, the *ex post* results of fiscal policy often differed considerably from the initial budgetary intentions, which were characterized by such labels as "neutral" and "positive." One reason for this is that actual tax revenue in Japan often exceeds anticipated revenue, and the increase in government service expenditures is likely to be more than offset by the unexpected tax-revenue increase.

Third, the temporary freezing of a part of the government fund (fiscal 1958), the suspension of expenditures (fiscal 1953 and 1957), and the discretionary increase in operating expenses (fiscal 1958) are of particular interest as examples of specific policy measures. The discretionary curtailment of expenditures in fiscal 1957 reached the magnitude of 54.5 billion yen, but was wrongly timed in terms of the criteria for the stabilization of both the external balance and the private sector. Other curtailments and postponements of expenditure programs were quantitatively of insignificant proportions.

Aside from the actual intentions of the government, we may conclude that, insofar as end results are concerned, Japanese fiscal policy has not been destabilizing vis-à-vis the private sector and the balance of payments. We may even go so far as to maintain that fiscal policy has, by and large, been stabilizing or neutral. In Japan one often encounters the criticism that fiscal policy does not pay sufficient attention to the goal of economic stability; our study suggests that this view is rather speculative and unsubstantiated by facts. The consistent annual increase in government spending on goods and services creates an impression of a chronically inflationary, expansionist policy; but much of the increase has been offset by adjustive changes in govern-

[5] Despite the balance-of-payments deficit in fiscal 1961, fiscal policy in that year continued to be excessively stimulative vis-à-vis the private sector.

ment revenues as well as transfer payments, with a resultant stabilizing (or neutral) overall effect.

The next section examines the automatic-stabilizing roles of tax revenues and transfer payments.[6]

EVALUATION OF AUTOMATIC STABILIZERS

Automatic stabilizers refer to those built-in systems and conventions within the economy which automatically tend to alleviate GNP fluctuations. In this section we evaluate the working of automatic stabilizers within the framework of National Income analysis similar to that employed in the preceding section.

We recall our previous equation (4) for the determination of the level of GNP (Y):

$$Y = \frac{a - b - c(R - T + V) + I + G + X}{1 - c + m} \tag{4}$$

Changes in GNP (Y) according to (4) may be thought of as consisting of two kinds: (1) exogenous changes, i.e., changes in private investment and exports, and discretionary policy-induced changes in the government sector; and (2) automatic changes in response to changes in exogenous variables.

The analysis of automatic stabilizers refers to the study of the second kind. We treat private investment, exports, and the government purchase of goods and services as variables that cause exogenous changes; government revenue (R), transfer payments (T), and business saving (V) cause automatic changes.[7] There are several different methods of gauging the effects of automatic stabilizers; we shall employ a slightly modified version of the Lusher method.[8]

We assume,

$$\left. \begin{array}{l} R = rY \\ T = tY \\ V = vY \end{array} \right\} \tag{5}$$

By substituting (5) into (4),

$$Y = \frac{a - b + I + G + X}{1 - c(1 - r + t - v) + m} \tag{6}$$

[6] Many useful ideas concerning the analysis of automatic stabilizers were drawn from E. C. Brown, "Federal Fiscal Policy in the Post-War Period" in R. E. Freeman, ed. *Post-War Economic Trends in the United States* (New York, 1960). In order to study the relationship between economic growth and stability, it is necessary to consider stabilization policies for the optimal rate of growth. This problem, however, is not dealt with in our paper.

[7] The following definitions are used. (a) Government revenue: total of personal, corporation, and indirect business taxes (inclusive of non-tax liabilities) and social-security contributions. (b) Transfer payment: total of transfer income, subsidies, and interest on government bonds. (c) Business saving: corporate retained earnings, public-enterprise surpluses, and capital consumption allowances.

[8] See D. W. Lusher, "The Stabilizing Effectiveness of Budget Flexibility," in *Policies to Combat Depression* (National Bureau of Economic Research, 1956).

Equation (6) differs from the Lusher formula in the following ways: first, business saving does not belong to the fiscal-policy sector but is classified in (6) as an automatic stabilizer; second, it is assumed in (6) that no automatic-stabilizing elements are found in government expenditures; third, exports are treated in (6) as exogenous whereas imports are assumed to be endogenous. Business saving is regarded as an automatic stabilizer in the broad sense of the term in order to evaluate the stabilizing effect of fiscal policy proper under the assumption of a symmetrical relationship between the two.[9] The assumed absence of automatic adjustments in government expenditures stems from the observation that in the context of present-day public finance in Japan the probability of contractive expenditure-policy is nil. The treatment of exports and imports as exogenous and endogenous, respectively, is believed appropriate in view of the weight of foreign trade in the Japanese economy.[10]

In order to gauge the impact of the stabilizers we have two periods (1 and 2), and calculate with respect to period 1.

$$Y_1 = \frac{a - b + I_1 + G_1 + X_1}{1 - c(1 - r_1 + t_1 - v_1) + m} \tag{7}$$

The subscript 1 refers to the period 1; and I_1, G_1, X_1, r_1, t_1, v_1 are all real values. Since c and a are the estimated parameters of the consumption function, the value of Y_1 in (7) does not necessarily equal the real value of GNP in the period 1.

Similarly, we calculate for the period 2.

$$Y_2 = \frac{a - b + I_2 + G_2 + X_2}{1 - c(1 - r_2 + t_2 - v_2) + m} \tag{8}$$

As in the case of (7), I_2, G_2, X_2, r_2, t_2, and v_2 are real values. Next we obtain Y_{12}, the hypothetical GNP, determined by the exogenous variables in period 2 under the assumption that r_1, t_1, and v_1 remained constant:

$$Y_{12} = \frac{a - b + I_2 + G_2 + X_2}{1 - c(1 - r_1 + t_1 - v_1) + m} \tag{9}$$

Y_1 and Y_2 are GNP's that correspond to the real values of investment, government expenditure, and exports in the periods 1 and 2, respectively, whereas $Y_1 - Y_2$ shows the actual change in GNP. Under the assumption that r, t, and v remain constant, the hypothetical

---

[9] Lusher uses throughout his study the coefficient of the regression, $V = d + vY$. The similar regression for Japan (1953–1960) was found to be: $V = 580.2 + 0.0866Y$
$$(0.0373)$$
($R^2 = 0.3860$). But the fit of the regression is very poor. If V cannot be treated as exogenous, we may consider it to be one of the automatic factors which offset GNP fluctuations.

[10] I am indebted to Professor Kenjiro Ara for improvement on this point. Exports and imports are treated as exogenous and endogenous, respectively, in the preceding section of this paper as well.

change in GNP is measured by $Y_1 - Y_{12}$.[11] The difference between the hypothetical and real GNP's equals

$$(Y_1 - Y_{12}) - (Y_1 - Y_2) = Y_2 - Y_{12} \qquad (10)$$

Since Y_{12} is the hypothetical GNP to be realized in the absence of automatic-stabilizing effects, and Y_2 refers to the actual GNP to be achieved by the normal working of the automatic stabilizers,

$$\phi = \frac{Y_2 - Y_{12}}{Y_1 - Y_{12}} \qquad (11)$$

indicates that extent to which GNP fluctuations due to changes in $(G + I + X)$ are offset by the automatic stabilizers. If $\phi = 0$, it shows the total absence of automatic-stabilization effects; $\phi = 1$ implies that fiscal policy has perfectly stabilized income changes. We may devise the following simple, computational formula for ϕ:

$$\phi = Y_2 \cdot \frac{c(\Delta r - \Delta t + \Delta v)}{\Delta(I + G + X)} \qquad (12)$$

in which $\Delta r = r_2 - r_1$, $\Delta t = t_2 - t_1$, $\Delta v = v_2 - v_1$. The above ϕ has an additive advantage in that the sum of ϕ's with respect to separate automatic stabilizers (e.g., personal income tax, corporation tax, and the like) equals the value of ϕ for the total stabilization effect.[12]

Table 10-2 gives annual data from which the values of ϕ in Table 10-3 are computed.[13] Were there no changes in the tax and transfer-payment systems, it would be possible to calculate directly from Table 10-3 the stabilizing effects of fiscal policy and business saving. There were, however, numerous such changes from 1955 through 1960, making a direct calculation impossible.[14] We shall therefore attempt a partial estimate of the stabilizers; given the unavailability of data on local taxes, our attention is focused on changes in the national tax system.

With respect to the national personal income tax, there were four reductions (in 1956, 1957, 1958, and 1959):[15]

(1) Fiscal 1956. Increase in the value of income deduction (the reduction value, 15.1 billion yen); increase in basic exemptions; increase in the tax rate.

[11] Lusher is not clear as to the classification of estimated parameters and whether Y_1 and Y_2 equal real values. Our interpretation is believed to be appropriate.

[12] Lusher's ϕ can easily be converted into α as proposed by R. A. Musgrave and M. H. Miller in their "Built-in Flexibility," *American Economic Review* (March 1948).

[13] The value of the marginal propensity to import is derived from the import functions (1953–1960): $M = 504.53 + 0.1199Y$. For the marginal propensity to consume, the same value (0.7) as in the preceding section is used. (See the note to Table 10-1.)

[14] For this point I am obliged to Professors Sei Fujita and Susumu Koizumi.

[15] See Ministry of Finance, *Zaisei Kinyū Tokei Geppō*, No. 110 (September 1960), pp. 82 and 85. Reduction values are estimated from Ministry of Finance, *Kuni no Yosan*.

TABLE 10-2

GOVERNMENT REVENUE, TRANSFER PAYMENTS, BUSINESS SAVING, AND GNP: FISCAL 1955–1960

(billions of yen)

	1955	1956	1957	1958	1959	1960
(1) Government Revenue (R)	1,613.3	1,853.6	2,103.8	2,145.8	2,467.6	3,106.9
(a) Personal tax and non-tax liabilities	415.4	449.3	421.3	436.2	468.3	602.8
Central	306.6	333.8	284.5	294.5	317.4	434.7
Local	108.7	115.5	136.8	141.7	150.9	168.0
(b) Corporation tax and non-tax liabilities	234.0	303.5	426.8	375.7	489.5	675.9
Central	206.0	266.4	375.3	329.1	430.2	592.1
Local	28.0	37.2	51.5	46.5	59.3	83.7
(c) Indirect business tax and non-tax liabilities	771.9	880.8	1,001.9	1,055.5	1,190.2	1,438.8
Central	460.3	518.7	582.7	619.4	699.8	831.1
Local	311.6	362.0	419.2	436.0	490.3	607.6
(d) Social-insurance liabilities	191.8	219.9	253.6	278.3	319.5	389.3
(2) Total of transfer payments, subsidies, interest on government bonds (T)	407.2	416.7	479.1	495.2	559.7	665.4
(3) Business savings (V)	985.8	1,390.0	1,500.5	1,521.4	2,160.2	2,760.8
(a) Corporate retained earnings	273.7	531.6	434.0	331.0	754.9	1,528.6
(b) Government-enterprise surpluses	61.6	64.0	134.2	137.1	143.9	173.4
(c) Capital depreciation	650.4	794.3	932.3	1,053.2	1,261.3	1,528.6
(4) Domestic capital formation (I)	2,086.6	2,955.1	3,210.1	2,831.6	4,404.7	5,607.0
(5) Government expenditures (G)	889.0	936.5	1,013.5	1,017.3	1,177.0	1,342.9
(6) Exports (X)	1,092.5	1,272.3	1,385.4	1,354.5	1,614.7	1,821.9
(7) Gross National Product (GNP)	8,235.5	9,292.9	10,149.7	10,394.7	12,572.4	14,664.8

SOURCE: Compiled mainly from Keizai Kikaku Chō, *Kokumin Shotoku Hakusho*, fiscal 1960, pp. 70–73, Table 8.

TABLE 10-3

The Values of Automatic Stabilizers
(ϕ)

	1955-1956	1956-1957	1957-1958	1958-1959	1959-1960
(1) Total government revenue	0.02275	0.15842	0.01556	−0.04878	0.10824
Personal tax and non-tax liabilities	−0.01319	−0.12252	−0.00889	−0.02266	0.02673
Central	−0.00835	−0.14092	−0.00611	−0.01483	0.03047
Local	−0.00484	0.01839	−0.00277	−0.00782	−0.00374
Corporation tax and non-tax liabilities	0.02715	0.18539	0.19951	0.01334	0.04971
Central	0.02326	0.16628	0.09839	0.01219	0.04283
Local	0.00388	0.01911	0.01111	0.00115	0.00687
Indirect business tax and non-tax liabilities	0.00663	0.07197	−0.05188	−0.03303	0.02402
Central	−0.00051	0.03928	−0.03928	−0.01887	0.00708
Local	0.00741	0.04179	−0.01204	−0.01416	0.01694
Social-insurance liabilities	0.00241	0.02357	−0.03317	−0.00657	0.00791
(2) Transfer payments	0.02938	−0.04215	0.00815	0.01493	−0.00590
Government revenue plus transfer payments	0.05213	0.11627	0.02371	−0.03385	0.10234
(3) Business saving	0.18997	−0.03143	0.02742	0.12225	0.11414
Total:	0.24210	0.08484	0.5113	0.08840	0.21648

SOURCE: Calculated from Table 10-2 by computational formula (12).

(2) Fiscal 1957. Decrease in the tax rate; increase in income deduction and basic exemptions (reduction value, 83.2 billion yen).

(3) Fiscal 1958. Introduction of the Savings Deduction System (reduction value, 5 billion yen); increase in basic exemptions.

(4) Fiscal 1959. Increase in dependents' exemptions (reduction value, 24.5 billion yen); decrease in the tax rate.

Since it was only in fiscal 1960 that no personal tax reforms took place, the value of 0.03047 (1959–1960) in Table 10-3 is the only value we can directly interpret to estimate the stabilizing effect of the national personal tax.[16] The remaining values of ϕ for the national personal tax in other periods are negative; this is perhaps not so much because the personal tax has had no automatic-stabilizing function at all as because the series of major tax reductions and the discretionary policy of the government have left little room for the personal tax to manifest its stabilizing effect. We can examine the effects of personal-tax reductions by the following formula which includes the dummy variables:

$$T_P = 108.4 - \underset{(0.040)}{0.023Y_{P0}} + \underset{(0.062)}{0.047Y_{P1}} + \underset{(0.04)}{0.10Y_{P2}}$$

$$- \underset{(104.4)}{72.1E_1} - \underset{(66.0)}{199.0E_2} - \underset{(66.3)}{206.7E_3} - \underset{(67.5)}{221.0E_4} \quad (13)$$

Degrees of freedom: 19, $\overline{R} = 0.9136$

In the above formula (13), T_P is personal-tax revenue; Y_P, personal income (seasonally adjusted, quarterly); Y_{P0}, personal income from fiscal 1955 through fiscal 1960; Y_{P1}, personal income in fiscal 1956; Y_{P2}, personal income from fiscal 1957 through fiscal 1960. These Y's are personal incomes of the periods in which there were no tax reforms.[17] E_1, E_2, E_3, and E_4 are dummy variables (1 or zero), corresponding to the exemption increases in fiscal 1956, 1957, 1958, and 1959, respectively. The coefficients of Y_{P0}, Y_{P1}, and E_1 in (13) were found to be insignificant; the equation, after dropping these three variables, becomes

$$T_P = 74.5 + \underset{(0.010)}{0.083Y_{P2}} - \underset{(19.7)}{165.1E_2} - \underset{(20.9)}{172.9E_3} - \underset{(24.9)}{187.1E_4} \quad (14)$$

Degrees of freedom: 16 $\overline{R} = 0.92766$

The equation (14) indicates that the tax reform of fiscal 1957 and the exemption increases in fiscal 1958 and 1959 had significant effects on tax revenue.

With respect to the national corporation tax, the following reforms took place:

---

[16] The corresponding value of Musgrave's α is: $\alpha = 0.090$. The weight of non-tax liabilities included in 0.03047 (Table 10-3) is negligibly small.

[17] The data for equation (13) are from *Kokumin Shotoku Hakusho*, fiscal 1960, pp. 29, 70. Equation (13) does not consider the tax reduction of 1959–1960; the reduction was applied to those income brackets near the exemption point and therefore its effect is assumed to have been small.

(1) Reduction in the tax rate effective since October 1, 1955 (reduction value, 6 billion yen).

(2) Fiscal 1956. Restriction on the retirement compensation allowances and expense accounts (tax-revenue increase, 8.8 billion yen).

(3) Fiscal 1957. Decrease in the tax rate and rationalization of Special Measures (tax-revenue increase, 7 billion yen).

(4) Fiscal 1958. Decrease in the tax rate, and Special Measures for Research and Development (reduction value, 13.4 billion yen).

(5) Fiscal 1959. Adjustment in discharge compensations, expense accounts, and reserves for price fluctuations of small and medium-size businesses (tax-revenue increase, 1.7 billion yen).[18]

In contrast to the personal tax, corporation-tax reforms meant tax reductions as well as tax increases. All values of ϕ for the corporation tax in Table 10-3 are positive. Since there were no reforms from fiscal 1959 through 1960, we may interpret the value of ϕ (0.04283) which corresponds to that period to be expressive of the stabilization effect of the corporation tax.[19] The value of ϕ (0.16628) for the period fiscal 1956–1957 reflects the tax-revenue increase due to the reform as well as the boom; similarly, the value of ϕ for the period fiscal 1957–1958 reflects the tax reduction due to both the reform and the recession. It is difficult to prepare dummy variables for the corporation-tax reductions; consequently, we did not calculate the adjusted corporation-tax formulas which correspond to (13) and (14) above.[20]

Next, a few words about transfer payments, which are assumed to

[18] Estimates are made from Ministry of Finance, *Kuni no Yosan*, various fiscal years.

[19] The value of α that corresponds to $\phi = 0.04283$ is: $\alpha = 0.125$.

[20] The corporation-tax reforms usually pertain to changes in tax rates and methods of calculating various expenses. If we connect the corporation-tax revenue $(T\hat{C})$ with the gross corporation profit (P) so as to examine the impact of the tax reforms on tax revenue by the following formula,

$$T_C = \alpha P + \beta$$

the change in the method of calculating expenses means change in the value of P, and $T\hat{C}$ cannot therefore be independent of P. For this reason it is not possible to introduce dummy variables similar to E_1, E_2, and so forth for the personal tax. As an experiment, the following equation was calculated on the basis of seasonally adjusted, quarterly data:

$$T_C = 18516 + 0.211P_0 + 0.061P_1 + 0.062P_2 + 0.012P_3 + 0.044P_4 + 152.2E_1$$
$$\quad\;\;\; (0.118) \quad\;\; (0.043) \quad\;\; (0.047) \quad\;\; (0.130) \quad\;\; (0.122) \quad\;\; (225.2)$$

Degrees of Freedom: 13 $\bar{R} = 0.9794$

P_0, P_1, P_2, P_3, and P_4 are gross profits in fiscal 1955–1960, fiscal 1956, fiscal 1957, fiscal 1958, fiscal 1956–1960, respectively; and E_1 (the fiscal 1958 reform that corresponds to the export-income exemption and is independent of P) is the dummy variable. However, all the regression coefficients except for that of P_0 were found to be insignificant; this may perhaps imply that tax-rate changes have little significant effect on corporation-tax revenue as a whole. The equation, recalculated after dropping all the insignificant coefficients, is as follows:

$$T_C = 11006 + 0.310P_0, \quad \bar{R} = 0.9668$$
$$\quad\;\;\;\; (0.018)$$

function as automatic stabilizers. The values of ϕ for transfer payments in Table 10-3 bear both plus and minus signs.[21] The components of transfer payments—health insurance, old-age pensions, unemployment compensations, welfare funds, and so forth—are not necessarily closely related to changes in the National Income. There have also been numerous reforms. For these reasons the results in Table 10-3 are not overly surprising. Some components of transfer payments, however, have a distinct, automatic-stabilizing characteristic despite their relatively small weights. Unemployment insurance is a representative example. The values of ϕ for unemployment insurance alone are: 0.00714 (fiscal 1955–1956); −0.00214 (fiscal 1956–1957); 0.02149 (fiscal 1957–1958); 0.00537 (fiscal 1958–1959); 0.00151 (fiscal 1959–1960). The increase in the maximum amount of daily dispensation from 460 to 590 yen in fiscal 1957 corresponds to the value −0.00214. Given the absence of reforms in the system in other periods, it is evident that unemployment insurance, despite its small weight, has consistently functioned as an automatic stabilizer.

It is not easy to appraise the overall effectiveness of fiscal policy as a stabilizer. The foregoing analyses seem to indicate, however, that much of its potential contribution to economic stability through corporation and personal taxes failed to be realized, chiefly because of the government's tax-reduction policies. In the private sector, business saving has shown a considerable, stabilizing effect (see column 3, Table 10-3). The recession-induced decline in profits has led to a concomitant fall in business saving, and conversely when a boom was in progress. This cyclical movement in business saving has been reflected in the stabilization mechanism of the corporation tax as well.

Conclusion

The results of our study may be summarized as follows:

First, one of the objectives of fiscal policy is to stabilize fluctuations in private economic activity. Although the Japanese government has not necessarily been explicitly conscious of such an objective in formulating its policy, our evidence suggests that Japanese fiscal policy on the whole has been neutral or stabilizing rather than destabilizing. In terms of the balance-of-payments criterion, of which the government has been very conscious, fiscal policy, by and large, has been successful.

Second, with respect to the working of automatic stabilizers, the corporation tax system has exerted some significant effect; but the normal, automatic-stabilizing function of the individual income tax system was largely paralyzed by the series of personal-tax reductions.

[21] Transfer payments (T) include subsidies and interest on government bonds (see footnote 7), but their weights are negligible.

Comment *by Sei Fujita*

Kaizuka's paper appraises recent Japanese fiscal policy from the standpoint of economic stability. Except for the last section, the income-determination model is used as the method of analysis. This particular approach has thus far been applied by few public-finance specialists in Japan; in this sense Kaizuka's efforts are to be commended.

The first section appraises the stabilization effect of fiscal policy as a whole. In this section he draws the interesting conclusion that Japanese fiscal policy has been more stabilizing (and neutral) than destabilizing. In other words, in his grading Kaizuka gives the Japanese government perhaps not an A, but a B. This is certainly blissful news to Japanese authorities in the role of examinees, but we have some doubts as to Kaizuka's grading criteria. In terms of his first criterion, changes in exogenous variables in the private sector $[\Delta I + \Delta X - c\Delta V]$ are offset by changes in exogenous variables belonging to the public sector, and the closer ΔY ($Y =$ GNP) approaches zero, the more effective fiscal policy is as an automatic stabilizer. This particular criterion does not seem appropriate for the stabilization problems of a growing economy. Let us assume that the average GNP growth rate for the period under observation is consistent with the long-run equilibrium in the balance of payments and the level of prices, and that the growth rate is warranted from the standpoint of optimal, intertemporal allocation of resources. To the extent that this assumption is permissible, we should interpret fiscal policy as destabilizing when the rate of increase in $[G - c\,(R - T)]$ is lower than the average GNP growth rate, provided that the rate of increase in $(I + X - cV)$ in a given fiscal year is considerably lower than the average rate of increase in GNP. Following this line of reasoning, government policy in fiscal 1954 and 1957, contrary to Kaizuka's appraisal, was actually destabilizing. The deflationary policy in those years was intended to restore the balance-of-payments equilibrium and to restrain excessive booms in the domestic economy. Aside from its professed intentions, the policy was still contradictory to the objective of stabilizing the home market.

According to Kaizuka's next criterion, the government should stimulate (suppress) private economic activity when there is a surplus (deficit) in the balance of payments; and he concludes that a correct fiscal policy was implemented only in 1953. His criterion implies that, as long as export expansion continues, one is allowed to drive at full speed, and, in the opposite case, one may apply the emergency brake as one pleases. It is questionable whether the passengers in such a car will think highly of their driver. No matter how important balance-of-payments problems might be to Japan, we find it hard to accept the notion that the external equilibrium should receive priority of consideration over domestic economic problems. True economic stability in the dynamic sense means that the growth rate is stabilized within a range consistent with the long-run equilibrium in the balance of payments, thus eliminating any need for the government to invoke rigorous, deflationary measures. In short, Kaizuka's approach to the problem in the first section of his study is enlightening in many ways, but his evaluation criteria are not free of difficulties.

In the second section Kaizuka attempts to apply the Lusher method to Japanese fiscal-policy problems. It is an interesting and highly suggestive study; the treatment of exports and imports as exogenous and endogenous, respectively, is quite appropriate. But we must remember that both works by Lusher and Musgrave were meant to examine only one phase of the built-in stabilizing function of fiscal policy—both studies were concerned only with the stabilization effect upon private consumption demand. A broader study should cover the stabilization effect on private investment as well. We must pay special attention to the effect of changes in the tax system (especially in the corporation tax) upon the availability of firms' internal funds as well as to the effect of fiscal-policy changes upon the money supply. Given the difficulty in identifying the determinants of private investment, it has been common practice to assume that private investment demand is exogenous and to concentrate on the stabilization effect of fiscal policy upon private consumption demand. With respect to the Japanese economy in the recent years, however, it seems reasonable to suppose that, even allowing for the disturbing effects of discretionary fiscal and monetary policies, the automatic adjustability of tax revenue has made a significant contribution to stabilizing private investments. To the extent that we allow for the internal-funds effect upon private investment activity, Kaizuka's contention that business saving has functioned as a built-in stabilizer must be discounted.

The values of tax revenues from the National Income statistics, of course, comprise the influence of the tax reforms. Consequently, as Kaizuka himself points out, the value of ϕ cannot be viewed as a direct index of the built-in stabilizers. A far more effective result would have been possible had he calculated the values of ϕ under the assumption that there were no reforms. Kaizuka is not to blame, however, since such adjustment would have involved enormous difficulties.

The first section includes an evaluation of discretionary fiscal policies in various years; but it is made up of only cursory remarks. This might have been due to space limitations. But he should perhaps have conducted a full-fledged econometric analysis of such discretionary policies as well as of public loans and investments. For example, a comparison of the initial budgets and public loan-and-investment plans with those following the revisions, and a study of their annual differences, might have provided an effective appraisal of the discretionary policies. Why those discretionary policies did not succeed in sufficiently preventing excessive booms and the balance-of-payments crises is another question yet to be answered. Kaizuka's silence on this problem leaves the reader rather discontented.

PART V

Management

I I

Kazuo Noda:

Postwar Japanese Executives

The London *Economist's* recent special series on postwar Japan[1] begins with a satirical note on Mr. Joseph Dodge, an extremely influential economist in the United States who came to Japan to instruct and advise on the economic policy of the Allied Occupation Forces. The *Economist* comments that despite the recommendations of Dodge, Japan continued to pursue those policies to which the American advisor was opposed; consequently, the real GNP persistently increased at an average annual rate of 9 per cent, industrial output and exports of industrial products more than quadrupled, and city residents had a taste of the age of mass consumption for the first time in Asia.[2]

On the surface it was the economic-policy makers of the Japanese government who chose a course of action counter to the Dodge recommendations, but the awesome achievement of Japanese postwar growth is attributable more to the energetic conduct of Japanese corporate managers. Inasmuch as Japan's accelerated growth has, to a large extent, been the result of the expansion of large corporations in the manufacturing sector, the roles played by and the characteristics of the decision makers in those corporations deserve careful study.

PREWAR FINANCIAL CIRCLES AND THEIR DISSOLUTION

Before we begin our discussion of postwar corporate executives, it is necessary to take a look at the general conditions that surrounded the prewar executives. Prewar Japanese industry, in general, was dominated by two groups: first, a group of Zaibatsu corporations active since the Meiji era, such as Mitsui, Mitsubishi, and Sumitomo; second, a group of new Zaibatsu firms which grew rapidly under the semi-wartime economy that developed after the Manchurian Incident. Table 11-1 shows that, as of 1946, the paid-in capital of the ten largest Zaibatsu firms constituted 35.2 per cent of total paid-in capital for all corporations, and the Zaibatsu concentration was particularly notice-

---

[1] "Consider Japan," *Economist* (London), September 1 and 8, 1962 (the Japanese translation by Atsushi Kawamura, *Odorokubeki Nihon,* Takeuchi Shoten, 1963).

[2] *Ibid.,* pp. 8–9 (the Japanese translation).

TABLE 11-1

PAID-IN CAPITAL OF THE TEN LARGEST ZAIBATSU CORPORATIONS[a]

Industry	Total of the four largest[b] (100 million yen)	Ratio to grand total[c] (per cent)	Total of the ten largest[d] (100 million yen)	Ratio to grand total[c] (per cent)
Finance:				
Banking	48	48.0	51	50.4
Trust	4	85.4	4	85.4
Insurance	9	51.2	10	60.3
Sub-total	60	49.7	64	53.0
Heavy Industry:				
Mining	87	28.3	155	50.5
Metals	101	26.4	160	41.8
Machinery	278	46.2	409	67.9
Ship-building	8	5.0	20	12.5
Chemicals	93	31.4	114	38.5
Sub-total	567	32.4	858	49.0
Light Industry:				
Paper	2	4.5	3	4.7
Ceramic	9	28.4	18	55.8
Textile	22	17.4	24	18.8
Agriculture, forestry, fishing, foods	3	2.7	12	10.4
Sundry	12	9.7	21	16.2
Sub-total	49	10.7	77	16.8
Others:				
Gas, electric	2	0.5	2	0.5
Land transport	5	4.9	5	5.6
Sea transport	60	60.8	61	61.4
Real estate, warehousing	14	22.7	18	29.4
Commerce, foreign trade	37	13.6	55	20.3
Sub-total	117	12.9	141	15.5
Grand total	794	24.5	1,141	35.2

SOURCE: Mochikabu Gaisha Seiri Iinkai, *Nihon Zaibatsu to Sono Kaitai: Shiryō*, pp. 468–469.

[a] As of 1946.
[b] Mitsui, Mitsubishi, Sumitomo, and Yasuda.
[c] Total paid-in capital of all corporations.
[d] The four in note *b* plus Ayukawa, Asano, Furukawa, Ōkura, Nakajima, Nomura.

able in the heavy-and-chemical industries. Since the leading Zaibatsu were highly selective in mergers with regard to the efficiency of other companies, their total influence upon prewar Japanese industry, when both the quantitative as well as qualitative aspects are taken into consideration, was much greater than the figures in Table 11-1 would indicate.

Intensity and manner of Zaibatsu control differed from one firm to another. But in general, a family-owned holding company wielded decisive control over the allocation of personnel and capital funds throughout the pyramid of member corporations. The Mitsui Zaibatsu is known to have been an example of a holding company with relatively weak control, under which member firms were given considerable freedom in decision-making. The methods of control by the Mitsui Parent Company were as follows:

(1) The important agenda for the directors' meetings at Mitsui Trading, Mitsui Mining, and Mitsui Warehousing had to be submitted to the parent company for approval. Actual cases of rejection, however, were very few. Mitsui Bank, Mitsui Trust, Mitsui Life Insurance, Mitsui Farming-Forestry and Tropical Industry, Hokkaido Coal Shipping, Nippon Steel, Shibaura Electric, and Sanshin Construction would submit to the parent company minutes of the directors' meetings. Records show that as a matter of regular practice the directors would obtain approval of the parent company before their meetings.

(2) From the late 1920's on, Mitsui Bank, Mitsui Trading, Mitsui Mining, Toshin Warehousing, Mitsui Trust, and Mitsui Life Insurance were periodically required to hold management-report meetings at which the presidents and chief executives of these six firms delivered reports on their activities to representatives from the Mitsui family and the parent company.

(3) Representatives appointed to the member firms by the Mitsui family and the Board of Directors of the Mitsui Parent Company acted as liaison officers.[3]

As long as activities of the member firms remained efficient and profitable, their managers were permitted to make decisions freely. But once there was any sign of managerial inefficiency, personnel transfers and other measures were rigorously invoked. New investments by the member firms, absorption of or merger with outside companies, and the launching of new projects were chiefly executed by the parent company, whose capital funds alone were sufficient to finance the majority of those undertakings.[4]

In contrast to the above example, the control of Mitsubishi and Sumitomo Zaibatsu is known to have been far more extensive and thorough. Other smaller Zaibatsu holding companies had fewer member firms, and their regulatory mechanisms were comparatively simpler; therefore, we may presume that the control of these smaller Zaibatsu tended to be more strict and comprehensive than that of the larger Zaibatsu.

Under such circumstances it is only natural that many executives of the member firms failed to develop a capacity for independent thought. Furthermore, Zaibatsu activities were concentrated in heavy-and-chemical industries, which were closely linked to government finance and military demand. This controlled economic environment, in which the main concern of Zaibatsu executives was not competition with other firms in the market but rather their dealings with government

---

[3] Hideo Edo, *Mitsui Zaibatsu ni tsuite* (1948), pp. 7–8.
[4] Kazuo Noda, "Kigyōka Gojūnen—Mukai Tadaharu," *Seisansei* (May 1963).

bureaucrats and military personnel, merely intensified the tendency toward development of executive personalities that were devoid of independent motives. In view of the fact that numerous companies which did not belong to any Zaibatsu line were nevertheless subjected to a multitude of indirect influences and pressures from the Zaibatsu, the number of corporate managers and executives throughout prewar Japanese industry who were forced by a relatively few Zaibatsu leaders to remain passive conformists must have been exceedingly large.[5]

The war and Japan's total surrender brought about a complete shakedown of such conditions. The United States government's mem-

[5] The following is my reply to Katsunosuke Moroi's comment on the role of Zaibatsu in prewar Japan discussed in this paper. It is after the Taishō period that Mitsui, Mitsubishi, Sumitomo, and other Zaibatsu came to exert extensive control over the Japanese economy; the study of the Meiji period does not reveal any evidence of their industrial domination. During the Meiji period, except for some sectors, there was still much room for founder-type executives to manifest their entrepreneurial spirit. In the absence of "bureaucratization" of the personnel structure which came into existence in later years, many new and young employees in the Meiji era could and did assume important positions, depending upon their abilities, and engaged in vigorous entrepreneurial activities, taking full advantage of the scale and might of the Zaibatsu system; and, at the same time, the growth of Zaibatsu itself was, to a large extent, attributable to those young executives. Toward the end of the Meiji period, the first generation of the corporations came to be replaced by a group of more conservative executives whose main interest lay not so much in expansion of the firms through new innovations as in preservation and consolidation of the corporate bureaucracy through market protection and absorption of other firms. The chemical industry provides an example of such passive Zaibatsu policy. Yūjiro Hayashi has observed: "Development of the chemical industry by old Zaibatsu firms was accelerated during the First World War, but once the postwar Depression began not a single adventurous step was taken by those firms. . . . When the new Zaibatsu, such as Nippon Chisso, introduced a new method of producing ammonium sulphate from synthetic ammonia, the old Zaibatsu continued to cling to the obsolescent method of making it from calcium cyanamide. The old Zaibatsu tended to keep up with new technology not through their own research and development but rather through absorption of other, newer firms. . . . Mitsui, Mitsubishi, Sumitomo, and other old Zaibatsu would refrain from adopting new production techniques until and unless their profitability was absolutely assured. They could realize sufficient profits by manipulating financial and commercial means, and the problem of introducing new technology was soluble by way of patents acquisition and absorption of other technologically progressive but financially vulnerable firms" (Yūjiro Hayashi, Nihon no Kagaku Kōgyō [Iwanami Shinsho, 1957], pp. 94–95, 104).

The above tendency was hardly confined to the chemical industry. The ultraconservativism and passivity of the old Zaibatsu even aroused hostility among the leaders of the military clique. As the Japanese military venture in the Chinese mainland became clear after the Manchurian Incident, however, many old Zaibatsu came to reverse their policy towards closer cooperation with and active participation in the military-economic operations on the Continent.

No doubt the old Zaibatsu contributed in various ways to Japanese economic growth. But it may also be argued that they hindered the process of growth to the extent that they were responsible for the development of a huge complex of corporate bureaucracy which discouraged creative management and suppressed the blossoming of the entrepreneurial spirit. For a more detailed discussion of this point, see Kazuo Noda and Tsuneo Murakami, Nihon no Keieisha.

orandum on occupation policy, issued as early as September 22, 1945, already indicated the forthcoming Zaibatsu dissolution. In reply, the Japanese government disclosed its own plan for the dissolution in November of the same year. The basic outline of the Japanese plan was accepted by the G.H.Q., and the liquidation of the four largest Zaibatsu (Mitsui, Mitsubishi, Sumitomo, and Yasuda) and the purge of Zaibatsu families and chief officers from their holding companies were announced. The G.H.Q. plan was far more comprehensive than was initially anticipated by the Japanese government, for it contained directives applying equally stern measures to industrial combines other than the four largest Zaibatsu. A large number of additional corporations were scheduled for abrogation prior to the forming of the Holding Company Liquidation Commission in August 1946. The dissolution measures, executed chiefly by the above commission under the strict supervision of the occupation authorities through March 1950, are summarized below.[6]

(1) Dissolution of 28 family-owned holding companies.

(2) Dissolution of Mitsui Bussan and Mitsubishi Shoji under the instruction and supervision of the above committee. Complete liquidation of the entire portfolios previously owned by those companies.

(3) Liquidation of stocks owned by 51 other holding companies and supervision of their activities.

(4) Freezing of assets owned by 56 members of the ten largest Zaibatsu families, liquidation of their stocks, and restriction on their corporate appointments.

(5) Application of the Excessive Economic Power Concentration Prevention Act (Shūchū Haijo Hō) in order to split or liquidate the assets owned by large corporations. As many as 325 firms were originally subjected to the act; but only 18 of them suffered actual application of the act.

(6) Liquidation of stocks owned by firms other than holding companies and supervision of their activities, as well as the activities of their subsidiaries and affiliated companies.

(7) Liquidation of stocks owned by certain corporations and the prohibition of the Zaibatsu trademarks and names under the Corporate Securities Ownership Restrictions Decree (Kaisha Shōken Hoyū Seigen Rei).

CHARACTERISTICS AND ROLE OF PROFESSIONAL MANAGERS

The fact that the Zaibatsu dissolution hardly applied to financial institutions has provoked much controversy. However, the aforementioned measures clearly brought to an end the complex human and capital relations which regulated all phases of corporate activity before the war. On the human side, a sweeping personnel reform took place after the war at the top-executive level of the old Zaibatsu. A total of

[6] For details, see Mochikabu Gaisha Seiri Iinkai, *Nihon Zaibatsu to Sono Kaitai* (1950), pp. 188–467.

2,210 officers of 632 corporations and 56 members of the Zaibatsu families were discharged from their previous posts. In addition, 2,500 high-ranking officers and major stock-owners of large corporations and banks, who were active during the war, were purged in January 1947 in accordance with the Revised Purge Decree based upon the cabinet decision concerning the Purge of Political and Economic Personnel (made in November 1946 under the G.H.Q. instructions). The above two measures resulted in a wholesale withdrawal of the highest echelon of prewar Japanese industrial and financial circles.

 Those who were promoted to fill the suddenly vacated, highest posts came for the most part from the upper-middle layer of the corporate structure, which, at the time of surrender, consisted of department heads, sectional vice-presidents, plant managers, divisional supervisors, and the like. Some of these so-called "third-class executives" were unable to withstand the depth of new responsibilities and had to resign after a short period of time; but the majority of them were quite successful in mastering their new jobs. The term "third-class executives" is a misnomer, for these individuals were not so much those who happened to be picked haphazardly in the days of postwar chaos, irrespective of their administrative skills and managerial competence, as those who were requested by their retiring supervisors to assume the higher posts because the latter recognized their abilities. The performance of those men, faced with the difficult tasks of recovery and reconstruction amidst the post-surrender confusion, indicates that they must have been equipped with indisputably high leadership qualities. The purge brought new and fresh opportunities for a younger generation of corporate managers.

The postwar generation of well-reputed company presidents includes: Chikara Kurata (Hitachi Seisakusho, director of Kasado Plant at the time of surrender); Kikuo Sodeyama (Tōyō Rayon, head of the ammunitions department of Shiga Plant); Yaichi Sasaki (Nippon Sekiyu, supervisor); Juichi Hirota (Sumitomo Kinzoku, the planning section chief in the engineering department). The list of those who became presidents as a result of abilities demonstrated during the pre-Korea period of financial crises and labor disputes includes: Toshio Dokō (Ishikawajima Harima Jūkō, became president in 1950); Taizo Odawara (Kubota Tekkō, 1950); Taizo Ishida (Toyota Automobiles, 1950); Taizo Ishizaka (Tō-shiba, 1949). All these men acquired knowledge, experience, and managerial competence in the process of climbing up from the bottom of the ladder in their respective firms; in this sense they belong to the category of "professional managers" as the term is used in the United States.

Despite the pronounced reversal in occupation policy after 1949, which brought about a considerable relaxation in the Zaibatsu dissolution measures as well as cancellation of many purges, few corporate leaders of the prewar generation returned to their former posts. There were two main reasons for this: first, after the war many corporations became independent and their top management consisted now of new and younger executives—there was little room left for the return of former corporate leaders (although the majority of former leaders did not express a desire to come back); second, a series of sweeping changes in the corporate environment after the war made the know-how of former executives critically obsolete (e.g., they were totally inexperienced in dealing with labor unions).

Up to the time of the Korean War it was still "possible" for some former executives to resume an active life. As purges were being cancelled around 1950, a certain number of them did return to their former posts, and some others joined the reorganized firms in the capacities of ex officio chairmen, consultants, and the like; but their numbers never became large enough to reshuffle the postwar formation of management in firms formerly affiliated with the Zaibatsu. With respect to 40 holding companies which escaped forced dissolution (out of 83 on the initial list), 9 companies had the same presidents (or chairmen of the board) in early 1952 as they had had at the time of surrender (cancellation of the purge was completed before the end of 1951), and the remaining 31 companies appointed new presidents (or chairmen of the board) during the same period. The breakdown of posts held by the new presidents at the time of surrender is as follows: 4 of them were executive supervisors or vice-presidents; 15 were supervisors; 11 held "other" posts; and the previous post for one is unknown. The relative youth of new presidents is indicated by the age statistics: the average age of those who were presidents at the time of surrender and of those who had become new presidents by early 1952 were 60.2 and 51.8 years old, respectively, as of 1948.[7]

One major characteristic of the postwar (as against prewar) corporate managers is that both the ratio of company stocks they own and the value of executive bonuses they receive are conspicuously smaller than they were before the war. In prewar Zaibatsu corporations, many executives, who were technically salary-earners, were regularly entitled to large amount of executive compensations (conventionally, 10 per cent of net profits) and to "status shares" of company stocks; consequently, there was a common tendency for them to become *de facto* owner-managers. This situation was radically changed after the war. Following G.H.Q. instructions, executive prerogatives and compensations were reduced by a sizable margin to become comparable to those of professional managers in the United States. A major revision (1950) of Japanese commercial laws included numerous provisions designed to promote professionalization of corporation managers in Japan, while the decision-making power of the directors was significantly increased (and that of the stockholders reduced). The corporate power structure was considerably decentralized, and many individuals, in addition to the directors, were allowed to participate in administrative control at different levels.[8] The prewar institution of "status shares" was naturally abolished. "Outside" buyers were given priority in acquiring newly

[7] *Ibid.*, pp. 6–22; and Diamond Sha, ed. *Kaisha Yōran*, second half of 1952.
[8] After the war it became possible for non-shareholders to be directors.

issued company stocks. Various social forces which tend to regulate and restrain corporate activity, such as labor unions, financial intermediaries, and institutional shareholders, became more powerful and complex than they had been before the war. These changes, together with the so-called "democratization of securities-ownership," made a decisive contribution to the separation of corporate ownership and control.

Most empirical studies conducted in Japan on control and ownership of postwar corporations have been based upon the classic work by Berle and Means.[9] These studies show that executives are capable of making decisions far more autonomously after the war than before the war.[10] Among similar works by economists, Yuichi Hirose's careful study of the 200 largest corporations in the major industrial sectors as of the first half of 1959 deserves mention. One of the significant contributions made by Hirose's study is the empirical demonstration of the fact that in the postwar period commercial banks and financial intermediaries have become leading buyers of corporate securities as well as predominant suppliers of loans to the major companies; they have, in fact, become formidable institutional stockholders capable of exerting a powerful influence upon corporate activity, although this fact, as Hirose points out, has been largely ignored by management scientists.

However, even in the light of Hirose's findings, the greater autonomy of postwar corporation managers in Japan relative to the prewar years is evident. Of 200 firms studied, only 33 are owner-controlled; approximately 40 which previously belonged to the Zaibatsu lines are "controlled" by financial institutions; and the remaining 107 are controlled by their own managers. The majority of those firms which were formerly members of the old Zaibatsu do not show today any sign of being controlled by stock-owners or outside financial institutions, nor is there evidence that inter-firm control exists. Hirose maintains, however, that "since there have developed complex and extensive links, through supply of and demand for investment funds, between many leading corporations and major financial institutions, it is only natural that the thoughts and actions of the executives of those corporations are bound to be conditioned by their external associations with financial institutions, i.e., they find it difficult to make purely autonomous, managerial decisions." [11] With respect to the managers who control firms, which is the case in about 50 per cent of the 200 leading corporations in major industrial sectors, Hirose writes: "The majority of them are hired managers with insignificant ownership of company stocks, and few are of the owner-manager type. Despite their technical employee status, they actively participate in managerial decision-making

[9] A. A. Berle, Jr., and G. C. Means, *The Modern Corporation and Private Property* (New York: The Macmillan Co., 1950).

[10] See, e.g., Kuniyoshi Urabe, *Keieisha* (Diamond Sha, 1958).

[11] Yuichi Hirose, *Kabushiki Gaisha Shihai no Kōzō* (Nihon Hyōron Shin Sha, 1963), p. 147.

of their employer firms. . . . However, the fact that a firm is controlled by professional managers does not necessarily imply that management of the firm can be independent of the supplier of capital.
Autonomy of the managers as such may be sustained as long as they
carry out the affairs of the firm without undue frictions, but it is
more than likely that once they make critical errors, the creditor banks
and the institutional owners of company stocks will collectively invoke
a tacit but effective instrument of control, say, by forcing policy
changes and dismissal or transfer of the managers in question." [12]

The postwar executives differ also from their prewar counterparts in
terms of the criteria by which they were promoted to their positions.
Table 11-2 summarizes the findings of a survey conducted in 1960 by
the Japan Committee for Economic Development (Keizai Dōyūkai)
with the cooperation of the Tokyo Economic Research Center. It is
evident from the table that the majority of postwar executives have
been chosen for their posts chiefly because of their knowledge, competence, and experience in general or sectional management.

The emergence of these postwar professional managers reflects his-
toric changes in Japanese industry. Before the war, few firms were
concerned with full-scale research in and systematic introduction of
modern managerial-control techniques; perhaps there was no need
then for management science in general. In many cases it would suffice
for prewar executives merely to carry out, as frictionlessly as possible,
routine procedures built upon a backlog of experience within firms.
Such methods were hardly operative or sufficient to maintain and
expand corporate activity in the postwar context, given the series of
revolutionary changes in Japanese political, economic, and social conditions. The rapid rise of labor unions and the concomitant multiplication of labor-management problems, the new and complex role of the
government vis-à-vis corporations, the new tax systems necessitating a
wholesale reorientation and revision of the accounting procedures of
business firms, the diversification as well as intensification of competition requiring firms constantly to engage in rationalization, product
development, and market research—all these meant a long list of
radically different qualifications demanded of the postwar generation
of corporation managers.

The most important of the newly demanded qualifications perhaps
was the ability to analyze and cope with the changed and changing
managerial environment. How did they acquire the knowledge and
technique necessary for the task? Many of them resorted to the methods
of American-style management control. The "management-science
boom," which began around 1955 with numerous publications introducing American management-science literature to the Japanese audience, is well known. Frequent management-control seminars, ubiqui-
tous lecture series on the subject, and incessant visits of Japanese
business groups to the United States (satirized as unprecedented since

[12] *Ibid.*, pp. 198–199.

TABLE 11-2

REASONS FOR EXECUTIVE APPOINTMENTS

Reasons	Total	Size of the firms (total assets)			
		More than 20 billion yen	10–20 billion yen	0.5–10 billion yen	Less than 0.5 billion yen
Major stock ownership	5.7	1.6	4.2	8.8	17.4
Representing financial institutions	2.3	1.1	2.7	3.1	3.1
Representing the government	0.3	...	1.3	...	...
Representing workers	0.0	...	...	...	0.4
Representing stockholders	3.7	2.3	3.3	5.3	5.4
Representing buyers	1.1	0.2	0.4	1.9	3.1
Representing suppliers of raw materials	0.3	0.4	...	0.4	...
Representing suppliers of parts, etc.	0.3	0.1	1.0	...	0.4
As financial consultants	0.6	0.5	...	0.7	1.3
As marketing consultant	0.2	0.1	0.4	0.1	0.4
As legal consultant	0.1	...	0.2	0.1	0.4
As engineering consultant	0.4	0.5	0.2	0.6	...
Comprehensive knowledge about business	37.4	43.5	42.1	30.1	23.1
Capacity for decision making	11.4	12.8	11.9	10.8	6.3
Capacity for handling employees	1.4	1.9	0.2	1.7	0.4
Professional knowledge about personnel	2.4	2.3	2.1	2.7	2.2
Professional engineering knowledge	16.0	15.4	17.1	14.8	17.4
Professional knowledge of liaison problems	0.8	0.9	0.6	1.0	0.4
Professional knowledge of marketing	8.5	8.7	6.3	10.5	9.4
No reply	7.1	7.5	5.9	7.3	8.9
Total	100.00	100.00	100.00	100.00	100.00

SOURCE: Katsutaro Miyashita, *et al.*, *Waga Kuni Kigyō ni okeru Keiei Ishi Kettei no Jittai*. Tokyo Economic Research Center Reprint Series, No. 4 (1960), p. 27.

the 7th-century Kentōshi Mission to China) all testify to the inde-
fatigable enthusiasm of postwar executives for modern-management
theory.[13]

What has been the outcome of importing this subject from the
United States? It is not easy to give a clear answer to this question,

[13] From the Japan Productivity Center alone, as many as 454 teams consisting
of 4,665 individuals visited the United States between May 31, 1955 and March 31,
1963.

and the following is largely a matter of speculation. The fact that the large corporations, acting as the spearheads of Japan's postwar growth, could and did manage to achieve not only quantitative expansion at an extraordinary pace but also qualitative improvement amidst the turbulent global waves of technological innovations might be attributed to the rapid introduction and digestion of modern managerial methods from the United States. In fact, we may go so far as to say that the kind of accelerated growth demonstrated by Japan would have been impossible had there been no importation of such methods. Table 11-3 gives a partial summary of surveys of 100 large corporations,

TABLE 11-3

CLASSIFICATION OF MAJOR MANAGEMENT PROBLEMS

Strengthening of and better planning in management	71
Mechanization of clerical work	13
Building staff for planning and research	18
Long-range planning	11
Management planning	8
Budget control, Cost control	8
Clarification of management objectives	3
Better organization of work, others	15
Modernization of the systems	65
Clarification of duties and rights	18
Systematizing and coordinating executive meetings	11
Adopting a new system of departments	6
Independent budgeting systems	3
Establishing committees	5
Better inter-departmental communications and cooperation	5
Establishing the line-staff system	3
Others	16
Improvement in Human Relations	34
Education and training of workers	11
Better human relations	8
Better labor management	3
Fairness of personnel appointments	3
Better labor-management relations	4
Better communication	2
Others	3
Improvement in production and engineering	26
New technology development	7
Product development	3
Automation, better production methods	5
Productivity increase, cost reduction	4
Quality control	4
Others	3
Marketing and Sales Promotion	14
Establishing the marketing system	4
Improving marketing efficiency	3
Better service, strengthening the service network	3
Others	4
Total	210

SOURCE: Tōyō Keizai Shimpo Sha, ed. *Nihon Keiei no Kaimei* (1961), pp. 277–278.

conducted from 1959 through 1960. The breakdown in the table of replies given by the middle level of management to the question, "What has been the most important problem you have confronted in your department during the postwar years?" is highly illustrative of the modernization of postwar management methods among large corporations.

While helping to modernize the management system through importation of new knowledge from the United States, professional managers of postwar Japan did not ignore the task of cultivating ideas and methods suited to the particular social and economic environment of Japan. The Japan Committee for Economic Development (Keizai Dōyūkai), organized by a group of young executives immediately after the war, has played a leading role in performing such a task. The committee's *Declaration on Social Responsibility of Executives,* in 1956, indicates the new character of the postwar generation of professional managers. Its preface states: "The task of modern corporation managers reaches far beyond that of profit making. From the ethical as well as practical standpoints, it is vital that they strive to produce and supply products of highest quality at the lowest possible prices, through better service and the most efficient utilization of resources in an atmosphere of harmony with the economy in general and society at large. It is the social responsibility of modern executives to become an effective instrument for establishing a corporate-management system capable of performing such a task." The declaration goes on to emphasize the importance of: (1) achieving social balance; (2) promoting fair competition in the home market; (3) technological progress and market development; (4) equitable distribution of corporate earnings; (5) training the future generation of executives.[14] Insofar as capitalism is presupposed, the above declaration seems to contain little that is objectionable to any sensible observer. However, the general reaction to it was rather unfavorable. Many academicians considered the declaration to be an overly idealistic piece of composition, while some industrialists called it an unrealistic essay by a group of egg-headed executives. This rather negative response to the declaration at the time of its publication (1956) indicates that there were still many people who remained skeptical about the potential conduct of "modern management," although they had never doubted the sincerity and conscience of postwar professional managers. During the following eight years Japanese economic society has experienced a series of rapid changes, including changes in the general public's attitude toward modern management concepts. What used to be considered as too idealistic and impractical has become the commonsense of today's industrialists. The membership of the Japan Committee for Economic Development, which comprised only 70 individuals at the time of its founding, has now reached the magnitude of 1,000, including numerous influential executives. The committee's voice in political and financial circles today is a strong one. In a way, growth of the Japan Committee

[14] Keizai Dōyūkai, *Keizai Dōyūkai Jūgonen Shi* (1962), pp. 391–397.

is a reflection of the growth of professional managers in postwar Japanese industry.

COMPETITIVE SOCIETY AND ENTREPRENEURSHIP

No essay on Japanese management after the war is complete without mention of the entrepreneurial spirit of Japanese executives. The topic is of particular importance in connection with economic growth. While most economists, Japanese as well as foreign, held a pessimistic view before 1955 on the future of the Japanese economy, corporate managers did not cease their aggressive activity; in retrospect it was their positive attitude that led and significantly contributed to the continual growth in the subsequent years. Many scholars (beginning with Max Weber) have pointed out the importance of entrepreneurship as a clue to economic growth; however, because of a relative retardation in behavioral science, no definitive, theoretical analysis of it has been thus far undertaken.[15] The present author is certainly not prepared to attempt a full-fledged, theoretical analysis in this paper of postwar Japanese entrepreneurship. However, after citing factors believed responsible for promoting interfirm competition, the remainder of this paper will take up two tentative approaches to this topic: (1) the emergence of founder-type executives, and (2) changes in the social environment surrounding managerial activity.

Factors Promoting Interfirm Competition

A flourishing of entrepreneurship presupposes the prevalence of sufficient competition in the market. The pace of accelerated growth of the Japanese economy suggests that various socio-economic changes after the war have helped to enhance competition in the home market. What follows below is a brief listing of factors believed responsible for having promoted competition in postwar Japan.

(1) The impact of the Zaibatsu dissolution and the purge of prewar financial leaders. Postwar corporation managers have had much greater freedom of decision-making than before the war.

(2) The impact of the anti-monopoly act. Prevention of excessive monopoly to the degree enjoyed by leading Zaibatsu before the war has afforded greater room for entry of new firms as well as for interfirm competition.[16] This factor, together with factors (6) and (7) below, has helped to reduce the interfirm technological gaps.[17]

[15] However, there have been some notable studies in recent years. For example, see D. C. McClelland, *The Achieving Society* (Princeton: D. Van Nostrand, 1961).

[16] Many firms became competitors, although they might have been of the same company before the anti-monopoly act. Some examples are given below (the first name is that of the "monopoly" firm before the split, and the names in parentheses are those of new, independent firms that became competitors after the split): Nihon Steel (Yawata Steel, Fuji Steel); Mitsubishi Heavy Industry (Higashi Nihon Heavy Industry, Naka Nihon Heavy Industry); Ōji Paper Products (Ōji, Jujo, and Honshū Paper Products); Daiken Sangyō (Marubeni-Iida, Ito-Chū, etc.); Dai Nippon Beer (Nippon Beer, Asahi Beer).

[17] Economic Planning Agency, *Gijutsu Kakushin to Kigyō Keiei* (Shisei Dō, 1958), pp. 58–61.

(3) A more even interfirm as well as interindustry distribution of technology and capital equipment than before the war. This tendency has been accelerated by the massive destruction of productive facilities, the stagnation in research and development during the war, and various postwar measures (e.g., termination of government subsidies to the military-goods industry, the Zaibatsu dissolution, and the like), the heaviest burden of which has been imposed upon the largest corporations.

(4) Shift of emphasis in corporate activity. New dimensions have been added to postwar corporate activity; in addition to the conventional task of supplying goods in response to market demand, it has become necessary to create demand for new products. An ever increasing emphasis placed upon research and development, modernization of marketing techniques, widening of the distribution network, and the like, are examples of the new problems faced by postwar corporations.

(5) Managerial innovations. It has become increasingly necessary to continuously introduce innovations throughout all phases of management (marketing, personnel, accounting, public relations, and so forth) in order to keep up with competition; at the same time these managerial innovations themselves have been reinforcing competition among firms.

(6) Lending methods of leading commercial banks. For a thorough discussion of this factor, the reader is referred to the recent study of Giichi Miyazaki.[18] The bilateral-oligopoly relationship between leading banks and major corporations in postwar Japan is believed to have helped intensify interfirm competition. Only one point needs to be added to Miyazaki's study; namely, it must be remembered that the initiative of investment decision has, by and large, been taken by corporate managers, and the role of commercial bankers has primarily been that of responding to the corporate demand for investment funds.

(7) The government's industrial policy. The Japanese government's protectionist policy with respect to Japanese foreign trade is well known. On the domestic scene, however, the government has consistently advocated a policy of promoting interfirm competition through legal (e.g., the anti-monopoly act), as well as administrative, means. A high degree of oligopolistic competition in postwar Japanese industry is, to a large extent, attributable to government policy. The acute concern of corporation managers in general with "market shares" is a uniquely postwar phenomenon.[19]

[18] Giichi Miyazaki, "Katō-Kyōsō no Ronri to Genjitsu," *Ekonomisto,* October 19, 1962.

[19] For an excellent discussion of the relationship between market shares and interfirm competition, see W. J. Baumol, *Business Behavior, Value and Growth* (New York: The Macmillan Co., 1959).

's

Founder-Type Executives

After the withdrawal of the prewar generation of executives, many professional managers who assumed new corporate responsibilities demonstrated extraordinary leadership and successfully carried out the enormous task of reconstruction and redevelopment. Some examples of these men are: Hōroku Andō (Onoda Cement); Yosamatsu Matsubara (Hitachi Zosen); Taizo Ishida (Toyota Automobiles); and, Isamu Saseki (Kinki Nippon Tetsudō). The list of those who started out as rank-and-file employees but, when given opportunities to assume managerial responsibilities, demonstrated remarkable abilities that led to rapid growth of their firms includes: Hideo Yoshida (Dentsu); Yatarō Nishiyama (Kawasaki Steel); Jirō Ueno (Sekisui Kagaku); Tokuji Mizushima (Taisei Kensetsu); Shiro Ohtagaki (Kansai Denryoku). Many executives became well known for their resiliency and viability during the postwar crises: e.g., Toshio Dokō (Ishikawajima Harima Jūkō); Katsuji Kawamata (Nissan Automobiles); Taizo Odawara (Kubota Steel); Shinzō Ohya (Teijin); Hitoshi Momose (Nippon Victor); Shigeru Kawai (Kawai Gakki). In the light of their performances and achievements, all these men may be said to have the characteristics of "founders."

One major postwar phenomenon in Japanese industry is the spectacular growth of new firms founded after the war or of firms which were only of insignificant size before the war. We shall call the founders of these corporations "founder-type executives" in contrast to the aforementioned category of "professional managers." The prewar generation of founder-type executives includes: Kōnosuke Matsushita (Matsushita Denki Sangyō); Shōjiro Ishibashi (Bridgestone Tires); Sazō Idemitsu (Idemitsu Kōsan); Tokuji Hayakawa (Hayakawa Electric); Ri-ichi Ezaki (Ezaki Guriko). Among the postwar generation of founder-type executives (although the majority of them had considerable amounts of business experience before and during the war) are found: Kiyoshi Ichimura (Rikko); Sōichiro Honda (Honda Giken); Toshio Iue (Sanyo Electric); Masaru Ibuka (Sony); Tsuyoshi Mitarai (Canon); Ryūichiro Enomoto (Nippon Gas Chemicals). These individuals are noted for their colorful "entrepreneurship," although their educational and business backgrounds are too diverse to be generalized.

In many ways economic conditions before the war were not conducive to the full working of entrepreneurship. Osamu Shimomura has written: ". . . before the war there were social, economic, and even historical restrictions as an underdeveloped country. The Zaibatsu domination is one example; it meant a formidable set of conservative and passive forces opposing new plans, positive ideas, and fresh ventures of entrepreneurs." [20]

Many suppressive conditions of the prewar period were removed

[20] Osamu Shimomura, *Nihon Keizai Seichō Ron* (1962), p. 297.

after 1945; moreover, there arose two new conditions which have favored entrepreneurial activity.

(1) Immediately after the war the majority of Zaibatsu and Zaibatsu-affiliated corporations found themselves in a state of massive confusion due to purges, the sudden termination of government subsidies, forced dissolution, the oversupply of labor relative to fallen demand, and so forth. This provided a setting advantageous to the growth and development of new firms.

(2) Many Zaibatsu corporations, having operated for so long under a controlled economic system geared towards the military industry, lacked knowledge and perception of modern marketing problems. Before the war these corporations operated chiefly in the heavy and chemical industries that catered to military demand. Marketing and distribution problems, as such, were routinely handled by separate companies belonging to the same Zaibatsu lines. The Strategic Industry Control Act of 1931 and the National Mobilization Act of 1938 intensified the cartelization of the Japanese economy, which covered, at its peak, 90 per cent of production and sales in the country. As the domestic demand structure shifted after the war toward the consumption-goods sector in which new firms could grow and operate with vigor and freedom, these prewar conditions constituted a serious handicap for many corporate managers who grew up in the Zaibatsu environment.

The number of founder-type executives among leading corporations in postwar Japan is extraordinarily large; only in the Meiji period does one find a similar phenomenon. Perhaps the phenomenon is rare even in the context of world business history. In his discussion of the mental attitudes and industry of men in the early stage of capitalism, Seiichi Tōhata makes a distinction between simple productive efforts and industrial creativity. According to him, the latter is possessed by only a few geniuses of the business world, and yet, the life of capitalism depends, to a large extent, upon it; those countries which bear many such geniuses are bound to develop and grow rapidly.[21] Following his vein of thought, we may say that postwar Japan has witnessed a rich crop of such industrial creativity. The positive influence of postwar executives on the entire industry is undeniable. These men began to take positive actions when many others were still in a state of stagnation and turmoil; they gave stimulus to the latter and helped to spread a cumulative, revitalizing influence throughout the entire economy. Economic consequences of their conduct have reached far beyond and above the immediate domain of their corporate activity.

CHANGES IN SOCIAL ENVIRONMENT

We shall briefly touch upon the impact of changes in the social, political, and cultural environment. Since the war, the prestige and

[21] Seiichi Tōhata, *Keizai Shutaisei Kōza III* (1960), p. 38.

power of industrialists as a social group have risen immensely, because of the disintegration of the military complex, the relative decline in the status of government bureaucrats, and the critical dependence of party politics upon private financial resources. The general public's image of industrialists has also changed; in lieu of "capitalist" and "financier," the term "executive" has come to be used as a common expression. These favorable changes have, in part, been generated by positive public-relations work such as that of the Japan Committee for Economic Development. A large number of founder-type executives have authored autobiographies and collections of essays, widely read by the general public. The popularity of their books is no doubt a reflection of the general public's greater interest in and respect for the business profession; this, in turn, as a nonpecuniary factor, must have motivated corporation managers toward more industrious conduct than ever before. D. Granick explains the stagnation of entrepreneurship in Great Britain, Belgium, and other countries in terms of the social climate vis-à-vis business executives in those countries.[22] In terms of Granick's thesis we might contend that the "social climate" in postwar Japan has been optimal to the blossoming of entrepreneurship. It has become quite common for able and ambitious young people to seek employment in business and industry. The ability principle, in place of the annual-proportional-promotion system, has been steadily gaining popularity, partly in response to the social trend of "democratization" and partly as a result of the practical need to cope with the ever-increasing interfirm competition. Technological innovations and economic growth are exerting pressure for the dissipation of the traditional lifelong-employment system and for greater interfirm mobility of human resources. The series of social changes mentioned above have, to a large extent, been the result of vigorous activities of corporation managers; and those changes in turn will undoubtedly cause a further flourishing of entrepreneurship in Japan.

Conclusion

This paper has been concerned with the role and characteristics of corporation managers in the course of Japan's postwar growth. We have discussed the two types of managers: professional managers and founder-type executives. The first group has richly contributed to the modernization of management-control methods and to the popularization of modern management concepts. The second group has contributed to Japanese growth not only through growth of their own firms but also by spreading the entrepreneurial spirit throughout Japanese industry. Of course, not all postwar Japanese executives can be classified into these two groups. However, the distinction between the two groups seems to provide an effective frame of reference in

---

[22] D. Granick, *The European Executive* (London, 1962).

discussing the management-science aspect of Japan's postwar economic growth.[23]

Comment I *by Katsunosuke Moroi*

The fact that the activity of corporation managers has been the engine of Japan's postwar growth has long been recognized; however, few systematic studies have been conducted to analyze the entrepreneurial contribution to growth in a historical setting. Noda's paper is to be commended because it is one of the first attempts to fill this research gap.

Noda distinguishes between professional managers and founder-type executives, and discusses their historical backgrounds as well as their roles in the course of industrial development. Noda's categorization provides a useful step that should lead to a new research area which one might call the theory of executives. However, his paper contains several points that require further clarification.

First, a more systematic and thorough comparison between prewar and postwar executives in terms of their strategic roles as promoters of economic growth seems necessary. As Noda points out, before the war the majority of corporation managers did not possess freedom of

[23] In their comments on this paper, both Katsunosuke Moroi and Yutaka Ōsawa complain that I fail to make a clear distinction between the founder-type executive and the professional manager. The former refers to someone who founded a firm for himself, played a direct and crucial role in expanding it, and (typically) remains as president or chairman of the company until his death or retirement. By the latter is meant someone who enters a firm founded by someone else as an employee and is promoted to a managerial position for his ability, competence, knowledge, personality, and the like. We may also consider a third category of "semi-founder-type executives," referring to those who did not found the firms but nevertheless played a leading role in transforming the firms into something radically different than before, say, in terms of the size or the diversity of products.

Classification of executives in this paper is made largely on the basis of personal-history criteria, and not on other alternative criteria such as "stock-ownership ratio," "behavioral characteristics," "job content," or "the manner of execution." Our criteria are applied only to those whom we can commonsensically evaluate as having made significant contributions to the growth of their firms and are not meant to be applicable to every single corporate manager. It is the author's view, however, that those executives whom we have discussed and classified under our method have been the true leaders of Japan's postwar industrial growth.

Ōsawa points out, "Executives' contribution to economic growth is . . . always indirect." No matter how ambitious the economic plans of political leaders (whose contribution to growth, Ōsawa implies, is more direct) might be, such plans are no more than mere blueprints without the incentive, will, and spirit of cooperation of corporate executives. To the extent that we recognize that Japan's postwar growth has centered around expansion of large corporations, the positive contribution to growth of the executives of those corporations is undeniable. It seems meaningless to ask whether their contribution has been direct or indirect.

action and thought under the extensive Zaibatsu control, whereas after the war the barriers against independent decision-making have been largely removed. Therefore, a meaningful comparison is not between those prewar managers without freedom and autonomy and postwar corporate leaders, but between the latter and the few "owner-type executives" of prewar days who did have freedom and independence. How the two groups compare in terms of their contribution to growth seems an interesting research topic. An international study in connection with the above prewar-postwar comparison should prove to be equally interesting. One frequently hears the remark that Japanese executives are obsessed with imitation of foreign technology and products, and lack independent creativity. What is the truth about this popular view in comparison with executives of other countries as well as in terms of prewar as against postwar periods?

My second point pertains to the relationship between Zaibatsu and economic growth. Noda contends that the Zaibatsu corporations represented a set of conservative and passive forces working against progressive ideas and ventures. Aside from the abnormal period of the wartime economy, however, it seems hard to deny that the Zaibatsu played an extremely important role in Japanese growth since the Meiji era. In the early developmental stages of Zaibatsu corporations, their "owner-type executives" must have been rather aggressive individuals. For example, Takuma Dan of Mitsui was noted for indecision in his later years, but it was the same individual who was largely responsible for transforming the Mitsui firm from a commercial enterprise to an industrial one in the Meiji period. In retrospect, the growth of Zaibatsu closely paralleled the growth of the Japanese economy. What is the explanation for once-progressive owner-type executives of Zaibatsu becoming conservative and passive individuals in later years? Monopolization may involve an inherent propensity towards rising conservatism within the firm. We must also remember that the decline in freedom and autonomy within the Zaibatsu was externally enforced by the rise of the military influence and the movement towards a controlled economy. Analysis of the behavior of prewar corporation managers should not discount the impact of nationalistic economic planning.

Third, Noda's distinction between professional managers and founder-type executives is rather vague. For example, in order for the postwar founder-type executives to succeed, they must presumably have had qualifications as professional managers as well. The former are distinguished from the prewar founder-type executives because the former have the qualifications of both categories of corporate leaders. In this sense, it seems that the concept of "professional manager" is so broad as to include that of the "postwar founder-type executives," although Noda is not clear on this point.

Finally, as Noda observes, the Zaibatsu dissolution, removal of government controls, and the like after the war, have resulted in a fuller manifestation of entrepreneurship throughout Japanese industry; and yet, in recent years, there has been a growing concern with the possible harm of excessive competition and the resultant tendency among large corporations to restrict their interfirm competition. I feel that this problem deserves careful scrutiny in any discussion of Japanese postwar growth based upon the theory of executives.

Comment II *by Yutaka Ōsawa*

Evaluation of the roles of executives in the process of Japanese economic growth is a difficult as well as important problem. One difficulty stems from the fact that the *ex post* behavior of executives is a function of both their own actions and thoughts as decision-makers, on the one hand, and external factors, such as the particular industrial structure and general trends in the national economy, on the other. While economic policy objectives of the government are usually explicitly stated, the behavior of corporate executives is generally not based upon a set of clearly defined objectives as such; and even if such objectives do exist, they are not, as a rule, disclosed to outsiders. In this sense, it may be held that the executives' contribution to economic growth, no matter what form it may assume, is always indirect —their contribution to the nation's economic growth is made only through the growth of their own firms. Various organizations of executives do attempt collectively to influence the government's economic policy; but the goal of these organizations usually amounts to an effort to alter the general corporate environment affecting their decision-making and does not have direct bearing upon the objective of economic growth itself. Analysis of executives' contribution to growth should comprise discussions of both the manner in which their contribution has been made and the particular corporate environment under which the executives have operated. The next task is to identify the guiding principles behind executive behavior, to examine how those principles have affected growth of the firms, and, finally, to clarify the relationship between economic growth and growth of individual firms.

Noda expounds the historical backgrounds of professional managers as against founder-type executives. The Zaibatsu Dissolution, purges, separation of ownership from control of corporations are cited as main causes of the emergence of professional managers, whereas the disproportionate share of wartime destruction imposed upon the Zaibatsu firms and radical changes in postwar patterns of demand from military to consumer goods to which the older corporations were not accustomed are cited as favoring the rise and success of founder-type executives. Noda's categorization provides a useful doorway towards further analysis of executive behavior and the aforementioned guiding principles. However, it is based solely upon the personal-historical backgrounds of executives and not upon their behavioral characteristics. Noda emphasizes the importance of contributions made by postwar executives in introducing and encouraging widespread use of modern managerial-control methods and concepts which are appropriate for an advanced economy. It is a fact that the number of so-called "professional managers" has increased after the war. It may also be true that modern managerial-control methods have been, and continue to be, applied by an increasing number of Japanese firms. But I do not believe that there is sufficient evidence to prove Noda's view that professional managers have been chiefly responsible for the introduction of these methods. Noda's conclusion that the *Declaration of the Japan Committee for Economic Development* has become common sense among Japanese industrialists seems rather farfetched. Japanese top management may certainly be conscious of their "social responsibility"; but whether it affects and conditions the decisions they make in the real world is another matter.

With respect to founder-type executives, Noda emphasizes the fact that the new socio-economic environment after the war has been conducive to the flourishing of entrepreneurship, which in turn has further improved the postwar environment. He relies upon the concept of "entrepreneurship" to differentiate founder-type executives from professional managers. Granted the postwar social climate has been favorable to uninhibited entrepreneurial activity, one is not certain whether (and why) this has been particularly true for founder-type executives. Noda's observation that these executives have stimulated many other corporation managers and that the entrepreneurial spirit is permeating the entire Japanese industry appears no more than a speculation. It is true that an increasing number of able young people have been entering business and industry as a result of the improved climate of opinion concerning the managerial profession; but it still seems too early to judge the precise effect of the new social climate upon Japan's economic growth.

The pace of Japan's postwar growth has been much faster than that of other countries. From this fact Noda draws a presupposition that there must be a set of unique contributions to growth attributable to Japanese executives and proceeds to compare prewar and postwar corporation managers. He paints a very clear picture of the historical backgrounds of the postwar executives, but most of what he has to say about their behavioral characteristics seems but a series of mere hypotheses.

Bibliography of Japanese Sources
with their English Titles

Andō, Hiroshi. "Kojin Chochiku no Shutai Betsu Suikei" (Estimates of Individual Savings by Occupational Group), *Keizai Bunseki* (Economic Analysis), December 1961.

Chochiku Dōkō Chōsa Hōkoku (Report on the Family Savings Survey).

Chochiku ni Kansuru Yoron Chōa (Survey of Public Opinion on Family Saving).

Chūshō Kigyō Kinyū Kōko (Small Business Finance Corporation). *Chūshō Kigyō Setsubi Tōshi Dōkō Chōsa Hōkoku* (Report on the Survey of the Equipment Investment of the Medium and Small-size Enterprises).

Daiichiji Tōshin no Shingi no Naiyō oyobi Keika no Setsumei (Explanation of the Contents and Process of Deliberations on the First Report).

Economic Planning Agency. *Gijutsu Kakushin to Kigyō Keiei* (Technological Innovations and Business Management), 1958.

————. *Keizai Hakusho* (Economic White Paper).

Edo, Hideo. *Mitsui Zaibatsu ni tsuite* (On the Mitsui Zaibatsu), 1948.

Endo, S. "Zaisei Tōyūshi no Taishō" (Objectives of Public Loans and Investment), *Kinyū Zaisei Kōza* (Monetary and Fiscal Policy Series), Vol. 3, Yūhikaku, 1961.

Fujita, Sei. "Kōsoku Shōkyaku to Kigyō Tōshi" (Accelerated Depreciation and Business Investment), *Osaka Daigaku Keizai Gaku* (University of Osaka Economic Papers), Vol. 9, no. 1, 1959.

————. "Seisaku Genzei ka Ippan Genzei ka" (Policy-Oriented versus General Tax Reductions), *Kinyū Journal,* April 1963.

————. "Shotoku Kazei no Seijiteki Genkai" (Political Limitations of Income Taxation), *Handai Keizai Gaku* (University of Osaka Economic Papers), Vol. 11, nos. 1–2, 1961.

Hashimoto, Tetsu. "Zeisei Kaikaku no Jakkan no Mondaiten" (Some Problems of the Tax Reform), *Keizai Gaku Ronkyū* (Journal of Economics), Vol. 13, no. 3, 1959.

Hayashi, Takashi. "Keizai Seichō to Rōdō no Bunpai Ritsu" (Economic Growth and Labor Shares), *Nihon Rōdō Kyōkai Zasshi* (Japan Labor Association Journal), August 1961.

Hayashi, Yoshio. *Sengo Nihon no Sozei Kōzō* (Tax Structure in Postwar Japan), Yūhikaku, 1958.

Hayashi, Yūjiro. *Nihon no Kagaku Kōgyō* (Chemical Industry in Japan), Iwanami Shinsho, 1957.

Hirose, Yuichi. *Kabushiki Gaisha Shihai no Kōzō* (The Structure of Corporate Ownership), Nihon Hyōron Shin Sha, 1963.

Hitotsubashi Daigaku Keizai Kenkyusho (The Institute of Economic Research, Hitotsubashi University). *Kaisetsu: Nihon Keizai Tōkei* (Japanese Economic Statistics: An Exposition).

Hōjin Kigyō Tōkei Nempō (Annual Report of Incorporated Enterprise Statistics).

Ikeuchi, Yasuhiko, *et al. Yushutsunyū Hendō Yōin no Bunseki* (Analysis of the Causes of Export-Import Fluctuations), Economic Planning Agency, 1962.

Ishizaki, Tadao. "Kaisō-betsu Shotoku Bunpu to Shotoku Saibunpai" (The Class-Distribution and Redistribution of Income), *Nihon Rōdō Kyōkai Zasshi* (Journal of Japan Labor Association), August 1961.

———. "Rōdō Shotoku Bunpairitsu no Teika to sono Yōin" (Decline in the Labor Share and Its Causes), *Keizai Geppō* (Economic Monthly), February 1962.

Ito, Mitsuharu. "Bukka Mondai no Tokikata" (How to Solve the Problem of Inflation), *Ekonomisto,* May 1, 1962.

Kaisha Yōran (Directory of Corporations).

Kakei Chōsa Nempō (Annual Report on Family Income and Expenditure).

Kanamori, Hisao. "Nihon no Chochiku Ritsu wa Naniyue Takai Ka" (Why the High Rate of Saving in Japan), *Keizai Geppō* (Economic Monthly), November 1961.

———. "Nihon no Yushutsu Kōzō to Hikaku Seisan Hi" (The Comparative Cost and the Composition of Japanese Exports), *Keizai Hyōron* (Economic Forum), March 1963.

Kawaguchi, Hiroshi. *Chochiku no Kōzō Bunseki* (Analysis of the Structure of Savings), Zenkoku Chihō Ginkō Kyōkai (National Association of Local Bankers), 1960.

———. *Chochiku Ryoku, Sono Riron to Jittai* (The Theory and Reality of the Savings Capacity), Zenkoku Chihō Ginkō Kyōkai (National Association of Local Bankers), 1954.

Keizai Dōyūkai (Japan Committee for Economic Development). *Keizai Dōyūkai Jūgonen Shi* (Fifteen Years of Japan Committee for Economic Development), 1962.

Keizai Kikaku Chō (Economic Planning Agency). *Kokumin Shotoku Hakusho* (National Income White Paper).

Keizai-tōkei Kenkyū Kai (Association for Research in Economic Statistics). *Keizai Shihyō* (Economic Indices).

Kensetsu Shō (Ministry of Construction). *1963-nen Kensetsu Hakusho* (The 1963 Construction White Paper).

Kigyō no Seichō to Shūekisei (Growth and Profitability of the Business Firms), 1962.

Kinyū Seido Chōsakai Tōshin (Monetary System Investigation Commission Report). *Overloan no Zesei* (Correction of Overloans), 1963.

Kōgyō Tōkei Hyō (Census of Manufactures).

Kōgyō Tōkei Hyō Sokuhō (Census of Manufactures—Prompt Report).

Kokumin Keizai Keisan Chōsa Iinkai Hōkoku (Report of the Social Accounting Research Committee).

Kokusei Chōsa (National Census).

Komiya, R. "Keizai Seichō to Bukka Mondai" (Economic Growth and the Problem of Inflation), *Nihon Keizai Shimbun* (Japan Economic Daily).

Komiya, R. "Sengo Nihon no Shihon Chikuseki Ritsu" (The Rate of Capital Accumulation in Postwar Japan), *Keizai Gaku Ronshū* (Journal of Economics), July 1963.

Kōsei Shō (Ministry of Welfare). *Kōsei Hakusho* (White Paper on Welfare).

Maigetsu Kinrō Tōkei (Monthly Labor Survey).

Ministry of Finance. *Gaikoku Bōeki Gaikyō* (Survey of Foreign Trade).

——. *Kuni no Yosan* (The National Budget).

——. *Tsūkan Tōkei* (Customs Statistics).

——. *Zaisei Kinyū Tōkei Geppō* (Public Finance and Monetary Statistics Monthly).

Ministry of International Trade and Industry. *Seisan Dōtai Tōkei* (Production Statistics).

Mitsubishi Economic Research Institute. *Hompō Jigyō Seiseki Bunseki* (Analysis of Business Earnings in Japan).

Miyashita, Katsutaro *et al. Waga Kuni Kigyō ni okeru Keiei Ishi Kettei no Jittai* (Facts Concerning Managerial Decision-Making in Japan), 1960.

Miyazaki, Giichi. "Katō-Kyōsō no Ronri to Genjitsu" (The Logic and Reality of Excessive Competition), *Ekonomisto* (special issue), October 10, 1962.

Miyazaki, Y. " 'Keizai Hakusho' no Approach ni tsuite" (On the Approach of the Economic White Paper), *Keizai Seminar* (extra edition), 1960.

Mizuno, Shōichi. *Nihon no Bukka Hendō* (Price Fluctuations in Japan), Tōyō Keizai Shimpo Sha, 1962.

Mochikabu Gaisha Seiri Iinkai (Holding Company Liquidation Commission). *Nihon Zaibatsu to Sono Kaitai* (Japanese Zaibatsu and their Dissolution), 1950.

Mori, Kei. "Minkan-Zaisei Kongō Model ni yoru Nihon Keizai no Kōzō Bunseki" (Structural Analysis of the Japanese Economy by the Mixed Private-Public Sector Model), *Riron Keizai Gaku* (Economic Studies Quarterly), May 1963.

Mori, Kei. "Nihon Keizai no Simulation Bunseki (I)" (Simulation Analysis of the Japanese Economy), *Keizai Bunseki* (Economic Analysis), June 1960.

Nakamura, Atsushi. "Kōgyō Seihin Kakaku no Cost Yōin Bunseki" (Analysis of Cost Elements in the Price of Manufactures), *Keizai Geppō* (Economic Monthly), November 1962.

Nakamura, Takafusa. "Bukka Jōshō Ron" (Theory of Inflation), *Chū-ō Kōron*, July 1962.

——. "Bunpairitsu no Teika to Shotoku Kōzō" (Decline in the Labor Share and the Income Structure), *Tōyō Keizai Bessatsu* (Oriental Economist, extra edition), Autumn 1961.

——. "Shotoku Bunpai to Shōhi Kōzō" (Income Distribution and the Consumption Structure). In M. Shinohara and T. Funahashi, eds. *Nihongata Chingin Kōzō no Kenkyū* (Studies in the Japanese Wage Structure), 1962.

1961-nen Zeisei Chōsakai Tōshin Bessatsu (The 1961 Report of the Tax System Investigation Commision, a separate volume).

Nihon Keiei no Kaimei (Exposition of Japanese Business Management).

Nihon Sozei Kenkyū Kyōkai (Japan Association for Taxation Studies). *Sengo Nihon no Zeisei* (Tax System in Postwar Japan), Tōyō Keizai Shimpo Sha, 1959.

——. *Zeisei Kenkyū Sankō Shiryō Shū* (Reference Materials for Tax Studies).

Nikkei-ren Rōdō Keizai Kenkyūsho Shiryō (Research Materials of the Japan Economic Federation Institute of Industrial Relations). *Seisansei, Chingin, Bunpairitsu no Kokusai Hikaku* (International Comparison of Productivity, Wages, and Labor Shares), 1961.

Noda, Kazuo. "Kigyōka Gojūnen—Mukai Tadaharu" (Mukai Tadaharu—A Half Century of Entrepreneurship), *Seisansei* (Productivity), May 1963.

Noda, Kazuo and Tsuneo Murakami. *Nihon no Keieisha* (Japanese Entrepreneurs).

Nōka Keizai Chōsa (Farming Household Economic Survey).

Ohkawa, Kazushi. *Nihon Keizai Bunseki—Seichō to Kōzō* (Analysis of the Japanese Economy—Growth and Structure), Shunju Sha, 1962.

Ono, H. "Rōdō Kumiai to Sangyō kan Chingin Kakusa" (Labor Unions and Interindustry Wage Differences), *Riron Keizai Gaku* (Economic Studies Quarterly), Vol. 12, no. 1, 1961.

Ozaki, Iwao and Keiichirō Obi. "Keizai Hatten to Shūgyō Kōzō" (Economic Growth and the Employment Structure), *Keizai Gaku Nempō* (Journal of Keio University Economic Association), no. 6, 1963.

Rinji Zeisei Chōsakai Tōshin (Special Report of the Tax System Investigation Commission).

Rōdō Hakusho (White Paper on Labor Conditions).

Rōdō Ryoku Rinji Chōsa (Labor Force Special Survey).

Rōdō Shō Chingin Chōsa Ka, ed. (Ministry of Labor, Wage Survey Section). *Nihon no Chingin Kōzō* (The Wage Structure in Japan), 1960.

Rōdō Sōgi Tōkei Chōsa (Labor Disputes Statistics Survey).

Rōdōkumiai Kihon Chōsa (Labor Union Basic Survey).

Samuelson, Paul A. "Tsuyoi Yen, Yowai Dollar" (The Strong Yen and the Weak Dollar), *Nihon Keizai Shimbun* (Japan Economic Daily), December 8, 1962.

Sasaki, Takao. "Seizōgyō ni okeru Seisansei, Chingin oyobi Kakaku no Suii" (Shifts in Productivity, Wages, and Prices in the Manufacturing Industry), *Keizai Bunseki* (Economic Analysis), no. 8, 1962.

Sasaki, Takao and Ryōhei Magota. "Sangyō Betsu, Kibobetsu Chingin Kakusa" (Interindustry and Interfirm Wage Gaps). In Ichiro Nakayama, ed. *Chingin Kihon Chōsa* (Basic Survey of Wages), Tōyō Keizai Shimpo Sha, 1956.

Sengo Nihon no Zeisei (Tax System in Postwar Japan).

Shimomura, Osamu. "Anzen Unten nitsuki Oshizukani" (Please Do not Disturb the Driver), *Ekonomisto,* June 20, 1961.

———. "Keizai Seichō no Tadashii Haakuno Tameni" (Towards a Correct Understanding of Economic Growth), *Nihon Keizai no Seichō Ryoku* (Growth Potential of the Japanese Economy), 1959.

———. *Nihon Keizai Seichō Ron* (The Theory of Japanese Economic Growth), Kinyū Zaisei Jijyō Kenkyū Kai, 1962.

———. "9% no Seichō ni Fuan Nashi" (Nothing to Worry about the 9% Growth), *Ekonomisto,* October 17, 1961.

———. "Watakushi no Egaku Nihon Keizai no Vision" (My Vision of the Japanese Economy), *Tōyō Keizai Shimpō* (Oriental Economic News Report), March 9, 1963.

Shin Chōki Keizai Keikaku ni Kansuru Keizai Shingikai Tōshin (Council for Economic Deliberation Report on the New Long-Range Economic Plan).

Shinohara, Miyohei. *Kōdo Seichō no Himitsu* (The Secret of Japan's Accelerated Growth), Nihon Keizai Shimbun Sha, 1961.

———. "Kōgyō ni okeru Bunpairitsu" (Capital-Labor Shares in the Manufacturing Industry). In Shigeto Tsuru and Kazushi Ohkawa, eds. *Nihon Keizai no Bunseki* (Studies on the Japanese Economy), Keisō Shobō, 1953.

———. *Nihon Keizai no Seichō to Junkan* (Growth and Cycles in the Japanese Economy), Sōbun Sha, 1961.

———. *Shōhi Kansū* (The Consumption Function), Tokyo, 1958.

Shokugyō Antei Gyōmu Tōkei (Employment Security Statistics).

Shūgyō Kōzō Kihon Chōsa Hōkoku (Report on the Employment Status Survey).

Sōgō Seisaku Kenkyū Kai (Association for Integrated Policy Research). *Bukka Seisaku e no Teigen* (Recommendation for Price Policy), August 1963.

Sōrifu Tōkei-kyoku (Bureau of Statistics, Office of the Prime Minister). *Kakei Shōsa Hōkoku* (Report on the Family Income and Expenditure Survey).

———. *Rōdō Ryoku Chōsa* (Labor Force Survey).

Suzuki, Takeo. *Gendai Zaisei Shi* (Modern History of Public Finance), University of Tokyo Press, 1960.

Tachi, Ryūichiro. "Keiki Hendō to Kinyū" (Money and Business Fluctuations), *Shisō* (Thought), November 1962

———. "Kinyū Seido Chōsakai 'Overloan no Zesei ni tsuite no Tōshin' o meguru Shomondai" (Some Problems surrounding the Report of the Monetary System Investigation Commission on Correction of Overloans), *Keizai Gaku Ronshū* (Journal of Economics), Vol. 29, July 1963.

———. "Sengo Waga Kuni no Kinyū Kōzō jō no Jakkan no Mondaiten ni tsuite" (Some Notes on Monetary Problems in Postwar Japan), *Suzuki Takeo Kyōju Kanreki Kinen Ronbun Shū* (Essays in Honor of Professor Takeo Suzuki), Tōyō Keizai Shimbun, 1963.

Tachi, Ryūichiro and Ryūtaro Komiya. "Wagakuni no Kinyū Seisaku wa Ikani Arubekika" (A Recommendation for Monetary Policy in Japan), *Keizai Hyōron* (Economic Forum), May 1961.

Takasuka, Yoshihiro. "Bukka Taikei Saihensei no Mechanism" (The Mechanism of Reorganizing the Price System), *Tōyō Keizai Bessatsu* (Oriental Economist, extra edition), Spring 1962.

———. "Seisan Kōzō Karamita Bukka Mondai" (Production Approach to the Problem of Inflation), *Ekonomisto*, April 4, 1962.

Tanaka, Hirohide. "Bunpairitsu Teika no Mechanism" (The Mechanism of Declining Labor Shares), *Rōdō Tōkei Chōsa Geppō* (Monthly Labor Statistics), Vol. 14, no. 8, 1962.

Tatemoto, Masahiro. *Bōeki no Keiryō-teki Bunseki* (Econometric Analysis of Foreign Trade), University of Osaka Social and Economic Studies Series, no. 17, 1963.

Tōhata, Seiichi. *Keizai Shutaisei Kōza* (Constituents of the Economy Series), 1960.

Tōkei Kenkyū Kai, ed. (Statistical Research Association). *Seisansei no Hendō to sono Eikyō* (Productivity Changes and Their Effects), 1958.

Tokyo Shōken Gyō Kyōkai (Tokyo Association of Security Dealers). *Shōken Gyō Hō* (Journal of Securities and Exchange).

Torii, Yasuhiko. "Nōka no Shūgyō Kōzō to Nōgyo Seisan Ryoku" (The Employment Structure and Production Capacity in Agriculture), unpublished.

Tsuchiya, K. "Kōdō Seicho ka no Keizai Seisaku no Kihonteki Shikaku" (Fundamental Viewpoint of Economic Policy in the Process of Accelerated Growth), *Kigyō Keizai Bunseki* (Enterprise Economic Analysis), 1962.

Tsuchiya, K. *et al.* "Dokomade Tsuzuku Neagarizo" (Will the Present Inflation Ever Stop?), *Bungei Shunjū*, May 1962.

Tsuru, Shigeto *et al.* "Bukka Mondai o Dō Tokuka" (How to Interpret the Recent Inflation?), *Ekonomisto*, June 26, 1962.

Uchida, Tadao and Kei Mori. "Nihon Keizai no Simulation Bunseki" (Simulation Analysis of the Japanese Economy). In Uchida *et al.*, eds. *Atarashii Keizai Bunseki* (New Economic Analysis), Sōbun Sha, 1960.

Uchida, Tadao and Tsunehiko Watanabe. "Nihon Keizai no Hendō" (Fluctuations of the Japanese Economy), *Riron Keizai Gaku* (Economic Studies Quarterly), Vol. 9, nos. 3–4.

Uchino, Akira. *Nihon no Kenkyū Tōshi* (Research Investment in Japan), Jitsugyō Kōhō Sha, 1962.

Urabe, Kuniyoshi. *Keieisha* (Entrepreneurs), Diamond Sha, 1958.

Yoshino, T., ed. *Keizai Seichō to Bukka Mondai* (Economic Growth and Price Problems), Shunjū Sha, 1962.

Zeisei Chōsakai (Tax System Investigation Commission). *Tōmen Jissensubeki Zeiseikaisei ni kansuru Tōshin oyobi sono Shingi no Naiyō to Keika no Setsumei* (Report on the Proposed Tax Reforms and an Explanation of the Contents and Process of the Deliberations).

Zenkoku Shōhisha Jittai Chōsa (National Survey of Family Income and Expenditure).

INDEX

Index